Identity by Dissociation

Copyright 2013 Hany Hannock Longwe

All rights reserved. No part of this publication may be reproduced, stored in a retrieval system or transmitted in any form or by any means, electronic, mechanical, photocopying, recording or otherwise, without prior permission from the publishers.

Published by
Mzuni Press
P/Bag 201, Luwinga, Mzuzu 2, Malawi

ISBN 978-99960-27-05-5
Mzuni Books no. 6

Mzuni Press is represented outside Africa by:
African Books Collective, Oxford
(orders@africanbookscollective.com)

Published with the assistance of a grant from the International Society for the Promotion of Christian Knowledge

Cover Design: Torben Ewaldt

Identity by Dissociation

A History of the Achewa Providence Industrial Mission

Hany Hannock Longwe

Mzuni Books no. 6

Mzuni Press
Mzuzu
2013

Mzuni Press
P/Bag 201, Luwinga, Mzuzu 2, Malawi
http://mzunipress@luviri.net

This book is part of Mzuni Press, which offers a range of books on religion, culture and society from Malawi. Other Mzuni Press titles are:

Johnathan Nkhoma, *The Use of Fulfilment Quotations in the Gospel according to Matthew*

Tito Banda, *Old Nyaviyuyi in Performance. Seven Tales from Northern Malawi as Told by a Master Performer of the Oral Narrative*

Brian Shaŵa and Boston Soko, *Tumbuka Folk Tales*

Hany Longwe, *Christians by Grace – Baptists by Choice. A History of the Baptist Convention of Malawi*

Rhodian Munyenyembe, *Christianity and Socio-Cultural Issues. The Charismatic Movement and Contextualization in Malawi*

John Ryan, *Science and Spirituality*

Tito Banda and Joshua Kumwenda (eds), *Reading Malawian Literature: New Approaches and Theories*

Klaus Fiedler, *Missions as the Theology of the Church*

Jonathan Nkhoma, *Significance of the Dead Sea Scrolls and other Essays: Biblical and Early Christianity Studies from Malawi*

Leon Spencer, *Toward an African Church in Mozambique: Kamba Simango and the Protestant Community in Manica and Sofala, 1892-1945*

Kenneth R. Ross, *Malawi and Scotland together in the Talking Place since 1859*

V.Y. Mgomezulu and F.A. Kalua, *A Guide to Academic Writing for Beginners*

Identity by Dissociation

A History of the Achewa Providence Industrial Mission

Hany Hannock Longwe

Mzuni Books no. 6

Mzuni Press
Mzuzu
2013

Mzuni Press
P/Bag 201, Luwinga, Mzuzu 2, Malawi
http://mzunipress@luviri.net

This book is part of Mzuni Press, which offers a range of books on religion, culture and society from Malawi. Other Mzuni Press titles are:

Johnathan Nkhoma, *The Use of Fulfilment Quotations in the Gospel according to Matthew*

Tito Banda, *Old Nyaviyuyi in Performance. Seven Tales from Northern Malawi as Told by a Master Performer of the Oral Narrative*

Brian Shaŵa and Boston Soko, *Tumbuka Folk Tales*

Hany Longwe, *Christians by Grace – Baptists by Choice. A History of the Baptist Convention of Malawi*

Rhodian Munyenyembe, *Christianity and Socio-Cultural Issues. The Charismatic Movement and Contextualization in Malawi*

John Ryan, *Science and Spirituality*

Tito Banda and Joshua Kumwenda (eds), *Reading Malawian Literature: New Approaches and Theories*

Klaus Fiedler, *Missions as the Theology of the Church*

Jonathan Nkhoma, *Significance of the Dead Sea Scrolls and other Essays: Biblical and Early Christianity Studies from Malawi*

Leon Spencer, *Toward an African Church in Mozambique: Kamba Simango and the Protestant Community in Manica and Sofala, 1892-1945*

Kenneth R. Ross, *Malawi and Scottland together in the Talking Place since 1859*

V.Y. Mgomezulu and F.A. Kalua, *A Guide to Academic Writing for Beginners*

Content

CHAPTER 1 .... **9**
THE BEGINNINGS: PIM IN CHIRADZULU AND LILONGWE DISTRICTS **9**
   Probably the Two most Prominent Students from Chilembwe's Schools 9
   Opposition to Colonialism 12
   The Formative Years of PIM in Mangoni 13

CHAPTER 2 .... **23**
THE ORIGIN AND EXPANSION OF ACHEWA PIM **23**
   The Re-opening of PIM at Mbombwe 23
   The Resumption of Ties between Chiradzulu and Mangoni 24
   The First Baptism Service Conducted by Malikebu in Mangoni ... 25
   Leadership Training under Malikebu 26
   Church Government of PIM in Mangoni 30
   Construction of Church Buildings 31
   Mpingo wa Mpatuko Breaks Ties with Chiradzulu 32
   Church Polity of Achewa PIM 43
   Kalemba's Divorces: Rather a Leadership Issue than a Moral One . 48
   Separation within APIM over its Future 50
   Kalemba's Death and the Beginning of Kamkalamba's Era 51
   Church Leadership Training after 1945 52

CHAPTER 3 .... **56**
ACHEWA PIM WORKING WITH FOREIGN MISSIONARIES **56**
   The Beginnings of Southern Baptist Convention Work in Malawi ... 56
   Leadership Training and its Results 61
   Women: Training and Church Planting: Bible Study and Songs ... 70
   Church Planting 71
   Kamkalamba and the Leadership Team 72
   APIM's Contribution to Baptist Work 75
   The Establishment of BACOMA 78
   APIM, BACOMA and Expansion 84

CHAPTER 4 .... **86**
INDEPENDENT AGAIN **86**
   Build-up to the Separation 86
   Resentment of APIM Pastors by BACOMA Leadership 87
   Achewa PIM Fighting against Suspicion: Competing for the Souls .. 90
   Schism: Some Congregations Leave APIM for BACOMA 94

    The Differing Positions of Albright and Scott 99
    Church Structure after Kamkalamba's Death 102
    APIM History: an Interpretation 108

CHAPTER 5 111
THE PRESENT STATE OF ACHEWA PIM 111
    Local Church Leadership 111
    Church Meetings 112
    Monthly Fellowship Meetings 112
    Annual Meetings 114
    Baptism Class and Service 120
    The Respect the Bishop Enjoys 128
    Original Quest for Education: What Happened? 132
    Gule Wamkulu: Kamchedzera's Case 132
    The Role of Women in Achewa PIM 134
    APIM and Children 135

CHAPTER 6 137
CONCLUSIONS 137
    Evangelism and Church Growth 137
    Achewa PIM Churches 139
    Theological Education 142
    Social Demand 145
    Practical Theology 150
    Achewa PIM: AIC or Baptist? 154
    A Religious Island 158
    Recommendations 161

BIBLIOGRAPHY 163

List of Abbreviations

AABF	All Africa Baptist Fellowship
ABA	African Baptist Assembly
AIC	African Instituted Church
APIM	Achewa Providence Industrial Mission
BACOMA	Baptist Convention of Malawi
BGCO	Baptist General Convention of Oklahoma
BCZ	Baptist Convention of Zimbabwe
BMCA	Baptist Mission in Central Africa
BMIM	Baptist Mission in Malawi
BWA	Baptist World Alliance
CCAP	Church of Central Africa Presbyterian
CCM	Christian Council of Malawi
CLAIM	Christian Literature Association in Malawi
DC	District Commissioner
DRCM	Dutch Reformed Church Mission
EC	Executive Committee
FMB	Foreign Mission Board
IBACOMA	Independent Baptist Convention of Malawi
IMB	International Mission Board
Inc	Incorporated
MCP	Malawi Congress Party
NBC	National Baptist Convention
NT	New Testament
PIM	Providence Industrial Mission
SBC	Southern Baptist Convention
SDB	Seventh Day Baptist
SS	Sunday School
TA	Traditional Authority
TC	Trading Centre
TEE	Theological Education by Extension
USA	United States of America
ZIM	Zambezi Industrial Mission

Editors' Preface

All know John Chilembwe as the National Hero, fighting for liberation. But he did that, and understood himself, as a missionary, a missionary to his own people. When the planning for the Rising was already in the advanced stages, late in 1914 he sent two of his trusted members to start a new branch of PIM in Mangoni, south of Lilongwe. He seems to have felt that, should PIM die in Chiradzulu, Migowi and Wallani, and all the other branches he had founded in the South, it should survive at least in Mangoni in the Centre.

The Church was banned indeed, but it survived both in the South and in the Centre. As Editors of Mzuni Press we are happy to be able to present the history of the Achewa PIM, which is one of the continuations of the early efforts of Peter Kalemba and his associates in Mangoni. Hany Longwe does not present the Achewa Providence Industrial Mission as an African Independent Church, but as the Baptist church it is. As a Baptist himself, the author discovered that affinity easily, though it is not reflected in the name of the church.

Earlier the Kachere Series published another book on the PIM Baptists, the *Church History of Providence Industrial Mission* by Patrick Makondesa, who argues that John Chilembwe foremost was a missionary and describes how the PIM was established not only in Mbombwe/Chiradzulu, and that it had its main strength in the Migowi area, but also some congregations in Zomba district.

Both books are the result of recent research at the University of Malawi, and as we are convinced that local research must be published localy, as Mzuni Press Editors we are happy to make Hany Longwe's research available as one of the Mzuni Books.

Mzuni Press Editors
May, 2013

Chapter 1
The Beginnings: PIM in Chiradzulu and Lilongwe Districts

The history of PIM, and of course that of Achewa PIM, begins with that of *Mbusa* (Pastor or Rev) John Chilembwe, a missionary to his own people. As a young person, Chilembwe was strong and aggressive: he knew what he wanted and went after it. His story highlights the rationale for the indigenization of Christianity. With the help of Joseph Booth, whom many called a friend of Africa; Chilembwe was able to leave Malawi for the United States of America where he studied theology at Virginia Theological Seminary from 1898.[1] While there he was made aware of the sociopolitical situation of black people in the USA, and also studied the self-help philosophy of their struggle.[2] Under the auspices of the Foreign Mission Board of the National Baptist Convention Inc, Chilembwe was able to set up and open Providence Industrial Mission at Mbombwe in Chiradzulu District in 1900. He was assisted between 1902 and 1906 by Afro-American missionaries Rev L.N. Cheek and Miss Emma DeLaney from the same FMB.[3] The team approach to missions lasted for about four years, after which Chilembwe had sole responsibility for the work at Mbombwe.[4] This he carried out successfully.

Probably the Two most Prominent Students from Chilembwe's Schools

Daniel S. Malikebu

Daniel S. Malikebu, a Yao like Chilembwe, was born about 1890. By 1901 Malikebu was one of the first students at PIM School under Chi-

---

[1] Harry Langworthy, "*Africa for the African*". *The Life of Joseph Booth*, Blantyre: CLAIM, 1996, p. 106.
[2] Leroy Fitts, *A History of Black Baptists,* Nashville: Broadman, 1985, p. 137.
[3] Langworthy, *Joseph Booth*, pp. 104, 224. See also Shepperson and Price, *Independent African*, p. 138.
[4] Leroy Fitts, *A History of Black Baptists*, Nashville: Broadman, 1985, p. 138.

lembwe. He grew up in Chilembwe's congregation.[5] Malikebu was employed as a house-servant and interpreter for Emma DeLaney. During her stay at Mbombwe DeLaney encouraged the young Malikebu to go with her to the USA. Malikebu's family did not support the idea. They made sure that when DeLaney was leaving, she went without him. Nevertheless, Malikebu was able to slip out of Malawi and walked almost 600 km to Beira.[6] From there he worked his way to England on S.S. Matebele and then on S.S. Saint Paul to the USA. Malikebu arrived in New York on 19 August 1905.[7] In 1915 Malikebu had started training at Meharry Medical College, Nashville, Tennessee.[8] In 1917, he briefly attended the Moody Bible Institute in Chicago. That same year Malikebu went to the University of Pennsylvania where he studied tropical medicine and took his internship at Mudgett Hospital until 1918. At the time he did not know of the events that were taking place in Malawi.[9]

Peter Kalemba

Peter Kalemba attended PIM School under Chilembwe at almost the same time as Malikebu.[10] His parents had left Kalumbu in Lilongwe District because of *nkhondo zakale* (wars of the past) between Ngoni and Chewa people and settled near Blantyre.[11] For several years Kalemba attended school at Blantyre Mission. It was his father who encouraged him to join a school which was run by an educated black *mzungu* (white man), Chilembwe, at Mbombwe.[12] Like Malikebu, Kalemba was bright and promising. After finishing school he was employed in one of the shops in Chiradzulu and he attended church at

---

[5] G. Shepperson and T. Price, *Independent African*, Edinburgh: University Press, 1987, first paperback edition, reprinted Blantyre: CLAIM-Kachere, 2000, p. 412.
[6] M. Mtewa, "Tribute to Dr Malikebu", *The Enquirer*, Vol. 1 No. (6 September 1993), p. 5.
[7] D.L. Saunders, "A History of Baptists in East and Central Africa", PhD, Southern Baptist Theological Seminary, 1973, p. 27. See also M. Mtewa, "Tribute", p. 5.
[8] G. Shepperson and T. Price, *Independent African*, Edinburgh: University Press, 1987, first paperback edition, reprinted Blantyre: CLAIM-Kachere, 2000, p. 142.
[9] M. Mtewa, "Tribute", p. 8.
[10] Int Velina Kaunde, Matapila, 9.6.1999.
[11] Int Eliamu Mlongoti Chijere Nyangu, Mchinji, 19.9.1999.
[12] Int Magi Kamunthu, Kalumbu, 26.10.1998.

the Mission.[13] During that period he became a prominent and trusted member of the Church.[14]

Kalemba was the first PIM convert from Mangoni. The second convert was Anderson Nyangu.[15] Nyangu's mother was Mwamtsindo in Kalumbu Village, across the main road from Nyangu Village. His uncle, a brother of Mwamtsindo, Chidampamba, was the first Chief Kalumbu. Nyangu's father was Msaiwala, known as Nyangu Mlidzo.[16] Nyangu had been to the Dutch Reformed Church Mission (DRCM) school at Nkhoma.[17] He went to Magomero in search of work. Nyangu was welcomed by Kalemba who shared his faith with him. It was Kalemba who took Nyangu to Chilembwe at Mbombwe. It is said that when Kalemba told Chilembwe that he had brought a candidate from Angoni who was also his nephew, Chilembwe rang the church bell and people gathered in the church building. Chilembwe told the congregation why he had summoned the church, and asked if anyone objected to Nyangu being baptized. Since no one objected, Nyangu was baptized by Chilembwe the same day. It was a special case because it meant that there were now two members who came from Mangoni out of the entire congregation at the Mission.[18]

Kalemba was aware of Chilembwe's opposition to foreign rule and of the preparations for the Rising. One of the things that Chilembwe did was to ask his followers at Mbombwe to make and burn bricks for future expansion work at the Mission. Instead of leaving the bricks on the kiln, Chilembwe ordered a pit be dug and the bricks put in it and covered with soil.[19] He anticipated the destruction of the Mission buildings by the colonial government in retaliation for his opposition to its rule.

Just as he had anticipated the destruction of the buildings, Chilembwe also foresaw his blood and that of his followers being shed. Some time before the 1915 Rising, Chilembwe ordered Kalemba and Nyangu to leave Mbombwe and escape to Mangoni *kuti Kalemba adzakhale mutu wa mpingo* (so that Kalemba would be the head of the church).[20] By preserving one of his own trusted products, Chi-

---

[13] Int Foulger Kafulatira, a son of Henry Kafulatira, one of Kalemba's first converts to PIM in Mangoni, Majondo Village, 21.5.1999.
[14] Int Numeri and Magi Kamunthu, Kalumbu, 26.10.1998.
[15] Int Eliamu Mlongoti Chijere Nyangu, Mchinji, 19.9.1999.
[16] Int Elenesi Kuthedze, Nyangu, 11.9.1999.
[17] That was later to be known as the Nkhoma Synod of the Church in Central Africa Presbyterian (CCAP).
[18] Int Eliamu Mlongoti Chijere Nyangu, Mchinji, 19.9.1999.
[19] Int Yosofati Ndege, Chalendewa, 13.6.1999.
[20] Int Foulger Kafulatira, Majondo, 21.5.1999.

lembwe believed that the future of PIM was secured no matter what was to become of him and the Mission.[21] He also encouraged Kalemba and Nyangu to commit their faith to at least one other person as soon as they would arrive in Mangoni. Time was running out and things had to be done instantly and in confidence.[22] Sometime in October 1914 Kalemba and Nyangu arrived at Kalumbu.[23]

Opposition to Colonialism

Hundreds of children were enrolled in PIM schools. The brick church that was completed in 1913 was very impressive. Nevertheless, there were growing problems. Chilembwe was short of money for his maintenance and the work of the Mission. Tension with the Bruce Estates, the Scottish agricultural development that owned most of the land around Magomero, was also mounting. The Bruce Estates wanted cheap labour. Many PIM members were "squatters" on Bruce's land. It appears the management burnt the grass-thatched churches that PIM members erected here and there near their dwellings. PIM, a church that did not hold extremist views, was being driven to radicalism by such colonial settlers.[24] Converts of Afro-American missionaries were linked to the Bambata Rebellion in British Natal. To many white people it was evidence that Africans were getting out of control.[25] Chilembwe's own nationalistic tendencies soon became so strong that they drove him to take the lead during the struggles of the African people in British Central Africa.[26]

During the First World War, Malawians could be dragged from their houses and be forced to carry *katundu* (headloads) for the *bwana* (boss) in an obnoxious system known as *mtengatenga* (helping to carry the load). Africans provided the muscle without which the British colonialists could not have stopped the Germans marching south from Tanzania. Over 50,000 porters, excluding Malawian soldiers, died. In November 1914 Chilembwe wrote a very strong letter of protest, which appeared in the Nyasaland Times.[27] Two months later Chi-

---

[21] Ezina Kamdolozi, a daughter of Harison Matapila, one of the first converts to PIM in Mangoni, Matapila, 20.5.1999.
[22] Int Litida Kakhobwe, Katantha, 26.5.1999.
[23] A.H. Kafulatira, "Ciyambi ca Mpingo wa Achewa Providence Indus¬trial Mis-sion Kudera la Lilongwe", n.p., n.d.
[24] Adrian Hastings, *The Church in Africa 1450-1950*, Oxford: Clarendon, 1996, pp. 486-487.
[25] G. Shepperson and T. Price, *Independent African*, p. 145.
[26] *Ibid*., pp. 143-146, 262-263.
[27] Adrian Hastings, *Church in Africa*, p. 488.

lembwe led the 1915 Rising against the British government. He was killed, together with some members of his leadership team. Chilembwe's political outlook and decision to resort to violence was believed by some to have been influenced by his experience in Lynchburg.[28] The Mission was closed and the buildings at Mbombwe razed. As a result, the British troops made several indiscriminate attacks against Malawian sympathizers and other churches, though they did not attack them physically, for their role in the Rising.[29] Chilembwe's Rising had significant ramifications for the NBC and Afro-Americans in general in relation to their missionary activities in Africa and especially in southern Africa.[30]

The Formative Years of PIM in Mangoni

One of the major results of Chilembwe's opposition to colonialism and the 1915 Rising was the establishment of PIM in Mangoni. Just as PIM began in Chiradzulu with a missionary to his own people, PIM in Mangoni also started with another missionary to his own people: Kalemba, who was assisted by Anderson Nyangu.[31] Without wasting time they shared their faith with Duncan and Salatiyele Mnthambala, and William Njawayawa who all lived in Kalumbu.[32]

In the process of witnessing, Kalemba and Nyangu found themselves wives. Kalemba married Magireti who came from across Linthipe near Chiipira in Dedza. Soon they had two sons, Robert and Aliyele, and a daughter whose name could not be remembered.[33] They made their home at Chasha, east of and not far from Kalumbu Traditional Court.[34] Nyangu's first wife was Anne from Chikumba. They were blessed with a boy and a girl, Jonathan and Janet respectively.[35] He stayed with her for a few years before he divorced her, and then married Milia, also known as Unice, of Tsoyo near Undi.[36]

---

[28] G. Shepperson and T. Price, *Independent African*, pp. 93-108, 112-113.
[29] *Ibid.*, p. 323ff.
[30] Leroy Fitts, *A History of Black Baptists*, Nashville: Broadman, 1985, p. 202.
[31] A.H. Kafulatira, "Ciyambi ca Mpingo wa Achewa Providence Indus¬trial Mis-sion Kudera la Lilongwe".
[32] Duncan later left PIM and joined *Mboni za Yehova* (Jehovah's Witnesses). When he was initiated as Chief Mnthambara, he stopped being *Mboni ya Yehova*.
[33] Int Eliamu Mlongoti Chijere Nyangu, Mchinji, 19.9.1999.
[34] Int Sefilina Mkhumbeni, Kalumbu, 26.10.1999.
[35] Int Velina Kaunde, Matapila, 9.6.1999.
[36] Int Emelesi Kuthedze, Nyangu, 11.9.1999.

They were also blessed with a boy and a girl. The boy was named Solomoni. The girl was popularly known by the name of Gelo.[37]

Immediately they knew of the Rising and its results, they met privately in Kalemba's home although several people there had already known of Kalemba's connections with Chilembwe.[38] During the witch-hunt that followed the Chilembwe Rising, Kalemba gave himself up to the police in Lilongwe, who later took him to Zomba. Before doing that, Kalemba entrusted Nyangu with the survival and development of PIM in Mangoni and in Malawi.[39]

The impact of the War and the Rising made the government accuse missions in general for what it called lack of adequate supervision over Africans, and for sometimes too much responsibility and freedom in the Africans' hands.[40] Since most missions feared accusations of disloyalty and subsequent termination of their work in the country, they felt obliged to participate in the war. African men, including church members, were being called up for military service against their will. Some were caught in their villages by the government officials before they could leave, but others managed to leave their work and their villages altogether. Following what others were doing, Nyangu ran away into Mozambique (commonly known then as Mpanyila), via Dzalanyama Range for fear of being forced into military service, and for fear of being persecuted for sympathizing with the Chilembwe Rising.[41]

Kalemba's case was heard before a magistrate or judge Jackson in Zomba.[42] Instead of being executed, Kalemba had over half of his right ear cut off during the torture applied to force him to say what he

---

[37] Int Eliamu Mlongoti Chijere Nyangu, Mchinji, 19.9.1999. It is common to find children who are called Gelo or Boyi (from girl or boy), just as for some women as Anti (aunt), takes the place of the real name. Sometimes the real name is forgotten for good, and the child continues to use the name Gelo or Boyi until she or he is old enough to know the meaning of the name and choose to change it especially if the child goes to school. Solomoni is said to have settled somewhere on the shores of Lake Malawi in Salima District, and was alive at the time of writing.
[38] Int Erika Matewere, Lilongwe, 28.5.1999.
[39] A.H. Kafulatira, "Ciyambi ca Mpingo wa Achewa Providence Indus¬trial Mis-sion Kudera la Lilongwe".
[40] Christoff Martin Pauw, "Mission in Malawi: The History of the Nkhoma Synod of the Church of Central Africa, Presbyterian 1889 -1962", PhD, University of Stellenbosch, 1980, p. 92; forthcoming as Zomba: Kachere, 2007.
[41] Int Daulosi S. Kuthedze, Nyangu, 11.9.1999.
[42] A.H. Kafulatira, "Ciyambi ca Mpingo wa Achewa Providence Indus¬trial Mis-sion Kudera la Lilongwe".

did not know. He was kept in prison for several years before being released. Kalemba was naked when he was let out of prison.[43] It was only when he got to Mandala at Dedza that he had *kansalu pathupi lake* (a piece of cloth on his body).[44] This was a very humiliating experience for an adult male Malawian and an educated one for that matter. *Akanakhala wina akanapenga misala* (If it had been somebody else he would have gone mad), but Kalemba maintained his composure.[45] He was able to get some clothing, which brought back his respect and dignity, in Lilongwe.[46] He was soon joined by Nyangu who had been keeping a low profile after his return from Mozambique.[47]

A Period of Secret Meetings

Kalemba was identified with PIM which was labeled as *mpingo wa nkhondo* (the church of war) because of the Chilembwe Rising.[48] Those who were interested in the teaching of PIM met with Kalemba in their homes at night. They had to meet at night because *amaopsyezedwa osati kubvutitsidwa kwenikweni* (they were intimidated not directly victimized).[49] Since the people had no candles or paraffin lamps, they used to pull off *nyenje* (reeds or some kind of grass tied together with poles to form doors), *mpakana zitseko kutha* (to the extent that the doors were destroyed).[50] Sometimes they *amayatsa dzinyasi they* (burnt trash) to provide light where they met.[51] Those who attended the meetings became *uthenga* (the communication) to others in the neighbourhood. The human communication spread into several villages across Diamphwe River into Dedza.[52]

Mpingo wa Mpatuko: From the Gospel of Modesty

When Chilembwe was in America, the fashion there was for women to cover their heads and wear floor length dresses, and for men to wear ties and jackets. He taught the local people of Chiradzulu to

---

[43] Int Adiresi Kampangire, Katantha, 26.5.1999.
[44] Int Ezina Kamdolozi, Matapila, 20.5.1999.
[45] Int Litida Kakhobwe, Katantha, 26.5.1999.
[46] Int Adiresi Kampangire, Katantha, 26.5.1999.
[47] A.H. Kafulatira, "Ciyambi ca Mpingo wa Achewa Providence Industrial Mis-sion Kudera la Lilongwe".
[48] Int Feliati Dirawo Kaunde, Matapila, 9.6.1999.
[49] Int Elikana Ngalawo, Mphindo, 7.6.1999.
[50] Int Adiresi Kampangire, Katantha, 26.5.1999.
[51] Int Velina Kaunde, Matapila, 9.6.1999.
[52] Int Dailesi P. Thole, Katantha, 26.5.1999.

dress "properly", as did Kalemba and Nyangu to the new converts to PIM in Mangoni. It was a time when *kubvala kunali kopelewera* (dressing was insufficient), *ena nguwo akadalinazo* (others still had animal skin-cloth).[53] Some of the people—especially the women—wore a piece of cloth wrapped around their bodies up to above their breasts and nothing covering their heads. Men put on at least a cover from the waist down, which was known as *nsalu mpamba* or *chikumba mseu* (a dirty white coarse khaki).[54] A few men wore short trousers probably with a shirt. Those who were employed in white peoples' households were given complete clothes in the form of uniforms so that they were "properly dressed". Apart from these were those employed in government institutions, Christian missions and schools who were also seen wearing ties and jackets, in many cases without shoes.[55]

It was in this setting that, despite holding secret meetings, members of PIM began to be identified in public by their clothing. Every female member wore *mpango ku mutu* (headscarf).[56] At that time women in the area did not wear headscarfs. They were still very new to the culture of the day. Wearing headscarfs has remained to date as *chizindikiro cha mpatuko* (identification of deviation), which causes the church to be commonly known as *Mpingo wa Mpatuko* (Church of deviation).[57] Women used whatever pieces of cloth they could find. It did not matter what type of cloth it was; so long as it was able to cover their heads.[58] They went to the extent of even tearing from their *zitenje* or old dresses or men's' shirts.[59] Headscarfs also led to the church being called *opha anthu* (those who kill people)[60] because the women were sneered at for carrying razor blades or knives under

---

[53] Int Eliamu Mlongoti Chijere Nyangu, Mchinji, 19.9.1999.
[54] Int Eliamu Mlongoti Chijere Nyangu, Mchinji, 19.9.1999.
[55] See Barbara Lamport-Stokes, *Blantyre: Glimpses of the Early Days*, Blantyre: Society of Malawi, 1989. See also pictures in Harry Langworthy, *Joseph Booth*, and, G. Shepperson and T. Price, *Independent African*, and the cover picture of John McCracken, *Politics and Christianity in Malawi 1875-1940*, Zomba: CLAIM, 2000.
[56] Int Ezina Kamdolozi, Matapila, 20.5.1999.
[57] Int Litida Kakhobwe, Katantha, 26.5.1999.
[58] Int Dalesi Lipenga, Mphindo, 7.6.1999.
[59] *Zitenje*, plural of *chitenje*, is a local name for pieces of cloth the women of Malawi and also Zambia, wrap around themselves over their dresses. The cloth is, in fact, multi-purpose. It can be used in place of a blanket, a mat or a handkerchief, and so on. It is usually worn at funerals.
[60] Int Ezina Kamdolozi, Matapila, 9.6.1999.

their headscarfs for killing people. They were also ridiculed as carrying *nyama ya anthu* (human flesh) *mu maduku* (under the headscarfs).

On the other hand *amuna amakulunga matayi* (men wound ties ie., they tied ties the way they knew best), or *kumanga zingwe pakhosi* (tying ropes on their necks, ie. the ties resembled ropes on the men's necks), and they also wore jackets. Most of these jackets were either not fitting or torn and dirty. Nevertheless, they wore them with pride and determination.[61] For many years in Mangoni people hardly knew the title PIM, instead it was popularly known as *Mpingo wa Mpatuko* by both Christians and non-Christians.[62]

Early Stalwarts of PIM in Mangoni

The second group of converts to PIM in Mangoni included Aaron Kamkalamba from Nyanje, and J. Kokha from Chikhanda.[63] These two men, especially, Kamkalamba, were to play a leading role in the founding and development of Achewa PIM. Chiphaka from Msondole was also to play a major role in the formative years of PIM in Mangoni.[64] He was a member of Nkhoma Mission[65] and had been to school there. He is known as one of the *zilimbilimbi* (stalwarts) of PIM in Mangoni.[66] Chiphaka was instrumental in the conversion of Harison Matapila and later his brother Joseph, and Aziri Kafulatira, all of whom were soon to become unwavering PIM leaders for a long time. They had all been members of Nkhoma mission.[67]

Harison Matapila, nicknamed "Kambanje", was a teacher at Matapila school under Nkhoma. He had also been a teacher at Bango and later at Chimango, also under Nkhoma.[68] Since Matapila was a teacher with Nkhoma he met with Chiphaka and Kalemba under the cover of the night at Mwachilolo. After a while he was able to convince his elder brother, Joseph, who was also a school teacher, to join Mpingo wa Mpatuko.[69] Although they met with Kalemba often, they did not officially join PIM for several years. They still went to Nkhoma to attend church. To leave Nkhoma would have meant losing their jobs

---

[61] Int Feliati Dirawo Kaunde, Matapila, 9.6.1999.
[62] Int Linesi Fulanki, Mphindo, 7.6.1999.
[63] Int Eliamu Mlongoti Chijere Nyangu, Mchinji, 19.9.1999.
[64] Int Foulger Kafulatira, Majondo, 21.5.1999.
[65] For its history see: Martin Pauw, *From Mission to Church. A History of Nkhoma Mission*, Zomba: Kachere, 2007.
[66] Int Litida Kakhobwe, Katantha, 26.5.1999.
[67] Int Foulger Kafulatira, Majondo, 21.5.1999.
[68] Int Ezina Kamdolozi, Matapila, 9.6.1999.
[69] Int Velina Kaunde, Matapila, 9.6.1999.

as teachers, which would also have meant loss of regular income, which would not have been easy for them and their families.[70]

Aziri Kafulatira, on the other hand, at first worked for *mbusa* A.L. Hofmeyr, a missionary at the Nkhoma Mission.[71] He lived at Nkhuwi Village on the other side of Nkhoma Mountain from the Hospital. By 1922 Kafulatira was a well respected and forceful teacher at Nkhoma. Though he continued to worship at Nkhoma, Kafulatira regularly met secretly with Kalemba and the other converts to PIM at Mwachilolo or at Matapila, mostly at night. It was only in 1924 that he officially left Nkhoma and joined Mpingo wa Mpatuko. In that very same year, Kafulatira was briefly arrested together with Kalemba and others. They were brought before the Lilongwe District Commissioner (DC), Foulger, who later released them.[72] When Kafulatira got home he found that his wife, Dareni, was with a baby boy, and they named him Foulger, after the DC. That marked the beginning of public meetings by PIM members.[73]

Public Meetings and Home Churches

From then on home churches began to flourish in Mangoni. Mpingo wa Mpatuko was now free to meet and worship openly during the day. Some of the men who immediately joined Mpingo wa Mpatuko included Dzoole from Mphanda, Nkhosa from Nkhosa Village, Tiopeyani from Msonthi, Chidoo from Chiumira, S. Kaphala from Msondole, Bizai Kachiwanda, and later his nephew, Andrew Mkute of Chiipira Village in Dedza District.[74] Kachiwanda never became a pastor, but just remained the leader (one who brought the church in the village, more or less thought of as the owner, *mwini wake wa mpingo*), but his wife, Magireti, became an elder.[75] Mkute was a deacon for a long time. The home churches were further strengthened by the message given by James Aggrey who spoke at Nkhoma and was attended by many people including these men.[76] People were hungry for new and

---

[70] Int Ezina Kamdolozi, Matapila, 9.6.1999.
[71] Int Foulger Kafulatira, Majondo, 21.5.1999.
[72] In that year several churches were able to petition the government to lift the ban on churches that followed the 1915 Rising. See also G.B. Shelburne, "History of the Church of Christ in Malawi", a paper presented in August 1978 at Namikango Bible School, p. 2.
[73] Int Foulger Kafulatira, Majombo, 21.5.1999.
[74] Int Linesi Bikisoni, Mphindo, 7.6.1999.
[75] Int Velina Kaunde, Matapila, 9.6.1999.
[76] Dr. James Aggrey was then Ghanain Vice Principal of Prince College at Achimoto. He was the white missionary's ideal black man, the educational

satisfying instruction. Kalemba's teaching was in a way endorsed by Aggrey's message, which made many more men *kupatuka* (to deviate or leave) instead of staying with Nkhoma. It was the opportune time for change.[77]

Two or more families would meet together in a home for worship and fellowship. The only church building was constructed at Nyangu instead of Kalumbu because Chief Kalumbu, who was Anderson Nyangu's *atsibweni* (mother's brother), did not want any trouble from the government.[78] Chief Nyangu Kabudula, Anderson's father's younger brother, accepted Mpingo wa Mpatuko in his village.[79] Despite this, it was 1928 before Eliamu Mlongoti Chijere became its first convert at Nyangu.[80] A small mud building with grass roof was erected there, east of present Mphanda church building. Sunday after Sunday members used to walk to and from Nyangu: for over five hours each way. That meant leaving home late on Saturday afternoon and returning late on Sunday afternoon. Soon services were being held from Saturday evening with an early Sunday morning worship service that ended early to allow the people to get home before dark. Most families were not able to attend church at Nyangu every Sunday. Some members were nursing mothers or had young children. With the introduction of house churches, all could attend meetings regularly. Their homes were accepted as chapels or houses of worship for the small bands of members of Mpingo wa Mpatuko.[81] In the late 1920s there were several home churches meeting; among these were Nyangu, Malapila, Mwachilolo, Nkhosa, Kampini, Senzani (near Mitundu TC), Nyanje and Nyangu in Dedza. Many more home churches were started and Mpingo wa Mpatuko was firmly established in Mangoni during the 1930s.

---

co-operator trusted on all sides, whose well-known idea of black and white cooperation to produce perfect harmony was exemplified by the black and white keys of the piano, that became the motto of Prince College. See also Adrian Hastings, *The Church in Africa 1450-1950*, Oxford: Clarendon, 1996, p. 604, and Baur, John, *2000 Years of Christianity in Africa: an African History 62 - 1992*, Nairobi: Paulines, 1994, p. 379. Dr Agreey visited in 1926 as a member of the Phelps – Stokes Commission on Education in Africa.

[77] Int Velina Khama, Mphindo, 7.6.1999.
[78] Int Emelesi Kuthedze, Nyangu, 11.9.1999.
[79] Int Letiya Dooko, Msemanjira, 10.6.1999.
[80] Int Daulosi Kuthedze, Nyangu, 11.9.1999.
[81] Int Lemia Yohane, Mphindo, 7.6.1999.

In-house Leadership Training

People in Mangoni respected and envied Kalemba because he was educated and knowledgeable beyond their expectations. He was welcomed in the area as a model of a successful African. Kalemba had taken advantage of the opportunities that Chilembwe and his school had offered and achieved a position very close to that of a white person. Many people began to encourage their children to study hard at school pointing to Kalemba's success as a goal.[82] With reference to his position and role in society and Mpingo wa Mpatuko, it was said, *Mphunzitsi akabwera, akaphunzitsa, anthu amamva* (When a teacher comes and he teaches, people listen).[83] That is exactly what happened when Kalemba introduced in-house training sessions for home church leaders and other interested parties.

These meetings were very informal and were held in the evenings, thus giving time for families to work on their fields or in their homes during the day. It was more like a chief summoning his *nduna* (counsellors) to a briefing before a public meeting.[84] That went down well with the people because they were used to such type of gatherings. In these meetings Kalemba taught what he thought his church leaders needed to know and practice. Nothing was written down: Kalemba used no notes and his students took no notes. Like in their culture, the participants were expected to memorize everything they learned from the teacher. What they learned was enforced as they put it into practice following the ideas and suggestions given to them by Kalemba. He also shared the Word of God and prayed with the church leaders. These meetings alternated between home churches.[85]

Relationship between Education and Culture

Gule wamkulu (also known as *Nyau*) has been one of the major obstacles affecting church growth and education in Mangoni.[86] *Gule wamkulu* is at the core of Chewa culture. Much of its teaching is centred on rites of passage which include the selection and appointment of chiefs.[87] Those who had not had some training through *Nyau* were treated as babies and harassed even to the point of death. *Gule*

---

[82] Int Anderson Chimlozi, Kalumbu, 26.10.1998.
[83] Int Velina Kaunde, Matapila, 9.6.1999.
[84] Int Yosofati Ndege, Chalendewa, 13.6.1998.
[85] Int Ezina Kamdolozi, Matapila, 20.5.1998.
[86] Christoff Martin Pauw, "Mission and Church in Malawi: The History of the Nkhoma Synod of the Church of Central Africa, Presbyterian 1889-1962", PhD, University of Stellenbosch, 1980, p. 85.
[87] Molly Longwe, *From Chinamwali to Chilangizo*, Zomba: Kachere, 2007.

wamkulu was further reinforced by the type of education system used by Nkhoma Mission that placed more emphasis on agriculture and village industries. Nkhoma resorted to training Africans for life in their villages, rather than the wider service for which they were prepared in Chiradzulu, and the other two Presbyterian Synods, Livingstonia and Blantyre. Their schools had six levels: Bolodi, Kaudzu, Mukeri, Mbiri ya Kale, Mbiri ya Tsopano, and Baibulo, all of which were taught in Chichewa. DRCM aimed at providing the masses with basic reading and writing skills to enable them to read the Bible, and only gave higher education to those who would be mission teachers. The DRCM was successful in the development of a widespread system of village schools, which became the backbone of DRC for many years, although objectively the educational value of such schools, whose Bible lessons constituted a large part of the daily school timetable, was not great.[88] Therefore *amati phunzireni, kenka kudambwe* (they used to attended classes briefly, and then went to the training centres for *Gule*).[89] That may be one explanation why Christians from Nkhoma Mission were not nearly so prominent in the national life as their counterparts from Blantyre and Livingstonia.[90] "*Adachi anatipusitsa*".[91] Nevertheless, with the arrival of Kalemba, education marked the advent of African independence in Mangoni. The hope for higher and better education was one causative factor for PIM in Lilongwe though the opposite materialized in the long run.

The Achewa community, in which mainly DRCM schools were established, had little or no share in the running of the schools and in the education of their children in these schools.[92] Children's experience in these schools was largely unrelated to the life of the community of their own background. It had little effect on the social development of his community as a whole. The Chewa people, like other African communities, were not called upon to contribute directly in any significant way to the development of the education of their children, except in such matters as helping in the construction or repair of school buildings. Parents simply left the running of the schools to the missionaries and the British colonial government, trusting that these Christian

---

[88] Christoff Martin Pauw, "Nkhoma Synod", pp. 153-155.
[89] Int Numeri Kamunthu, Kalumbu, 26.10.1998.
[90] John Weller and Jane Linden, *Mainstream Christianity to 1980 in Malawi, Zambia and Zimbabwe*, Gweru, Mambo, 1984, p. 115.
[91] Int Numeri Kamunthu, Kalumbu, 26.10.1998.
[92] Int Magi Kamunthu, Kalumbu, 26.10.1998. See also Erasto Muga, *African Response to Western Christian Religion: A Sociological Analysis of African Separatist Religious and Political Movements in East Africa*, Nairobi: East African Literature Bureau, 1975, p. 90.

missionaries were competent to deal with the educational affairs involved. The educational system was not geared to the needs of Africans as conceived by the Africans themselves.[93]

Before the introduction of DRCM schools, the education of a Chewa child was the responsibility of the parents in the family, clan and the tribe: and that embraced the fundamental moral, religious, cultural, economic, social and political elements that were in accord with the Chewa traditional way of life. New values, skills and concepts, unknown to the Achewa people, were introduced by the new educational system from the West. Though that was not entirely bad, it forced the child to be divorced from his own value system and adopt those values that were foreign. *Gule wamkulu* reacted strongly against Western education to the extent of using force against children who joined foreign systems of instruction.[94]

Through Kalemba, Chilembwe was successful in spreading his nets for both educated and uneducated converts outside the Yao and Lomwe tribes. In Mangoni, Kalemba's first move was to attract people of influence to join him in the work of evangelizing the neighbourhood. He shared with the people what he had learnt from Chilembwe which they saw and admired. Through his lifestyle and teaching, Kalemba attempted to offer to the people better living standards, and a new kind of relationship through the Word of God. Unfortunately, the Chilembwe Rising slowed down the process as the church went underground. The demolition of New Jerusalem Church did not end Chilembwe's missionary enterprise. During the next five years Kalemba was able to win a handful of faithful men, some of whom had received education from a CCAP Nkhoma Synod schools. They could be compared to Duncan Njilima, David Kaduya and Gray Kufa who availed themselves for admission into Chilembwe's church. Kalemba also won the loyalty and adherence of members of his extended family. As time went on, more people, both educated and non-educated, young and old, joined Mpingo wa Mpatuko. Kalemba spent considerable time in leadership training and fellowship. Despite lifting of the ban on church meetings by the government in 1924, both black and white people were still suspicious of African-led and other small churches. Until very recently, Chilembwe's church in Mangoni was called Mpingo wa Mpatuko.

---

[93] Erasto Muga, *African Response*, p. 92.
[94] This is not the full historical truth about DRCM educational system (see Pauw, *Nkhoma Synod*,) but this is how it was seen from the point of view. the Chewa people.

Chapter 2
The Origin and Expansion of Achewa PIM

The Re-opening of PIM at Mbombwe

Nobody at Chiradzulu thought of informing Malikebu about the 1915 Rising until late in 1919, when he was ready to return to Malawi. That was when he learned of the destruction of the Mission at Mbombwe and the disappearance of Chilembwe. In spite of the troubles at home, Malikebu was determined to join his people. Some church members in the USA were not ready to help him in his preparation for the journey back to Chiradzulu because they fear for his: life, nevertheless those who did not know about the Rising assisted him. In 1924 Malikebu and his wife, Flora, left the USA for Malawi through Beira to Nsanje. There they were asked by an immigration officer to surrender all their correspondence, passports, certificates and diplomas from all the colleges they had attended in the USA. These were sent to the Governor in Zomba while they waited in Nsanje. The Malikebus were denied permission to enter Malawi and re-open the Mission because of their link with Chilembwe. In spite of this, they were given 5 to 6 days to visit the country.[1] The Malikebus then went to Cape Town where they stayed for about 9 months before going to Liberia under Lott Carey Baptist Foreign Mission. Malikebu had become acquainted -with Lott Carey FMB during his travels between 1919 and 1921.[2] They joined NBC Inc in 1924 as a way of smoothing disagreements between Lott Carey and NBC FMB.[3]

In the meantime Chilembwe's PIM and several other Churches such as the Churches of Christ and the Seventh Day Baptists that had been closed by the colonial government, continued to meet in secret. Some devout followers of Chilembwe who had remained in the country had been meeting quietly in their homes just as in Mangoni. It was in 1924, after permission had been sought from the Government,

---

[1] Mtewa, "Tribute to Malikebu", p. 8.
[2] Saunders, "A History of Baptists", p. 28.
[3] M. Mtewa, "Tribute to Dr Malikebu", *The Enquirer*, Vol. 1 No. (6 September 1993), p. 5.

that PIM started to operate openly again.⁴ This marked a new era of PIM's growth. Leaders of PIM wrote to NBC requesting them to send missionaries to Chiradzulu. In 1925 Malikebu and Flora were in the USA under the NBC Inc FMB. They arrived in Chiradzulu in 1926.⁵

On 3 June of the same year, Malikebu convened a meeting of the followers of Chilembwe and other interested persons. At the end of the discussions they decided to re-establish the Mission of John Chilembwe on the very site and continue the work that he had begun.⁶ The people began to mold bricks and immediately commenced work on the construction of a church building and the Malikebus' house. A number of people were converted and baptized and some later became prominent members of PIM. These included L.C. Muocha.⁷

The Resumption of Ties between Chiradzulu and Mangoni

In 1926, as members at Mbombwe were engrossed in making bricks for the rebuilding and expansion of the Mission, they were somehow reminded of the bricks that had been made and hidden away before the Chilembwe Rising. Those present were not sure of the location but were very positive of the large number of bricks that, if they were found, would make life easier for them, as well as hasten the re-establishment of the Mission.⁸ The extent of the destruction of the Mission and the debris on the area made it difficult for people to locate the bricks. They decided to get some help from outside the Mission from those who were there before the Rising. Efforts were made to send word around in search of those who might have some clue as to where the bricks were hidden. Soon requests for help reached Kalemba. Instead of going to Mbombwe himself he sent Kamkalamba with a sketch showing the location of the bricks. Before Kamkalamba left, Kalemba briefed him well.⁹ With the help of those who were at Mbombwe, Kamkalamba was able to locate the site of the bricks. That episode marked the beginning of another chapter of the rela-

---

4 Patrick Makondesa, *The Church History of Providence Industrial Mission*, Zomba: Kachere, 2006, pp. 160ff.
5 Leory Fitts, *A History of Black Baptists*, p.139.
6 Patrick Makondesa, *The Church History of Providence Industrial Mission*, pp. 160-172
7 Makondesa, Patrick., "The Life and Ministry of Rev and Mrs Muocha of Providence Industrial Mission", BA, University of Malawi, 1996, p. 2.
8 Int Magi Numeri, Kalumbu, 26.10.1998.
9 Int Yosofati Ndege, 13.6.1998.

tionship between Chiradzulu and Mangoni. Kalemba and Malikebu began to work closely together.[10]

The First Baptism Service Conducted by Malikebu in Mangoni

In the same year Malikebu visited Mangoni. This became an annual event except when he was outside the country. From its beginning up to this time, no Mpingo wa Mpatuko convert had been baptized: Kalemba only welcomed them into the new church. Most of the Mangoni PIM members were baptized on this trip by Malikebu in Linthipe River.[11] No young person was baptized during this first baptism by PIM in Mangoni.[12] Immediately Malikebu was recognized as the head of the church both in Chiradzulu and Mangoni. His position and acceptance as the head of PIM in Malawi was further strengthened by his having one of Chilembwe's first students at Mbombwe, and that Malikebu had been to America where Chilembwe had been, that he had brought with him an Afro-American wife, and that he was driving a car and not walking like Kalemba, and that he had financial support just as Chilembwe had from the American church. Kalemba placed himself and his congregations under the leadership of Malikebu who was then re-building Mbombwe whence both men could trace their roots.[13] For him that was the best thing he could do for Mpingo wa Mpatuko since he knew what Chiradzulu, and of course Malikebu, would offer in terms of spiritual, moral and material support. He had no doubt Mpingo wa Mpatuko was PIM as were those churches growing in and around Mbombwe. Kalemba was invited to visit Chiradzulu to see what was going on and for fellowship.

In 1927 another group of converts were baptized, but the most interesting baptism was that of 1928. That was as a result of the introduction of a Bible School in which men systematically learnt the word of God through those who had had some training under Malikebu. The meeting was held at Kalumbu, and the baptism was done in a dug-out *chitsime* (pool),.where, Malikebu baptized three hundred candidates in one day.[14] There were more women than men baptized on that day, a trend that has remained so till today. It was a cold day, so some members collected *mapesi* (maize stalks) and put up a fire for Malikebu to warm himself half way through the baptism ceremony. He baptized 150 in the morning and the other half in the after-

---

[10] Int Lositala Vizi, Phatha, 20.10.1998.
[11] Int Ezina Kamdolozi, Matapila, 20.5.1999.
[12] Int Adiresi Kampangire, Katantha, 26.5.1999.
[13] Int Magi Kamunthu, Kalumbu, 26.10.1998.
[14] Int Eliamu Mlongoti Chijere Nyangu, Mchinji, 19.9.1999.

noon.[15] In 1930 and 1931, Malikebu baptized in a *dziwe* (pool) in Namanyanga Stream and in Linthipe River at Chiipira respectively. Some of the first young people to be baptized during the 1930s included John Mkomba, William Njawayawa, Lindadi Tambala and Eliyamu Nyangu. They were from the Kalumbu-Nyangu area.[16]

Children and Baptism

Right from the beginning, children were never baptized.[17] Most of the converts were old men and women, later followed by young adults. There was no question of baptizing young children, though many had been members of Nkhoma Mission before joining Mpingo wa Mpatuko. People were serious about conversion. Baptism was only for those who had made a decision to divert from the ordinary and join this strange church. Most children followed their parents. One of the differences between Nkhoma and the new church had been established and accepted, and that was baptism by immersion and regenerate church membership. Children were brought to Malikebu and he blessed them.[18] Among the many things that happened in the five or so years of good working relationship that passed, was leadership training.[19]

Leadership Training under Malikebu

Kafulatira interpreted for Malikebu on his first trip to Mangoni. He made such an impression that Malikebu invited him to study at the Mission. Before the end of 1926 Kafulatira was studying at Mbombwe under Malikebu. He was there for a year studying *ulaliki* (preaching).[20] In 1926 Aliyele Biswick Kakhobwe went to Nyangu to study under Kalemba, but in 1927 he went to Chiradzulu. Kakhobwe was already married and had several children.[21] From then on he assisted Kalemba in in-house teaching of church leaders. In 1928 Kafulatira, Chiphaka and two other men, who could only be remembered as Msuzi and Mfumu Village headman Salima, attended a meeting that was called for the laying of the cornerstone of the New Jerusalem Baptist Church

---

15 Int Daulosi Kuthedze, Nyangu, 11.9.1999.
16 Int Adiresi Kampangire, Katantha, 26.5.1999.
17 Int Ezina Kamdolozi, Matapila, 20.5.1999.
18 Int Eliamu Mlogoti Chijere Nyangu, Mchinji, 19.09 1999.
19 Int Yosofati Ndege, Chalendewa, 4.6.1998.
20 Int Foulger Kafulatira, Majondo, 21.5.1999.
21 Int Eliamu Mlongoti Chijere Nyangu, Mchinji, 19.9.1999.

at Mbombwe.²² While the rest returned home after the meeting, Kafulatira remained there to study under Malikebu until 1933. During that period he only visited Mangoni a couple of times during vacation. In that same year the entire Kafulatira clan moved to Kalumba south of Bunda College of Agriculture and east of Mitundu TC. He later took his family out of Kalumba and built his own village, which he called Majondo. Kafulatira's reason for this was that he wanted to have the freedom to preach what he believed. His parents were still members of Nkhoma Mission while the majority of the people of Kalumba participated in *Gule wamkulu*.²³ Although he worked as a court clerk at Chadza from 1936, Kafulatira was very committed to preaching and teaching. His first assignment in Mangoni was that of a home missionary. In fact Kafulatira became known as *mlaliki wa kumudzi* (village preacher).²⁴ He was also a talented teacher. Some of his outstanding students were Matthew Ndalama, Feniasi (also known as Peter) Kalonga, Charles Kamchiliko, Peturo Chimpesa and Anderson Zingano.²⁵

In the same year, following the success of Kafulatira in his training, Kalemba sent the first group of six people to study for ministerial and teaching offices under Malikebu. Some of the men dropped out of the course altogether while others failed to qualify. When they went back to Mangoni the men did not help Kalemba as was expected of them. Another group of six men was sent to Chiradzulu for training, and like the first team, nothing good materialized from the courses.²⁶ One reason might have been that Malikebu was very selective and only ordained one or two candidates at a time as a way of letting people believe that the courses were of high standard; and therefore that only those who worked hard deserved the recognition.²⁷ It might have helped if Malikebu had been sensitive to the events in Mangoni and allowed a fen from Mangoni to qualify because there was a great need for more workers there who had the backing of Chiradzulu as Kalemba and Kafulatira had. Mpingo wa Mpatuko was surrounded by other churches that were involved in the training of their church members, who were recognized and given support as they spread the word in their areas. Mangoni PIM had put all their hope in

---

²² Int Ezina Kamdolozi, Matapila, 21.5.1999. See also Sauders, "A History of Baptists", p. 31 and Patrick Makondesa, *The Church History of Providence Industrial Mission*, Zomba: Kachere, 2006, pp. 168ff.
²³ Int Foulger Kafulatira, Majondo, 21.5.1999.
²⁴ Int Yosofati Ndege, Chalendewa, 13.6.1999.
²⁵ Int Peturo Chimpesa, Nkhulawe, 23.10.1998.
²⁶ A.H. Kafulatira, "Ciyambi ca Mpingo wa Achewa Providence Indus¬trial Mis-sion Kudera la Lilongwe".
²⁷ Patrick Makondesa, "Muocha", p. 12.

Chiradzulu, and this was not what they had expected to get from there: failures and drop-outs. School or no school certification, these men should have continued to serve the church as before they went to Chiradzulu.[28]

Mpingo wa Mpatuko and Women

Although many women came on their own, a good number followed their husbands to Mpingo wa Mpatuko with little or no to say in the decision.[29] The first faithfuls moved from Nkhoma Mission and joined Mpingo wa Mpatuko. They were the foundation upon which the new church was built. Despite not being recognized publicly, the wives were, in the hearts of most men, appreciated as having contributed to the founding and development of Mpingo wa Mpatuko.[30] On the other hand, the public physically saw and understood Mpingo wa Mpatuko by the presence of women and girls wearing *maduku*.[31] Women were the ones who unimpededly stood up against ridicule and intimidation, and they should be considered as the real foundation of the church during its formative years. In spite of that, they were not immediately included in the training programmes which Kalemba and/or Malikebu conducted, and therefore, not included in the government of Mpingo wa Mpatuko.[32] Women were thought of as being inferior, both intellectually and physically and that their right place was considered to be child rearing and homemaking, and listening to their men teach in church or speak in public places. In spite of women out-numbering men, they were expected to act in the background, not as co-players, but as support teams or caring teams or even observers.[33] *Ndi zokhumudwitsa kuti mpingo wa tonse amuna akhala akuutenga ngati wa iwo okha* (It's annoying that men have taken charge of the church that belongs to us all).[34] In a way that is why *mpingo unapulukira* (the church went astray): because it left the women behind without education and without participation in church government right from the beginning.[35] "*Mphunzitsani mkazi ndipo*

---

[28] Following Baptist principles, Malikebu could easily have ordained men irrespective of their educational attainments
[29] Int Letiya Dooko, Msemanjira, 10.6.1999.
[30] Int Oliva Chisemphere, Kalumbu, 24.10.1998.
[31] Int Letiya Dooko, Msemanjira, 10.6.1999.
[32] Int Erika Matewere, Lilongwe, 28.5.1999.
[33] Int Elikana Ngalawo, Mphindo, 7.6.1999.
[34] Int Velina Kaunde, Matapila, 9.6.1999.
[35] Int Litida Kakhobwe, Katantha, 26.5.1999.

mwaphunzitsa mtundu wonse" (Teach a woman and you have taught the whole nation).[36]

In the Chewa culture the teaching of important things in a woman's life was entrusted to special female teachers called *anankungwi*. These were highly respectable, elderly and experienced members of society.[37] With the girls coming of age, older women in the church acted as *anankungwi* who were later to be known as *alangizi* (counsellors). Their main task was to counsel the girls who had come of age.[38] They had no uniform or any other attire to identify them as counsellors, as the role became part of APIM from the beginning of the 1940s, when all the women wore floor length white dresses with long sleeves.[39]

Mpingo wa Mpatuko and Children

Children were and still are woman's responsibility, in church and elsewhere, and at home.[40] The church provided no activities specifically for children. They were seen as the extension of the families and *mpingo* in the long run. Despite supposedly being the future of the church, nothing serious was being done to prepare them.[41] While at home children were taught and encouraged to participate in the activities around the home, Mpingo wa Mpatuko did not apply that rationale with the children who came to church.[42] Although there were several former Nkhoma Mission teachers, Mpingo wa Mpatuko never considered starting their own schools and using these teachers to teach the children. They went on to attend Nkhoma Mission schools or Roman Catholic schools which were also beginning to penetrate the area. That was the best Mpingo wa Mpatuko could do for their children.[43] As time proved, not many of these children went further than four years in secondary school because of lack of encouragement

---

[36] Int Beti Chalinda, Falls Estate, 3.10.1998.
[37] For more discussion on this see Isabel Apawo Phiri, *Women, Presbyterainism and Patriarchy*, Blantyre: CLAIM, 1997, pp. 34-36.
[38] For details see: Molly Longwe, *From Chinamwali to Chilangizo*, Zomba: Kachere, 2007.
[39] Inter Velina Kaunde, Matapila, 9.6.1999.
[40] Int Velina Khama, Mphindo, 7.6.1999.
[41] Int Peturo Chimpesa, Nkhalawe, 23.10.1998.
[42] Int Magi Kamunthu, Kalumbu, 26.10.1998.
[43] Int Feliati Dirawo Kaunde, Matapila, 9.6.1999.

and participation in the world around them where they could have otherwise used what they had learnt.[44]

Children of members of Mpingo wa Mpatuko were living in a different era from that of their parents. The period of their parents was described as *nthawi yakumva* (a period of listening and doing).[45] The children had less faith than their parents had. At the same time *mpingo umayenda mmdima* (the church met secretly); it was a difficult time so parents could not think of the education of their children.

Church Government of PIM in Mangoni

For efficient management and operation of PIM churches, Malikebu grouped them into sections, which were directly under the central church, New Jerusalem Baptist Church, the Mission. Congregations in Lilongwe/Dedza were designated as one section. Though Kalemba was not an ordained pastor, Malikebu recognized him as the leader of Lilongwe section, but the mission did not financially support him.[46] The Mangoni section had its central church at Nyangu. A supervisory committee which was composed of Kalemba and church leaders was responsible for the affairs of the section. Each church leader reported to the committee on the daily activities of the local congregation under his supervision. Any issue that the local congregation failed to agree upon or solve was referred to the section supervisory committee.[47] This committee was also responsible for ensuring that all the funds collected from the local churches were forwarded to Mbombwe on time.[48]

Each local congregation was called an out-station and was under the leadership of a *mkulu wa mpingo* (elder), who was a mature man, respected and expected to be knowledgeable. He was the one who guided the congregation and he was supposed to teach and nurture the church. The elder was assisted by a church monitor whose responsibilities included the collection, counting and recording of local church funds, which he later sent to Mbombwe via the central church at Nyangu. One or two women were also part of the local church

---

[44] Up to 1998 only one family, the Kamchedzeras, managed to produce college graduates because of the father's interest in education and insistence that his children learn, in order that they take up their rightful positions in life though he himself never had much education.
[45] Int Velina Kaunde, Matapila, 9.6.1999.
[46] Int Magi Kamunthu, Kalumbu, 26.10.1998.
[47] Int Peturo Chimpesa, Nkhulawe, 23.10.1998.
[48] Int Alexina Lenadi, Gondwa, 10.10.1998

leadership as *alangizi*. That was purely from Chewa culture; *kulangiza kwake kunali kwa chikunja* (the counselling was done from a purely cultural perspective).[49] These women participated in the decision making process at the local and sectional church levels, but the final resolution lay in the hands of the elders.[50]

Construction of Church Buildings

Chiefs were not consulted regarding the founding of churches in their areas until after 1924 when PIM and other churches were free to operate again. From then on chiefs were always consulted in the establishment of congregations and in the construction of church buildings in the areas under their control. Section leaders first approached the chiefs for permission to hold meetings in their areas. When permission was granted the chiefs were also responsible for allocating land to erect a church building. The chiefs who accepted Mpingo wa Mpatuko in their areas often assisted in informing the villagers about the meetings. Some churches were established through evangelistic meetings, while others began with requests from a member living in the area. In some cases there were churches within walking distance, but some members were isolated because there were no churches nearby. In every the case, chiefs were consulted, since the ground on which the people were to meet and later build was under their jurisdiction.[51] Once the chief had allocated APIM a site, a day was chosen and announced on which the church building profile was going to be set out. The pastor or pastors of the section in which the building was going to be built were responsible for all the arrangements concerning the setting out of the building profile On the day of the setting, Scriptures that related to church building were read and explained, then the leading pastor would tell the people to hold hands as a form of measuring tape. This was also a sign of unity among the member.[52] Once the pastor had drawn the size of the building on the ground, other men followed and marked the border with hoes. A few days later the builder would lay the foundation and build the church.[53]

---

[49] Int Velina Kaunde, Matapila, 9.6.1999.
[50] Int Yosofati Ndege, Chalendewa, 4.6.1998.
[51] Int W. Thomasi, pastor, Mwase church, 21.10.1998.
[52] Int Feliati Dirawo Kaunde, Matapila, 9.6.1999.
[53] See Plate 2 for the common design of the church buildings since then.

A typical APIM church building

Mpingo wa Mpatuko Breaks Ties with Chiradzulu

The success and growth of Mpingo wa Mpatuko was possible because of the personal relations and close social ties that Kalemba could provide. He also provided basic first aid to the sick, probably from his experience and training at Mbombwe.[54] He was a pastor at heart. Kalemba's lifestyle led the followers to love him so much that they called him *mtsogoleri wodabwitsa* (a wonderful leader).[55] His style of authority was very informal, a "camaraderie". And he was very patient even when his instructions were not carried out.[56]

Kalemba saw his accomplishments in Mangoni as PIM achievements. He understood himself as a member of PIM, and therefore, a Baptist.[57] Throughout the years of his relationship with Mbombwe, Kalemba followed PIM church polity. He led the church in Mangoni under the leadership of Malikebu such that Kalemba had no final authority on certain issues such as church offerings and tithes. These had

---

[54] Int Foulger Kafulatira, Majondo, 21.5.1999.
[55] Int Ezina Kamdolozi, Matapila, 20.5.1999.
[56] Int Linesi Bikisoni, Mphindo, 7.6.1999.
[57] Int Foulger Kafulatira, Majondo, 21.5.1999.

to go to Mbombwe without fail. This was not new to Kalemba, since he had learnt it from the Chilembwe era. It was then taught and implemented in the Mpingo wa Mpatuko following Malikebu's visit in 1926.[58] Kalemba was not on the payroll of PIM because he was not an ordained minister: and yet, there were other Mission workers, such as teachers, who received some salary.[59] Malikebu could have paid Kalemba as a teacher or any other worker under the Mission as a way of showing appreciation for what he had done and was still doing for the congregations in Mangoni on behalf of PIM. At his age, Kalemba would not have gone back to school: instead he sent younger men to study under Malikebu who was probably his age mate. Though Mpingo wa Mpatuko wanted to assist their *mtsogoleri* using church funds when he had a need, they could not do it. That forced some church members to begin to question the reasoning behind sending all the offerings to Chiradzulu and not keeping some for the local ministry and support for their leadership.[60]

This extreme centralization is a feature of PIM, but it contradicts worldwide Baptist principles.[61] It is also a feature of NBC Inc, with its history of strong presidents. The president serves as the chief executive officer, and over the years this office has acquired enormous power. The president almost single handedly controls the convention. Usually the presidents serve for life or until poor health sidelines them.[62] NBC is more centralized than SBC who are shaped and identified by their commitment to the autonomy of the local church.[63] SBC does realize, however, that as with all biblical principles, there is the potential for distortion and misapplication. The principle understood correctly gives no justification for church teaching or practice that is unorthodox and destructive. Baptists have for long not found theological and/or historical support for ecclesiastical hierarchy. They contend that passages of Scripture suggest that God's design and intent for the local church was that it functions under the direct authority of God and without any outside authoritative ecclesiastical body. That is to say, the whole congregation: under the Lordship of Jesus Christ: has the final say over its life and affairs, including the appointment of its lead-

---

[58] Int Yosofati Ndege, Chalendewa, 4.6.1998.
[59] Int Feliati Dirawo Kaunde, Matapila, 9.6.1999.
[60] Int Yosofati Ndege, Chalendewa, 4.6.1998.
[61] See "Civil Case No. 319 of 1977", p. 6; and H. Leon McBeth, *The Baptist Heritage: Four Centuries of Baptist Witness*, Nash-ville: Broadman, 1987, pp. 121-122.
[62] H. Leaon Mcbeth, *Baptist Heritage*, pp. 786-787.
[63] Robert A. Baker, *A Baptist Source Book with Particular Reference to Southern Baptists*, Nashville: Broadman, 1966, p. 214.

ers. While the Bible depicts the local church as independent of outside human authority, it also presents evidence that God designed his church to function as part of a larger fellowship, so all churches joined in the bond of Jesus Christ. Therefore churches have the opportunity and obligation to relate to each other as partners on various levels. The core of Baptist heritage is the recognition of the Lord's authority over each autonomous local church. Baptist churches are ready to cooperate with other churches in broad ventures and to be accountable for biblical fidelity.[64]

In 1934 an opportunity came for Mpingo wa Mpatuko to challenge PIM church government. Kalemba was in need.[65] His home life was in such difficulty so that he borrowed some money from the church what was known as the "Poor Saints Collection". It was Nkhosa, Fanuel Senzani and Chikumba who asked Kalemba, "*Musauka ndi njala bwanji?* (Why are you afflicted by hunger)?[66] They were saying to Kalemba that they saw no reason why he should go without the basic necessities of life while the resources were at his disposal. Kalemba concurred, and each man borrowed £2. In addition Mpingo wa Mpatuko bought a bicycle for Kalemba to use as a means of transport since he was walking long distances visiting the congregations.[67] Kalemba was perceived as a poor saint' who deserved the support of the church. Mbombwe was seen as *kugwirilira* (oppressing) Mpingo wa Mpatuko.[68] Nkhosa, Senzani and Chikumba went behind Kalemba's back and quietly informed Mbombwe of what had transpired in Mangoni; and when the money did not arrive as usual, Malikebu, as the leader of PIM, accused Kalemba of mismanaging church funds.[69] Malikebu also felt the action taken by Mangoni churches as *mipingo kugalukira* (churches usurping [the power of]) Mbombwe.[70] Immediately Kalemba paid a part of the credit back, and promised to pay the rest as soon as he could, but that was not acceptable to Malikebu.[71]

---

[64] Morris H. Chapman, president and chief executive officer of the Executive Committee, SBC, "Local Church Autonomy", SBC life, December 1997, pp. 4-5. See also C. Maritn Pauw, "Nkhoma Synod", p. 283, and compare. The PIM practice, though, differed from general Baptist practice and the churches in Mangoni, had to come to terms with that.
[65] A.H. Kafulatira, "*Chiyambi cha Achewa PIM*".
[66] Int Eliamu Mlongoti Chijere Nyangu, Mchinji, 19.9.1999.
[67] Int Foulger Kafulatira, Majondo, 21.5.1999.
[68] Int Ezina Kamdolozi, Matapila, 20.5.1999.
[69] Int Yosofati Ndege, Chalendewa, 13.6.1998.
[70] Int Foulger Kafulatira, Majondo, 21.5.1999.
[71] Int Kafulatira, "*Chiyambi cha Achewa PIM*".

Instead he sent a team from Mbombwe, led by Kanyore to sort out the matter with Mpingo wa Mpatuko, and especially with Kalemba himself. The team from Mbombwe met with the Mpingo wa Mpatuko that was at the time meeting at Chivuluvulu, upstream Diamphwe in Dedza. They excommunicated Kalemba and took away the bicycle Mpingo wa Mpatuko had bought for him.[72] Kalemba failed to understand why Malikebu was fussing over such a little amount that had been used with the blessing of those who had donated the money. Almost the entire Mpingo wa Mpatuko was not happy with the way Malikebu had handled the issue. According to Kalemba, Malikebu's action showed no appreciation for the work that he was doing in the life of PIM, and in particular for Mpingo wa Mpatuko.[73]

Up until that time Malikebu had established himself as the sole owner of PIM. His name meant PIM; there was no PIM without Malikebu.[74] He had absolute authority over PIM, as opposed to Kalemba who was a servant leader. It may be seen partly because people at Mbombwe had respected Malikebu so much that he took advantage of their lack of knowledge of the world around them. Probably Malikebu's love for self-glorification and money caused him to not let go of what he thought was his responsibility, for example the use of some church funds to support his immediate helpers such as Kalemba.

Perhaps Malikebu was reacting from an American set of expectations. It should not have been a strain for Malikebu to remind himself of the significant factors of an African point of view.[75] He had forgotten that he was in a different logic system with a different order of priorities. Instead of being slow to act, Malikebu acted in haste. He did not even have time to sit down and talk things out with Kalemba who was the founder and leader of the church that Malikebu was now heading. Malikebu made a serious mistake when he used confrontation as a way of pointing out deficiencies of another leader. Consider the proverb, *"Njovu zikamamenyana umabvutika ndi udzu"* (When elephants fight, the grass gets hurt). That is exactly what happened to

---

[72] Int Foulger Kafulatira, Majondo, 21.5.1999.
[73] A.H. Kafulatira, *"Chiyambi cha Achewa PIM"*
[74] See John Parratt, "Mbombwe Revisited: Dr. Daniel Malikebu and the Sec¬ond Era of the Providence Industrial Mission", a history seminar paper, University of Malawi, 29 January 1985, p. 3; and Patrick Makondesa, "Muocha", p. 2, 3.
[75] A white man with a black skin, a black person who behaves like a white person.

Mpingo wa Mpatuko, they were abused and wounded by Malikebu; directive.

The issue of money was later discussed and resolved.[76] Kalemba was asked to come back into the church for the sake of PIM in Mangoni. After his return, Kalemba divorced Magireti and married Elineti from Chikumba, across Linthipe in Dedza District, before Mayani. Elineti was formerly a wife to Samsoni Makunganya, who had gone to Zimbabwe in search of work and had remained there ever since (*kuchona*).[77] When Malikebu heard about this he urged Kalemba to leave Elineti and remain with Magireti. Kalemba had given no reason for divorcing her, therefore, it was not acceptable. Above all it was sin. Before the issue could be discussed, Kalemba wrote a letter *kulawira* (taking leave of) Malikebu in which he said he had left Mpingo wa Mpatuko and was going to join Dachi Rifometi (Dutch Reformed; DRCM at Nkhoma, now Church of Central Africa Presbyterian [CCAP], Nkhoma Synod).[78] He wanted to be among Christians (despite not following Christian teaching on marriage and divorce), while he decided what to do next and Nkhoma was his choice. Kalemba did not go to Nkhoma Mission as a new convert but as *mkristu wakugwa* (transgressed Christian) needing reconciliation with the church. Elineti was a member of Nkhoma. It is not known why she was not disciplined them by.[79] It is unclear whether Kalemba was reconciled with Nkhoma Synod, but it is known that he was there for several months. Nevertheless there is a hint that he became involved, since he was not new to Nkhoma and the people.[80]

Mpingo wa Mpatuko could not accept losing Kalemba just like that after all that he had done and all that he meant to them. Kamkalamba and Kokha approached Kalemba *kuti asalekane nawo anthu ake* (he should not separate from his people). Kalemba told them that he was not going to go back to Mpingo wa Mpatuko; he had had enough of Malikebu and the people across the Shire River. He told Kamkalamba and Kokha that *aganizire njira ina* (that they should think of another way) to overcome the problem.[81] Kamkalamba, Kokha, Kafulatira, the two Matapila brothers Joseph and Harison, Chiphaka, and other leaders decided to organize themselves into a new

---

[76] Int Daulosi S. Kuthedze, Nyangu, 11.9.1999.
[77] Int Eliamu Mlongoti Chijere Nyangu, Mchinji, 19.9.1999.
[78] Int Lositala Vizi, Phatha, 20.10.1999. See also A.H. Kafulatira, "*Chiyambi cha Achewa PIM*".
[79] Int K.J. Mgawi, Kasungu, 2.6.1992.
[80] Int Foulger Kafulatira, Majondo, 21.5.1999.
[81] Int Eliamu Mlongoti Chijere Nyangu, Mchinji, 19.9.1999.

church. That meant that no offering money was to go to Mbombwe, and that they were going to use it as they felt fit.[82] *Pafupi fupi mpingo wonse unagumuka* (Almost the entire church left PIM).[83] They beseeched Kalemba to leave Nkhoma Synod and lead the new church as before, without the interference of Malikebu and others across Nyanja (Shire River). Mpingo wa Mpatuko choose Kalumbu as the interim central church since it was Kalemba's home and that would signal to him how serious the people were about the new church.[84] They kept petitioning Kalemba *tichite wathu mpingo* (let us pattern our own church).[85]

Realizing what he had already achieved and the support he still enjoyed amongst Mpingo wa Mpatuko membership, Kalemba yielded to their wish. Nkhoma knew what had happened and what was going on because it was the talk of the day. At last, when Kalemba decided to leave, he was asked to pay 10 British shillings to Nkhoma. To Mpingo wa Mpatuko it was like *kusudzula pa gulu* (breaking the relationship in public) *tambala wawo* (between their rooster [leader] and Nkhoma).[86] The idea behind a public denunciation was that all present were witnesses and that, Kalemba wanted to come back to Nkhoma he would have to say so in public. Nevertheless if things had reached that far, there was no sign of return.[87] Mpingo wa Mpatuko was prepared to pay because Kalemba was the only one they had who could lead the group; he was knowledgeable and respected by all. The time was ripe and the separation from Mbombwe was a foregone conclusion. Kalemba's move back to his church was the final step of separation.[88]

In 1935 Kalemba and his leadership team had a series of discussions with chiefs Mazengera and Kalumbu at which the issue of separation from PIM in Chiradzulu was discussed. Both parties later met with the DC, of Lilongwe. Mpingo wa Mpatuko initially chose "Ache-

---

[82] Int Anderson Chimlozi, Kalumbu, 26.10.1998.
[83] Int Velina Kaunde, Matapila, 9.6.1999.
[84] Int David Tsokonombwe, Nyanje, 20.6.1998.
[85] Int Numeri Kamunthu, Kalumbu, 26.10.1998.
[86] Int Lositala Vizi, Phatha, 20.10.1998.
[87] This was done only after all the avenues of reconciliation had been exhausted, because after a public denunciation, a return to normal friendship was never in sight. One was called a fool (*chitsiru*) if ever one tried to come back after having rejected the other in public. Matters of relationship between spouses were expected to be done *mu nyumba yomata* (in a plastered house, that is, with sound-proof walls). What was discussed in private was not for public consumption.
[88] A.H. Kafulatira, "*Chiyambi cha Achewa PIM*"

wa" as its name but that was not accepted; they had to add PIM at the end of the name.[89] This was deliberate on the part of the DC who wanted to remind Mpingo wa Mpatuko of their roots. On 19 October 1937 the Achewa PIM (APIM) was registered with the Lilongwe DC who represented the government.[90] Kalemba chose Nyanje as the site for APIM's central office.[91]

The Name "Achewa"

The name "Achewa" is said not to be tribal, but to be inclusive of all people.[92] It may basically represent the people who founded the church, or the people among whom the church was planted. It may be compared to the Catholic church, which is described as "Roman"; and the Reformed Church, which is described as "Dutch". Although APIM does not restrict its membership to Achewa only, there are not many people from other tribes who are members. Non-Chewa members of APIM are there mainly because of marriage. APIM might also be compared to the Anglican Church in Malawi which, for a long time was perceived as *mpingo wa anthu aku Likoma* (the church of the people from Likoma Island).[93] Another example is that of the CCAP Harare Synod, which was started by and exists for Malawians

---

[89] Int Lositala Vizi, Phatha, 20.10.1998.
[90] A.H. Kafulatira, *"Chiyambi cha Achewa PIM"*. There is no record of APIM'S registration with the Registrar General's office in Blantyre. Frank Chibisa, the Chief Examination Officer in the Registrar General's office agreed that registration of organizations were done either by the DC of the area or by the Governor of the Protectorate. There being no registration no records in the Registrar's office does not mean that APIM was never registered. The Lilongwe DC's office may have not submitted all the documents on registered organizations to Blantyre. Some of the documents may have been in such poor condition that moving them destroyed them further this and could not then be reproduced. *Chiyambi cha Mpingo wa Achewa mu Dela la Lilongwe* is sure proof of good record keeping on the part of APIM. It has also been used when APIM's beliefs and practices were questioned in Dedza where they are not well known. The latest was during the 1999 voter registration exercise when APIM women refused to be photographed without their headscarfs on, for identity. After the production of the *Chiyambi cha Achewa PIM* by Kamchedzera as proof of their identity as a recognized church and not as a sect, APIM women were immediately permitted to be photographed with scarfs on their heads.
[91] Int Foulger Kafulatira, Majondo, 21.5.1999.
[92] Int Yosofati Ndege, Chalendewa, 13.6.1998.
[93] Bishop Dr James Tengatenga of the Anglican Church in Malawi, Nantipwiri, 13.5.1999.

who wanted to keep in touch with their roots. They do not bar people of other tribes becoming members, but the use of Malawian languages in Zimbabwe reduces the possibility. That is very tribal. Using the name "Achewa" limits the church from growing outside the Achewa area, just as "Tumbuka", "Sena", or any other tribal title would bar those outside the tribe named.[94] Despite calling themselves Achewa PIM as opposed to PIM, they were still popularly known by the people as Mpingo wa Mpatuko; even today, they are still called by that name.[95] It made no make any difference what changes had taken place in their church polity: they were still seen as a church that had deviated from the standard.[96]

The Result of the Separation

Anderson Nyangu emerged as the sole leader of Mangoni PIM. He did not leave PIM despite the departure of 2nd formation of new church by his mentor's and other Mangoni PIM stalwarts' departure and the formation of a new church.[97] He was not an ordained minister as was Kalemba. Nyangu was seen just as *mtsogoleri basi* (a leader only). Together with Kalemba, *anali eni mpingo* (they were the owners of the church). Now that Kalemba had left PIM, Nyangu emerged the sole leader of the PIM section in Mangoni. Stewart Kampa was sent from Chiradzulu to pastor the church at Nyangu which took its name from the hills nearby: Mphanda.[98]

Before he ended his 1933 visit, Malikebu chose the site for the construction of a modern central church near Mphanda Hills. He also promised financial help from the Mission and the builder. Members in Mangoni were very excited. In 1935 members of Mpingo wa Mpatuko molded and burnt bricks for the construction of the Mangoni Mission Station at Nyangu. The first mud building was close to the Chinsale tree east of the present building: and in 1928 it was rebuilt close to *mphambano yopita kwa Nyengwe* (the junction leading to Nyengwe).[99] The foundation of Mphanda church was only laid in 1937

---

[94] Int Frank Chibisa, Blantyre, 23.4.1999.
[95] To differentiate one from another, from this point on I will use the names "APIM" and "PIM" because both churches were commonly known by the people by the, Mpingo wa Mpatuko.
[96] Int Adiresi Kampangire, Katantha, 26.5.1999.
[97] Int Eliamu Mlongoti Chijere Nyangu, Mchinji, 19.9.1999.
[98] Int Eliamu Mlongoti Chijere Nyangu, Mchinji, 19.9.1999.
[99] Int Ezina Kamdolozi, Matapila, 20.5.1999.

by Richard Chiwayula.[100] Between 1938 and 1944 Malikebu was in the USA and no work was done on the building. People were waiting for his directive and the financial support he had promised. It took the people so long because they told themselves *kapena abwera kapena abwera* (maybe he is coming).[101] It was on 18 January 1960 when the church building was completed.[102] The building team was headed by Namate, and it included Che Kapanire and Mbwana all of whom had been sent from Chiradzulu.[103] They were not well experienced but they did the job under the overall leadership of Chijere Nyangu.[104]

The financial support that Malikebu gave to Mangoni PIM was not much when all the work the people did is valued in monetary terms. It was a self-help project for the members. Chief Batiwelo Matapila was one of the people who were influential in the construction of Mphanda Church.[105] Amayi Dofa Masula, from Lunguzi south of Phatha, was one of the women who encouraged more people to participate in the construction of the church building. *Amachita chamuna kuocha njerwa* (she worked like a man burning the bricks).[106] She carried the logs and fired them throughout the night without sleeping. Nyangu died in 1960 and was buried by Kampa at Kalumbu. In that same year, Kampa was succeeded by Sam Mapakata as pastor at Mphanda. He had been a student of Malikebu at Mbombwe. There is no *chiriza* built for him because *manda anafafanizika* (his grave was levelled over), and no one could correctly identify correctly the site.[107]

Evangelism and Church Growth

Between 1938 and 1945 Achewa PIM experienced remarkable growth in terms of numbers of individual members with only one new church started in 1941.[108] This was as a result of the preaching of such men as Kafulatira, Kamkalamba and Ndalama. Though they did not go outside their home ground, they walked for kilometres through vil-

---

[100] Richard was a younger brother of Chiwayula, who was head builder at Mbombwe. Their home was towards Chiradzulu Mountain from Mbombwe.
[101] Int Emelesi Kuthedze, Nyangu, 11.9.1999.
[102] Int Eliamu Mlongoti Chijere Nyangu, Mchinji, 19.9.1999.
[103] Int Eliamu Mlongoti Chijere Nyangu, Mchinji, 19.9.1999.
[104] Int Emelesi Kuthedze, Nyangu, 11.9.1999.
[105] Int Elenesi Wisikoti, Nyanje, 20.6.1998.
[106] Int Emelesi Kuthedze, Nyangu, 11.9.1999.
[107] Int Eliamu Mlongoti Chijere Nyangu, Mchinji, 19.9.1999.
[108] Int Foulger, Majondo, 21.5.1999. The new church was at Msendere.

lages teaching about redemption and challenging people to accept Jesus as Lord and Saviour of their lives.[109] Soon more and more families identified themselves with APIM. The harvest was ready but the workers were few.[110] Those who gathered together needed someone to nurture them. Those who went about preaching were not prepared to stay in one place and teach the new converts until they were mature enough to take care of themselves, and then move on to the next place to preach again. As a result large numbers of people were baptized without proper teaching about what it meant to be a Christian, and in particular a Baptist.[111] They were joining *mpingo* (a group of people), *anthu a Mulungu* (people of God) whose teaching, and probably their way of dressing, appealed to their hearts and minds. Whatever the reason, *ntchito inachuluka* (the work became too much) for the evangelists, many of whom were not prepared as pastors.[112] The preachers themselves felt *kuti anachepa nayo ntchitoyo* (they were ill equipped for the work).[113] Several preachers saw the future of APIM as being limited or difficult without organized leadership training and outside help. Kalemba was not systematically preparing his followers for ministry as was done by PIM through Chilembwe and Malikebu. It seemed as though Kalemba. was letting the ministries take their own course.[114]

Kalemba's Ordination

With so many people joining APIM. there was need for them to be baptized into the membership of the church. Although *analandira ubatizo wa John Chilembwe* (he had been baptized by John Chilembwe) in the early 1900s and had been the head of the Mpingo wa Mpatuko for almost a quarter of a century, Kalemba had never baptized any convert before because he had not been ordained for the ministry: neither by his church, PIM, now by APIM. Kalemba had been faithful to the teaching of PIM that barred anyone not ordained to administer ordinances (baptism and the Lord's Supper).[115] Now he

---

[109] Int Yosofati Ndege, Chalendewa, 13.6.1998.

[110] See Matthew 9:37. This is a problem that was identified long back by Jesus which surfaces all through the history of the Church. Many churches were started and never grew or died altogether because of lack of leadership.

[111] Int Yosofati Ndege, Chalendewa, 13.6.1998.

[112] Int Foulger Kafulatira, Majondo, 21.5.1999.

[113] Int Ezina Kamdolozi, Matapila, 20.5.1999.

[114] Int Yosofati Ndege, Chalendewa, 13.6.1998.

[115] As a primary leader, Kalemba was expected to baptize and preside over they believed that the Lord's Supper. New Testament churches were more

had no choice but to get around it and baptize the converts and preside over the Lord's Supper because there was no one else who was going to do that for him, as did Malikebu had time from 1926 until the separation. While he denied that baptism was necessary to salvation, Kalemba insisted that baptism was essential for the life of the church. He encouraged his converts to learn first the truths of the Bible; and after they understood what it meant to be a believer, they were to be baptized like him into PIM. Kalemba also believed that baptism was at the same time essential for one to be a true follower of Jesus Christ. That meant that baptism was an initiatory sign of a committed disciple, demonstrating one's commitment to Jesus and to fellow believers in the church.[116]

Sometime in 1938 Kalemba asked *mbusa* Kanguru of the Seventh-Day Baptist Church at Jorijo near Makhanya to ordain him so as to enable him to baptize his converts by immersion as practiced by other Baptists.[117] The SDB at Jorijo were the nearest like-Christians to PIM who practice baptism by immersion. There were other groups in the area that practiced *ubatizo wa mu Yorodani* (baptism in the Jordan), i.e., by immersion, including *Mpingo wa Zioni wa Bata* (the Zion church that does not beat drums), but Kalemba did not approach them because he knew that they were not like his assembly, which was a Baptist church. Therefore, *anachita kupempha ubatizo* (he asked for baptism) from another Baptist church.[118] What this meant administratively is that Kalemba asked for authority from another Baptist church to enable him to baptize and preside over the Lord's supper.[119]

The first baptism took place that same year at Kalumbu. It was conducted in a dug-out pond (*Yorodani yochita chokumba*).[120] One of Kalemba's first baptism candidates was Jese, was Kamkalamba's sister. Although he was ordained by a SDB minister, Kalemba's baptism was known as *ubatizo wa John Chilembwe* (baptism of John Chi-

---

concerned with function in ministry than with position and status. The Holy Spirit called people to carry out certain tasks on behalf of the community of believers. One example is the case of Phillip. The emphasis in the New Testament is not upon rights or powers or even authority", but upon service to God, to the Gospel, and to the community of faith. For further discussion, see Brackney, *Faith, Life and Witness*, pp. 318-320. In the *original* Baptist tradition, too, ordination is not required for the administration of the ordinances

[116] Int Yosofati Ndege, Kakwere, 5.7.1998.
[117] Int Foulger Kafulatira, Majondo, 21.5.1999.
[118] In general Baptist tradition, ordination is not really required.
[119] Int Yosofati Ndege, Kakwere, 5.7.1998.
[120] Int Yosofati Ndege, Chalendewa, 13.6.1998.

lembwe) simply because he had received his baptism from Chilembwe; and that he was going to pass it on to his followers not as his own baptism, but as the founder's (Chilembwe's) baptism.[121] Evangelicalism, being transdenominational, provided Kalemba and his followers with a superb opportunity to co-operate with another Christian church—in this case Baptist—for the sake of the kingdom of God.[122]

Church Polity of Achewa PIM

The way Kalemba related to different ministries, the way they all functioned under APIM, and when they started, is not easy to understand. In general it is agreed that the church polity was a result of experience, rather than of special study.[123] Most of the time Kalemba made choices on the basis of what he thought Jesus or Chilembwe would have done in the same situation and in the light of what he thought the Bible taught.

Church Government

As *mtsogoleri*, Kalemba was looked to for leadership and guidance. He made the final decisions on matters pertaining to doctrine and practice.[124] During that period, Kamkalamba emerged as *mtsogoleri wa chiwiri* (the second leader, or the second in command) because he proved himself as a leader in his own right.[125]

Baptist church polity in general supports servant leadership rather than authoritarian roles. It recognizes the importance of oversight of the community of believers, *episkope (utsogoleri)*, as a gift of Christ to his church for the care and discipline of the people of God. The community has both the responsibility and freedom under God to commission certain persons to fulfill particular aspects of *episkope*, especially the ministry of preaching, pastoral care and teaching. By calling Kalemba *mtsogoleri* and Kamkalamba, *mtsogoleri wa chiwiri*, APIM did not distinguish between the function of the two leaders. Both men were leaders, invested with *episkope*, which they fulfilled as servant leaders: a biblical challenge that is facing Christian leadership

---

[121] Int Foulger Kafulatira, Majondo, 21.5.1999.
[122] Dee Morcom, "What Do We Stand for as Baptists and as Evangelicals?", in Desmond Hoffmeister and Louise Kretszchmar, Towards a Holistic, Afro-centric and Participatory Understanding of the Gospel of Jesus Christ, Jo-hannesburg: Baptist Convention of South Africa, 1995, p. 87.
[123] Int Feliati Dirawo Kaunde, Matapila, 9.6.1999.
[124] Int Yosofati Ndege, Chalendewa, 13.6.1999.
[125] Int Elenesi Wisikoti, Nyanje, 20.6.1998.

today.[126] Generally Baptists cannot justify in the light of Scripture the development of monarchical, metropolitan bishops, and archbishops or patriarchs, or any other forms of the episcopate.

Local Churches

Local churches began as home churches in which the members learnt worship of God, the importance of the Bible, and content and church membership. They were also taught some church history beginning with that of Chilembwe. Everyone needed to know that and tell others even if they were not members of APIM or PIM.[127] People presented themselves for membership of APIM in a local church. Local churches were like home churches, centres of fellowship and mutual support. They were viewed as *mpingo*, which meant a group of people with a common cause or calling. Although children were seen as part of the home and then the local church, Kalemba did not baptize them into membership:[128] membership APIM was officially open to adults only. Baptists only baptize when an individual has made a personal confession of faith. It was risk taking for anyone to declare that they were a member of APIM (including PIM). In the local churches members met for worship, proclamation, evangelism and education.[129]

The idea of total independence from other local churches never existed and was never taught and thought in APIM. All the churches needed each other and had to share together their joys and sorrows as one church. Since all the churches were facing similar problems, they looked to area leaders who in turn reported the matters to Kalemba, who was *mtsogoleri* of APIM. Issues that were affecting any part of APIM were discussed by all the leaders present from the local churches, and they agreed on the best possible solution available to them.[130]

Monthly Fellowship Meetings

Apart from the usual Sunday meetings, Kalemba introduced monthly fellowship meetings at which all the congregations met as one church. These began late in the afternoon on Saturday and ended in

---

[126] Gottfried Osei-Mensah, *Wanted Servant Leaders: The Challenge of Christian Leadership in Africa Today*, Achimoto: African Christian Press, 1990, pp. 9-21.
[127] Int Adiresi Kampangire, Katantha, 26.5.1999.
[128] Int Yosofati Ndege Kakwere, 5.7.1999.
[129] Int Feliati Dirawo Kaunde, Matapila, 9.6.1999.
[130] Int Foulger Kafulatira, Majondo, 21.5.1999.

the afternoon on Sunday. It was a time of fellowship during which members met at meals and worship. The meetings were like large family reunions because they were attended by many people from all APIM congregations. It was the only time when baptism and the Lord's Supper were administered. That attracted members and members-to-be to attend these meetings.[131]

Church Leadership at the Central Church at Nyanje

Even though Kalemba chose Nyanje as the central church for APIM, he did not move from Kalumbu to settle at Nyanje. It was the opposite of PIM where the leader, Malikebu, ministered from the central church at Mbombwe. Kalemba served from Kalumbu while *mtsogoleri wa chiwiri*, Kamkalamba, was at Nyanje. Early in 1945 Kalemba ordained Kamkalamba as pastor. Kalonga, a brother-in-law to Kamkalamba, was ordained *mlaliki* (preacher).[132]

Kalonga was from Mcholoma.[133] He had been to a DRCM school and he later became a member of Nkhoma Mission, and he could read and write very well He had been introduced to PIM during 2-year stay in Zimbabwe in the early 1940s..[134] When he came back home he met with Kamkalamba, who introduced him to APIM. Kamkalamba also influenced Kalonga to get interested in his sister, Kelita, who was by then pregnant by man called man, Tsokonombwe. Tsokonombwe had left for the mines in South Africa and never communicated with or supported her. Though Kelita, dejected she still kept her composure such that it did not take long for Kalonga to marry her. He became a *mkamwini* at Nyanje.[135] Kalonga took care of Kelita and she gave birth to a baby boy, David, also known as Pindepinde, who was later to become another pastor at Nyanje.[136]

Another man who was active at Nyanje at that time was Lazaro Dooko. His mother was from Kalumba while his father was from Dooko, which Village neighbours Nyanje. Dooko went to a DRCM school at Mzama near his home. He could read and write very well and had grown up as a member of Nkhoma Mission. Dooko married Letiya, who was a member of Makolo Church (the Church of our Ancestors).

---

[131] Int Yosofati Ndege, Chalendewa, 4.6.1998.
[132] Int David Tsokonombwe, Nyanje,13.6.1998.
[133] Int Dalesi Lipenga, Mphindo, 7.6.1999.
[134] Several people were introduced to PIM in Zimbabwe.
[135] *Mkamwini* means "he belongs to someone". When a Chewa man marries, he goes and settles at his wife's home. He is not seen as one of them but as a foreigner: and hence he belongs to another village and to some family there.
[136] Int Linesi Fulanki, Mphindo, 7.6.1999.

He moved and lived with her at her home village, Msemanjira, west of Dooko Village.[137] Letiya could not read and write because she had had only one year of primary school education. They were both introduced to Mpingo wa Mpatuko by Kamkalamba. Letiya did not join initially but followed Dooko after he was ordained *mkulu wa mpingo* (deacon). At the same time Kalonga was ordained *mlaliki* and Kamkalamba, *mbusa*, at Nyanje.[138] The membership at Nyanje increased tremendously from about 230 to over 500 during the period in which Kamkalamba joined with Kalonga and Dooko as *mbusa*, *mlaliki* and *mkulu wa mpingo* respectively.[139]

Church Leadership at Kumisu

Ndalama was from Kumisu and was married to a woman from Chipysela. Instead of remaining mkamwini, they chose to live at Kumisu.[140] Ndalama was a mlaliki trained by Kafulatira in the late 1930s. Like Kafulatira, he had a gift of preaching. Coupled with this was the gift of visitation. He not only visited members of Kumisu, but of the entire Mpingo ya Mpatuko, especially those in the area of Chief Chadza.[141] Ndalama was ordained by Kalemba as pastor in 1950

Church Leadership at Mphindo

The church at Mphindo traces its origin to Gilison Gumbi. He was from Nkhuwa and had married his cousin, Matilesi, of Mphindo where they made their home.[142] He had been to Zimbabwe, where he came into contact with PIM. When he returned home Gumbi met with Kamkalamba who encouraged him to join PIM and he did. Gumbi and Matilesi were members of Nyanje church for several years until 1932 ndi pamene anapempha gome (when they asked for the pulpit, that is, authority from Nyanje the mother church, to start a daughter church at Mphindo church).[143] Though Mphindo had a DRCM school, soon several people joined PIM; as evidenced by the number of

---

[137] Int Elenesi Wisikoti, Nyanje, 20.6.1998.
[138] Int Letiya Dooko, Msemanjira, 10.6.1999.
[139] Int. David Tsokonombwe, Nyanje, 20.6.1998.
[140] Int Sandifolo Kamchedzera, Nsabwe, 4.9.1999. In the Chewa culture, when a *mkamwini* remembers his home, he asks for *chitengwa*. This means that *mkamwini* asks his wife's relatives to allow him to take his wife and live with her at his home. He gives them a chicken, and the wife becomes a *mtengwa* (one who is taken).
[141] Int Yosofati Ndege, Gondwa, 11.10.1998.
[142] Int Lemia Yohane, Mphindo, 7.6.1999.
[143] Int Linesi Bikisoni, Mphindo, 7.6.1999.

women wearing *maduku kumutu* (headscarfs covering their heads) and long dresses.

APIM members were supposed to be smart in every area of their lives. Instead of allowing the people to continue using the bush as toilets, Gumbi pleaded with his fellow members to have pit latrines for Each household. Before long most households at Mphindo, especially APIM members, had pit latrines.[144]

PIM was soon replaced by APIM. Gumbi by then was being assisted by Josiya and Nelson Chalinda, Maliko Tsekani, Simoni Mpakasa and Hezekia Khama who formed the backbone of Mphindo.[145] The Chalindas were brothers of Matiresi.[146] Early in the 1940s Gumbi went to Kasungu were he was employed as a *kapitao* (gang leader/foreman) on a tobacco farm. Yosiya and the others met with the village headman, who refused to give them a place on which to erect a church building. The headman was a member of DRCM, which was meeting in the village. The men did not stop there: instead they went and met with T/A Chadza, who later referred the matter to the DC. Permission was granted and they constructed the building.[147]

Financial Support for Church Leaders (Pastors)

Generally Baptists have been known to have aggressive programmes on giving including tithes and offerings which are basically used to support ministry. That includes payment of the pastor, one who cares for the faithfuls at a local church. Only those elected into the denominational offices of the convention or union receive payment for their services to the churches that form that organization. School teachers and other workers are paid through appropriate boards or committees responsible for the institutions under the conventions or unions. On the other hand, the founding and the re-opening of PIM was done by Chilembwe and Malikebu who were paid as missionaries to Malawi by FMB of NBC Inc After their departure the FMB continued to pay stipends of PIM ministers and other church workers including school teachers, as well as funding certain mission projects.[148] Kalemba did not receive any financial support from the FMB because, firstly, Mpingo wa Mpatuko was started FMB's knowledge; and secondly:

---

[144] Int Dalesi Lipenga, Mphindo, 7.6.1999.
[145] Int Velina Khama, Mphindo, 7.6.1999.
[146] Int Beti Chalinda, Falls, 30.9.1999.
[147] Int Lemia Yohane, Mphindo, 7.6.1999.
[148] John Parratt, "Mbombwe Revisited: Dr. Daniel Malikebu and the Second Era of the Providence Industrial Mission", a history seminar paper, University of Malawi, 29 January 1985, p. 3.. See also Patrick Makondesa, "Muocha", p. 20.

Malikebu did not recognize Kalemba for mission support since he had not received any official training from PIM.

In light of this, Kalemba did not consciously take time to teach his followers to give generously to the church.[149] He did not ask APIM churches to give a monthly financial support.[150] The opposite has been the church imposing on the pastors the "keep them humble; keep them poor" syndrome. In part it is linked with the pressure of image. The pastor is expected to be and has to be seen to be a saint. He is supposed to set an example of holy poverty.[151] Kalemba left it to his followers to decide when to assist him, he could not be sure of getting help when he needed it. That became the standard for future leaders and their support.[152]

Kalemba's Divorces: Rather a Leadership Issue than a Moral One

Kalemba is known to have married at least four times. After he divorced Magireti, he married Eleneti. She was followed by another woman, Dabwani, from Mtandamula at Mwachilolo, and they had a daughter named Ethelo.[153] His last wife was Malita, popularly known as Shuwa, from Lingodzi at Salima Village after KamPhatha on the way to Blantyre from Lilongwe. They had no children.[154] She was a member of DRCM. Shuwa did not move her membership to APIM even after she married Kalemba. She lived with Kalemba the longest of all his wives, until his death. Shuwa anachita kusudzulidwa (was set free) by Kalemba's relatives to live her life as she pleased.[155] Shuwa became a sing'anga wa azimayi (namwino, which means is midwife). She went to Nsanje where she practiced for a years and then returned to her home where she later died and was buried.[156]

---

[149] Int Yosofati Ndege, Chalendewa, 13.6.1998.

[150] This is common among BACOMA pastors who do not want to talk about money or fear that their churches will call them lovers of money and therefore satanic. Yet they fail to realize the biblical teaching about church members supporting their pastor/teacher. See Galatiyans 6:6; 1 Corinthians 9:1-12.

[151] William H. Brackney, with Ruby J. Burke, *Faith, Life, and Witness: The Papers of the Study and Research Division of the Baptist World Alli¬ance - 1986-1990*, Birmingham, AL: Sanford University, 1990, p. 377.

[152] Int Yosofati Ndege, Chalendewa, 13.6.1998.

[153] Int Elikana Ngalawo, Mphindo, 7.6.1999.

[154] Int Eliamu Mlongoti Chijere Nyangu, Mchinji, 19.9.1999.

[155] Int Emelesi Kuthedze, Nyangu, 11.9.1999.

[156] Int Peturo Chimpesa, Nkhulawe, 23.10.1998.

Kalemba was described as *wokwatira kwatira* (one who married frequently).[157] As soon as he felt that he no longer wanted to live with the woman, he involved the church leadership and members. In order to protect God's work, as he put it, Kalemba would ask them to approve of his divorce. The spouse was described as a stumbling block to God's servant, and therefore also to God. Kalemba had learnt to work extra hard and could go for days without proper meals, which was not easy for the wives. Everyone who could not work as hard as he did, Kalemba described as being as lazy and unworthy of God's blessings. He was looking for something impossible: his own—self in the form of a woman. In general APIM did not perceive Kalemba's marriages and divorces as being un-Christian.[158]

However according to Baptist teaching, Kalemba's *kukwatira kwatira* is seen as un-Christian and therefore a sin. No one is allowed to divorce and remarry while the other partner is still alive[159]. When he married Elineti, Magireti was still alive, as was Eleneti's husband. She was then divorced and Dabwani took her place. Kalemba again married Shuwa while Dabwani was still alive. Kalemba might have taken divorce as his sole right which was also accepted by his family and followers, and the divorced women also had the right to marry someone else if they so wished. Like other Evangelical churches, Baptists believe and hold on to God's ideal of marriage that each man has one woman with whom to live in union throughout life. The idea of "open-ended" marriages is incompatible with Christian principles. If two people enter into marriage with the thought that it may not be permanent, they are sowing the first seeds of discontent and may expect ultimate dissolution of the union.

There are no easy solutions to problems related to divorce. While a categorical solution to every problem would be wonderful, the attitude and actions of Jesus toward divorce help a lot. Christ respected the personality of each individual and sought to enrich life for every person, regardless of their situation. If that is our attitude, then we will walk with other Kalembas in their dark moments and seek to point them to the way that will bring greater contentment and ultimate glory to God's kingdom.[160]

---

[157] Int Magi Kamunthu, Kalumbu, 26.10.1998.

[158] Int Peturo Chimpesa, Nkhulawe, 23.10.1998.

[159] That the *reality* is different in the Baptist Convention, is shown by Rachel Nyagondwe Banda, *Women of Bible and Culture*, Zomba: Kachere 2005, p. 169ff.

[160] James E. Giles, *Biblical Ethics and Contemporary Issues*, El Paso: Carib, 1994, p. 127.

Separation within APIM over its Future

From around 1944 the lack of a well-defined sense of direction in APIM, some APIM leaders begin to wonder where was heading. They were happy that the church was growing, but they were equally troubled about the way the leadership was carrying on its work of caring for the church. They saw no bright future for APIM.[161] There were several alternatives from which to choose.

The first one was to turn the church back to PIM. If they went back to PIM they were sure of financial support for all pastors who had had some training and had been ordained and for other mission workers, which was not the case with APIM. They lived in very poor villages where cash incomes were meagre. There was no way APIM could keep people in ministry if they were not going to pay them a salary.

Not only that, there was not enough teaching of the Word. APIM leadership kept teaching what many of its members already knew. Since the leaders they were not learning any more than their members, spiritual apathy that would result in the disintegration of APIM was though of as creeping in. They needed to go back to PIM where people would study the Word of God step by step, which would make them grow into maturity in faith in Jesus Christ.

Another issue was that there was no deliberate training to multiply the church leaders even if there was no money to pay them.[162] Without education one cannot talk of freedom and development. People remain *mbuli kapena opulukira* (foolish or ignorant).[163]

Another option was to quit APIM altogether and not even return to PIM. Advocates of this possibility felt that those they had left in PIM would tease them or think of them as not being true believers. So their preference was to be an unbeliever by choice rather by the accusation of someone else.[164] However this was a helpless situation in which to find oneself; why not accept the error and be part of a successful church.

There were those who made the problems even more complicated by arguing the credibility of using "Achewa" as a name of a church that was supposed to welcome people of all tribes and nations. "Achewa" ndi *fuko* ("Achewa" is an ethnic group), and a church

---

[161] Int Velina Kaunde, Matapila, 9.6.1999.
[162] Int Foulger Kafulatira, Majondo, 21.5.1999.
[163] Int Litida Kakhobwe, Katantha, 26.5.1999.
[164] Int Ezina Kamdolozi, Matapila, 20.5.1999.

needs to not be of a particular *fuko*, but for *mafuko onse* (all the ethnic groups).[165]

The concern over the magnitude of the ministry that APIM was facing, the anxiety of what the future held for him and his family in APIM, and the implication of using "Achewa" in the title, forced some to leave APIM and return to PIM. In 1945 Kafulatira and his family went back to PIM. The Kafulatira family stood before the congregation at PIM's central church in Mangoni, Mphanda, and asked the church to forgive them and welcome them back into the fellowship. The church gladly welcomed them back and they were reinstated as members of Mphanda church from where Kafulatira continued to preach and teach. The number of people who left APIM were not significant despite faithfuls like Kafulatira leaving.[166] Kamkalamba and Kalonga at Nyanje, and Ndalama at Kumisu vowed not accept any form of leadership from across the Shire again no matter what happened to APIM.[167] Eight APIM churches were clearly identified at that time: and these were Nyanje, Kalumbu, Mphindo, Chiuzira, Phatha, Katunga, Msenjere and Dziwe. A few of these had actual church buildings standing.[168]

Kalemba's Death and the Beginning of Kamkalamba's Era

Kalemba died on 18 August 1945. He was buried at Kalumbu about 400 metres north-east of Kalumbu Traditional Court. Kalemba's *chiriza* (memorial pillar) does not truly represent the person who was buried there. It is a chiriza for *munthu wamba* (an ordinary person) of *dziko lakale* (the days gone by).[169] It is of a simple design. It takes the form of a pyramid made of about 12 lines of 230 x 105 mm burnt bricks with a thin coat of weak cement/sand plaster. The front is crowned with a pillar about twice the height of the triangular-shaped sides. It is on this pillar that Kalemba's name and date because the plaster has been flaking off. At the rear end is a shorter pillar that stands as a guard to the rest of the chiriza.

Before his death Kalemba had ordained Kamkalamba as pastor. Kamkalamba was the first member of APIM to be ordained as pastor by APIM.[170] He was *munthu zedi; wa mphamvu zake* (a person of

---

[165] Int Velina Kaunde, Matapila, 9.6.1999.
[166] Int Foulger Kafulatira, 21.5.1999.
[167] Int Yosofati Ndege, Chelendewa, 13.6.1998.
[168] Int Sandifolo Kamchedzera, Nsabwe, 20.10.1998.
[169] Int Feliati Durawo Kaunde, Matapila, 9.6.1999.
[170] Int Yosofati Ndege, Gondwa, 11.10.1998.

good repute; and hard working).[171] Kamkalamba worked very closely with his wife Alenesi, who was a *mtengwa* from Dooko Village.[172] She was a serious person committed to excellence.[173]

Church Leadership Training after 1945

Ndalama took over from Kafulatira as a teacher of alaliki (preachers). One of Ndalama's students was Yosofati Ndege from Chalendewa. Though he had been to a DRCM school in his area, Ndege did not become a Presbyterian. He married Jolita of Mphindo but divorced her in 1932. And Immediately, Ndege moved back to Chalendewa. In 1934 he was a mkamwini at Kayabwa Village, where he was married to Buthu.[174] Ndege moved back to Chalendewa with Buthu in 1939. Before long, he had married a second wife from Mbewa.

A Chewa PIM Congregations in 1945

---

[171] Int Velina Khama, Mphindo, 7.6.1999.
[172] Int Letiya Dooko, Msemanjira, 10.6.1999.
[173] Int Enita Kamchedzera, Nsabwe, 4.9.1999.
[174] That was not her real name. A little girl is called *buthu*. For some reason, *buthu* became a personal name instead of a title. This could have been because she was of small body structure.

Her name was Achenjakwapi, also known as Abiti Kalinda.[175] It was during the early 1940s that Ndege was introduced to an APIM congregation that met at Mphindo. Though he was interested, he did not become a member of APIM right away.

Between 1945 and 1947 Ndege worked at a stone-crushing plant just outside Johannesburg towards Pretoria in South Africa for a while and then moved on to a commercial farm near Sinoia in Zimbabwe. In the following year, the Achewa PIM congregation at Mphindo held a meeting at Chalendewa at the invitation of one of its members, Ndege's long time friend Yohane Chikadula, who was married to a woman at Mpindo. Chikadula and his wife made Chalendewa their home. Chikadula had become a member of Achewa PIM while he was a *mkamwini* at Mphindo.[176]

Peter Kalemba's grave (with chiriza) at Kalumbu.

---

[175] *Abiti* means "daughter of".
[176] Int Yosofati Ndege, Nsabwe, 4.9.1999.

Ndege was attracted to Achewa PIM, and to really show his commitment *anasudzula Achenjakwapi* he divorced Achenjakwapi, and remained with Buthu. They were baptized a few months later from which time Buthu was given the name of Esitere, by Achewa PIM.

The Ndeges and Chikadulas used to go to and from Mphindo for worship. They were soon joined by Ndege's younger brothers Akim and Daniel and their wives, and Isaka Malaka and his wife, as members of Achewa PIM at Chalendewa. Soon all of them felt *mtunda kutalika* (the distance to be long), and they asked for permission to establish a congregation at Chalendewa separate from Mphindo. At that time, the congregation at Mphindo looked to the pastoral leadership of Kamkalamba at Nyanje. Gumbi and his brothers-in-law, Jesiya and Nelson Chalinda, were the deacons who were the leaders at Mphindo. After permission was sought from Chief and DC, the members at Chalendewa erected for themselves a mud church building.[177] Two years later Ndege was appointed a church monitor, and a year later he was ordained a deacon at Chalendewa. From 1953 to 1954 he studied preaching under Ndalama. After the training Ndege was designated *mlaliki* at the same church, a position that he held until 22 November 1963

Think-tank: Bungwe la pa 15 or Chififitini

Kamkalamba introduced a monthly meeting for the leaders of the local congregations. The Bungwe (committee) met at the central church at Nyanje and it was open to all in positions of leadership from all congregations.[178] They met on the 15 of every month or thereabouts, and thus the branding, Chififitini. It was during these meetings that the leaders discussed developments in their local congregations. Issues were tabled and decisions made. No local church leader made resolutions on issues that would later affect the entire Achewa PIM without the matter being discussed at Chififitini. It was also a time of building relationships.[179] Issues of discipline, forgiveness and restoration of members who had fallen in their churches were equally tabled at Chififitini. The committee was responsible for excommunicating any member from the church if there was enough evidence to do so. No one local congregation could excommunicate a member unless his or her case was heard by the committee and approved. Nevertheless cases leading to excommunication were very rare because the

---

[177] Int Linesi Fulanki, Mphindo, 7.6.1999.
[178] Int Peturo Chimpesa, Nkhuluwe, 23.10.1998. See Plate 4 for a sample of names of women and men who formed such a committee in 1964.
[179] Int Lexina Lenadi, Gondwa, 10.10.1998.

committee did all it could to restore and unite its members. Once decisions were made all APIM members were expected to abide by them. What was agreed by Chififitini was made known to the local congregations at APIM's monthly fellowship meetings.[180]

The re-opening of PIM at Mbombwe and the re-establishment of ties with PIM in Mangoni further strengthened Mpingo wa Mpatuko and Chilembwe's legacy. Several men who received training from Mbombwe alighted Mangoni's enthusiasm Chilembwe's type of education and his intent for African independence. Unfortunately, Malikebu's treatment of fellow workers was a departure from John Chilembwe's method of working with auxiliaries. Malikebu did not show appreciation of co-workers such as Kalemba, who had kept the Church since the time of Chilembwe. Although he had not been jailed for life, hanged or killed, Kalemba had suffered at the hands of the Government and the people. Malikebu needed to recognize that and value Kalemba by working with him as an equal who was worthy worth of some pay. His monopoly over church offerings showed that Malikebu had dictatorial attitudes that contributed to the formation of Achewa PIM. Although the Church in Mangoni desperately needed the education, spiritual and moral support that Mbombwe was providing, a decision had to be made between having one pastor ministering under PIM, and several pastors sharing the load and the benefits. Until 1937 Malikebu had performed all the baptisms and celebrated all marriages. This extreme centralization contradicted worldwide Baptist principles

---

[180] Int Shadreck Chinsera, Nyanje, 20.6.1998.

Chapter 3
Achewa PIM Working with Foreign Missionaries

The Beginnings of Southern Baptist Convention Work in Malawi

In July 1959 two SBC missionary couples: Leroy and Jean Albright, and William and Blanche Wester left Zimbabwe under the Baptist Mission of Central Africa (BMCA) to start new work in Malawi. They both took up residence in Blantyre. In 1960 the Albrights moved to Lilongwe while the Westers remained in the City. In September of the same year, they were joined by another couple straight from America, Gene and Beverly Kingsley.[1]

The BMCA and SBC Foreign Mission Board were aware of the presence of other Baptist groups in Malawi before SBC missionaries came to the country.[2] Early in 1961 BMCA representatives who included Marvin L. Garrett and his wife, the Kingsleys and the Westers visited PIM at Mbombwe, where they held bilateral talks with Malikebu on how best they could help PIM.[3] During the discussions Malikebu requested from the SBC (through BMCA) personnel and funding to meet the growing needs of PIM. After feedback and comments from SBC missionaries, BMCA concluded that they were going to help only as advisors to the member churches of PIM and other Baptist groups in Malawi. If there was going to be a request for assistance in education, BMCA was prepared to consider that very seriously.[4] Nevertheless the FMB (IMB since mid 1998) cautioned its missionaries to tread carefully in light of the history of PIM, its achievements and the involvement of the NBC Inc In other words, BMCA was to keep clear of PIM if possible.[5] BMCA heedfully avoided direct organizational rela-

---
[1] Baker J. Cauthen and Others, *Advance: A History of Southern Baptist Foreign Missions*, Nashville: Broadman, 1970, pp. 163-164.
[2] An excerpt from a letter to BMCA families, which was given to me by the Kingsleys.
[3] Marvin L. Garrett, an excerpt from a letter to BMCA families, Gatooma (now Kadoma), 29.1.1961 - supplied to me by the Kingsleys.
[4] Garret, an excerpt of a letter to missionary families in Malawi, Kadoma, 20.3.1961.
[5] H. Cornell Goerner, FMB secretary for Africa, Europe, and the Near East from 1957 to 1963, an excerpt from a letter to BMCA, 6.2.1961 - a copy that was provided to me by the Kingsleys.

tionships with PIM but accepted invitations to speak at their assemblies.[6]

The Role of an Expatriate in Achewa PIM

Though SBC reported that members of Achewa PIM approached Albright and asked him to be their adviser and teacher, there is no evidence for this from the members themselves.[7] In fact it was Albright who started the relationship.[8] Since he had known knew about them, Albright made an effort to locate the leadership of Achewa PIM. A certain civil servant, Chidzanja Nkhoma from Nathenje, is said to have met Albright in his search and helped him to find the APIM leadership at Nyanje.[9] After introducing himself, Albright told APIM leadership that he wanted to fellowship with them because they were all Baptists. He showed them pictures of Chilembwe, some of which were from a book, presumably *Independent African*. The Achewa PIM leadership was very excited and when they asked Albright to give them the book, he promised to find them another copy, which he never did.[10] Albright invited APIM leadership to his house in Lilongwe Town. Kamkalamba, Ndalama, Karonga, and Ndege visited Albright at the appointed time. What transpired after the visit was a gentleman's agreement to work together. That was an opportunity for Albright to reach the people of the area with the Word of God through already established Baptist churches.[11]

In addition, the partnership was also an opportunity for Achewa PIM to link with other Christians, especially Baptists outside their community. That was going to make them get involved in cross-cultural ministry for they were going to work side by side with a foreign white missionary. APIM was already confident in itself as a church, having survived since the late 1930s outside any form of partnership. Achewa PIM was creating an interpersonal relationship with Albright. It was not a one way relationship; APIM was not dependent on an expatriate nor on foreign donations. One cannot deny the fact that they would have loved to have some moral and financial support from outside

---

[6] The 1962 Annual Session of the National Baptist Assembly of Africa, Nyasaland Inc which was made available to me by the Kingsleys.
[7] "Adviser in Malawi", an excerpt from a story in a SBC magazine which was given to me by Barbara Workman, a former SBC missionary to Malawi now based in South Africa.
[8] Gene Kingsley, a note to Hany Longwe, n.d.
[9] Int Velina and Feliati D. Kaunde, Matapila, 22 June 1999.
[10] Int Yosofati Ndege, Chalendewa, 4.6.1998
[11] Gene Kingsley, a note to Hany Longwe.

donors just as PIM at Mbombwe and other churches in the country were enjoying. Probably the most important thing they were looking for was external reinforcement of what they believed and practiced. They respected the expatriate who in turn was expected to respect.

Opposition to the Partnership between APIM and BMIM

Not all the members of APIM were happy with its leadership's move for partnership with a foreign white missionary. A small group led by Peturo Chimpesa, Tanalute Kampheta and a woman by the name of Elite Gorombe, felt that their independence as an African church was in jeopardy. They challenged the leadership saying, "Simumati mpingowu ndi woima paokha? Bwanji tsono mukulandira mzungu?" ("Did not you say that this church was independent? Why then are you receiving a white man?")[12] The concerned members began to boycott meetings that Albright attended, and branded APIM as not Achewa eni (true Achewa). The group perceived Kamkalamba as having sold Achewa PIM to Albright.[13]

MCP Membership Cards: a Symbol of Political Involvement

With gradual transfer of power from the colonial authority to national leadership, a national symbol of political involvement was the "party card", which signified membership in the MCP.[14] The relationship between the grumbling group and the rest of Achewa PIM was further strained when Kamkalamba succumbed to MCP's demand for all Malawians to buy party cards. Since the beginning of the MCP Kamkalamba had refused the obligation of that Achewa PIM members buy MCP membership cards. So that MCP viewed Achewa PIM as kapirikoni.[15] Anyone labelled as such was in trouble with the MCP. The persecution of non-compliant Malawians started even before official in-

---

[12] Int Peturo Chimpesa, Nkhulawe, 23.10.1998; Yosofati Ndege, Chandewa, 25.10.1998.
[13] Int Peturo Chimpesa, Nkhulawe, 23.10.1998.
[14] Klaus Fiedler, "Power at the Receiving End: The Jehovah's Witnesses' Experience in One Party Malawi", in Kenneth R. Ross (ed.), *God, People and Power in Malawi: Democratization in Theological Perspective*, Blantyre: CLAIM, 1996, pp. 153-154.
[15] The term *kapirikoni* meant one who was against black rule or a neocolonialist. It was coined at the coming of MCP and was commonly used during the struggle for independence. The word was used to mean a person of double standards or of bad motives. The original meaning goes back to the Capricorn Society, promoting a multiracial Central Africa.

dependence.[16]. Like most people in Lilongwe, Dowa and Ntchisi, Kamkalamba was not sure of the reliability and continuity of MCP as a political party that was challenging the atsamunda (colonial government) in the country.[17] When the MCP formed the first African government of Malawi, Achewa PIM had no choice but to go along with the rest of the citizens. To safeguard his members Kamkalamba went to the MCP office and requested to buy sufficient membership cards for his church members, but was turned down. Instead they agreed on MCP officials to sell the cards at APIM's monthly church meeting, which was scheduled for 4 July 1964 at Chiuzira.[18] Most APIM members who were present at the meeting bought MCP membership cards except for those who did not have money on them, and a group that was opposed to the whole idea of buying any party membership cards. Chimpesa, Kampheta, Gorombe, and akazi a Mbeta (Mrs Mbeta), plus a few others, refused to buy MCP cards accusing Kamkalamba of double play. Although Kamkalamba tried to reason with them, the concerned group did not accept his defence. As a

---

[16] MCP supporters threatened to burn the PIM mission station when Malikebu's message was interpreted by church members to mean no to party cards. That led to PIM members sleeping outside their homes for several weeks for fear of their lives. Though the church at Mbombwe was spared, some churches in Thyolo district were set on fire for members not buying MCP party cards. Youth Leaguers from the MCP were being sent as spies to attend some PIM worship services. Some members were killed before independence for not buying MCP party cards. See Makondesa,

[17] It took them time to believe that an African could really fight the white men and take over the government. The British colonial administration policy imposed a functional state structure on diverse African societies lacking a common tradition of centralized authority long before independence. The British ruined traditional forms of civil association and cemented their rule in diverse ways through pacts with local leaders who continued to administer indigenous law under external authority. The British also succeeded in confining rural populations to the realm of tribal existence where ethnicity and kinship became the primary basis of identification. Within the context of the colonial socialization process, "ndale" (politics) was defined as a field of venture reserved for those who ruled. See J.R. Minnis, "Prospects and Problems for Civil Society in Malawi", in Kings M. Phiri and Kenneth R. Ross, (ed.)*Democratization in Malawi: A Stocktaking*, Blantyre: CLAIM, 1998, pp. 136-138.

[18] *Ufulu* (freedom) that Kamuzu emphasized became clear after that it meant to support what Kamuzu chose and that MCP demanded the allegiance of all Malawians. See Klaus Fiedler, "Power at the Receiving End: the Jehovah's Witnesses' Experience in One Party Malawi", in Kenneth R. Ross (ed.), *God, People and Power in Malawi: Democratization in Theological Perspective*, Blantyre: CLAIM, 1996, pp. 149-150.

result the group began to meet separately and called itself the "true" Achewa PIM.[19] Though records of persecution of those who refused to buy MCP membership cards go back to 1963, Chimpesa and his colleagues were not persecuted.[20] Not many members of APIM were influenced to join the breakaway group. Chimpesa was known by many as not being in consistent, therefore, unreliable as a leader.[21]

In order to clear themselves from being labelled *kapirikoni*, the Achewa PIM leadership summoned Chimpesa and his colleagues to chief Tsabango's court. In the presence of the chief and one of his *nduna*, Dzuwa, Kamkalamba told the chief that his church had nothing to do with Chimpesa and his companions who called themselves true Achewa PIM. He emphasized the fact that Achewa PIM had decided to go along with the rest of the country in supporting MCP in its fight against colonial rule. Every APIM member was encouraged to support the cause through the buying of MCP membership cards. Any member of Achewa PIM who did not buy the cards did so at his or her own choice and not following a directive from Achewa PIM.[22]

The judicial system was not free to protect those who did not buy MCP membership, therefore, Chimpesa and his colleagues, like all Malawians who wanted to avoid persecution, were forced to buy cards. When Chimpesa moved from Namakwa to Lilongwe town, he was quick to befriend one of the MCP branch chairmen. By mid-1965 Chimpesa was one of the many people *amene ankabvutitsa anthu opanda makhadi a chipani* (who used to trouble the people without party cards). He had changed from refusing to buy party cards to being a staunch MCP supporter.[23] Through his relationship with the MCP, Chimpesa had a letter typed that stated that he was a pastor of Achewa PIM and that he was entitled to preach the Gospel and to bury the dead. In order to practice what he had always wanted to but was not given the opportunity under Kamkalamba, Chimpesa moved to Nkhulawe under Chief Tsabango where he and his followers started a church that was also called Achewa PIM. The group misinformed members of nearby Chiuzira congregation, some of whom immediately joined Chimpesa and formed another church there. Other small congregations were meeting at Chinsamba and

---

[19] Int Sandifolo Kamchedzera and Yosofati Ndege, Chalendewa, 25.10.1998.
[20] Int Lositala Vizi, Phatha, 20.10.1998. See Patrick Makondesa, "Muocha", pp. 18-19.
[21] Int Linesi Fulanki, Mphindo, 7.6.1999.
[22] Int Peturo Chimpesa, Nkhulawe, 23.10.1998.
[23] Int Sandifolo Kamchedzera, Nsabwe, 25.10.1998.

Mphombwe also in Lilongwe district.[24] By November 1974 the congregations under Chimpesa had opened a savings account under the name of Achewa PIM with the Post Office Savings Bank. (See Plate 7)

The Disintegration of the "True" Achewa PIM

In 1988 Chimpesa went to Mzimba in search of land for commercial farming. His departure to the Northern Region created a leadership vacuum. There was no one of Chimpesa's character who could lead the three "true" Achewa PIM churches in the area north-east of Lilongwe Town. Sooner or later the members began to fall back and scatter like sheep without a shepherd. Some of the members joined mainline churches like CCAP, while others were enlisted in AICs like African Abraham and Zion churches, or stopped worshipping altogether. As things turned out Chimpesa was not able to fulfil his ambition and he returned home in 1994 to a church that had almost folded due to lack of leadership. In addition to those who had left his church, two of his children, a daughter and a son, had joined Chingira Baptist Church. which was near their home.[25]

Nevertheless, that did not move Chimpesa and his wife to abandon their church. Together with one of their sons, they continued to meet for worship services in their home. In spite of being renounced by the people they thought were with them all the way, they were instead strengthened to remain "true" Achewa PIM *mpakana imfa* (till death).[26] They were not bitter against their former members, but they were sorry for what they had done out of ignorance. The truth for which they were searching was there in the "true" Achewa PIM.

Leadership Training and its Results

The First Lay Pastors' Training Institute Organized by BMIM

By the end of 1961 the Baptist Mission in Malawi had established relationships with several individual Malawians and a couple of indigenous churches. The discussions throughout 1960 and 1961 then resulted in the organization of a lay pastors' "training institute" in 1962. The students who attended the training by BMIM included the Achewa PIM leadership of Kamkalamba, Ndalama, Kalonga and Ndege. Also there were Thomas Kachaso Gama of Zion Church in Zomba District, Dafren Makhaya from Ntcheu who was working in as an interpreter

---

[24] Int Peturo Chimpesa, Nkhulawe, 23.10.1998.
[25] Int Lefani Chibwinja, Chingira, 23.10.1998.
[26] Int Peturo Chimpesa, Nkhulawe, 23.10.1998.

with the BMIM: Stephen Galatiya from Mwanza, who had became a Baptist white working in Sommerset West in near Cape Town, Donald Kaduya from Chiradzulu District who had been a Baptist in Harare since the time he had been working in Zimbabwe: And Bonzo and Zuze from Lilongwe town.[27] Galatiya first met with Wester in Blantyre while selling vegetables in the suburbs of the town.[28] These men were thought to be good preachers who needed some instruction. One of the instructors at the meeting was Abel Nziramasanga, a pastor from Waterfalls Baptist Church in Harare. He was brought to Malawi, not only to teach in the school but also to discuss with students at the "institute" and other interested Malawians on what it meant to be a Baptist.[29]

All along APIM valued leadership training. The first lay pastors' training institute was an answer to their quest for continued theological training since they had broken their relationship with Mbombwe. They received free Bibles and tracts, which they were supposed to use in their local churches and in witnessing. Their desire to win more people to Christ was rekindled.[30] They were reminded of the big task of winning souls to Christ and the possibility of multiplying the harvest if they worked together with other Christians. Through the school Achewa PIM leaders were encouraged to study the Word of God, which also compelled them to improve their reading skills.[31] The teaching they received confirmed their Baptist roots and emphasized the position of Jesus Christ in the Christian faith. In addition, the school connected them to the outside world.

The First Baptist Church in Malawi Associated with BMIM

Achewa PIM felt that they were not alone, but that they were part of a very large Baptist family.[32] As a result, Achewa PIM felt important; they too could have friends from outside the country who visited

---

[27] What is known of Bonzo is that he had worked as Albright's clerk. He was neither a *mlaliki* nor a *mbusa*. The last thing people know of him is that he moved to Blantyre in the same year. Almost nothing is remembered of Zuze. See also the note from Gene Kingsley to Hany Longwe.
[28] Int Stephen Galatiya, Lilongwe, 13.4.1997. See also D.L. Saunders, "A History of Baptists in East and Central Africa", PhD, Southern Baptist Theological Seminary, 1973, p. 126.
[29] See Gene Kingsley's note to Hany Longwe.
[30] Int Yosofati Ndege, Chalendewa, 4.6.1998.
[31] Int Wiscot Thomasi, Mwase, 13.6.1998.
[32] Int Sandifolo Kamchedzera, Nsabwe, 4.9.1999.

them, not only in their churches, but also in their homes. They felt respected and worthy of recognition as a church.³³

One of the 1961 Baptist Bible School Classes

A permanent church building was constructed at Ndalama village in Zomba District through BMIM funding. The Zion church became a Baptist church by choice, and the first Baptist church associated with the SBC through BMIM.³⁴ At the close of the "school", Kachaso, Kaduya, Galatiya, Wester and Kingsley went to Ndalama Village where they taught Baptist beliefs and practice to the Zion church members. As a result of the teaching, the church at Ndalama unanimously decided to become a Baptist congregation.³⁵ Those present were re-baptized that same day.³⁶ The rest of the church members and all

---

³³ Int Enita Kamchedzera, Nsabwe, 4.9.1999.
³⁴ See D.L. Saunders, "A History of Baptists", p. 125.
³⁵ The Zion church at Ndalama was one that is termed *Zioni ya Bata* (calm), meaning that they do not beat drums in their worship services.
³⁶ The SBC missionaries decided to accept the faith of Zion Christians, but not their baptism. Though there is no Baptist principle that requires re-baptism of

who joined later were baptized into the Baptist family whenever they were ready.³⁷

Unfortunately for BMIM, the church at Ndalama progressed as a Baptist church for about two years, only after which it reverted to Zion.

The participation of Zion church leadership in the lay pastors' school had some impact on Achewa PIM leadership. They realized that they were not the only black led church that was seeking mutual partnership with outside organizations and individuals. Together they laid the foundation of the Baptist Convention of Malawi. While Ndalama church became the first Baptist church in the country that was associated with BMIM, some of APIM's congregations became part of BACOMA and Ndege became a member of its Board of Trustees.

The First Malawian to Go for Further Training under SBC

In 1963 Galatiya became the first participant of the first lay pastors' training school to go for further theological studies at a SBC-funded seminary outside Malawi. He would have not gone if it were not for the institution of the short-lived Ndalama Baptist Church. For one to go to a seminary funded by SBC one had to be a member of and have an endorsement from a Baptist church that was in good standing with SBC through its missionaries in the country.

Since Ndalama was the only church that met SBC requirements, Galatiya had to place his membership there in order for him to qualify for theological training. He was at Gweru with his family for about three years and returned to Malawi at the end of 1965.³⁸

Bible Study: the Vehicle for Spiritual Growth

---

believers baptized by another church after confession of their faith, this has become a frequent practice in Malawi.

³⁷ Int Stephen Galatiya, Lilongwe, 3.6.1998.

³⁸ Galatiya later became the first associate pastor of the multi-racial, English-speaking BMIM church in Blantyre. As an evangelist, he started New Jerusalem Baptist Church near Newlands in Limbe, South Lunzu Baptist Church, Mwanza, and Senzani in Ntcheu were he now makes his home with his wife and family. He was also instrumental in the establishment of several churches in Chikwawa, Thyolo and Chiradzulu. He served for many years as an officer of the Blantyre Baptist Association and as an officer of the Baptist Convention of Malawi (BACOMA) which was a result of SBC's FMB work in the country. Galatiya's biggest contribution was probably in the area of teaching stewardship in BACOMA congregations.

Kamkalamba, Ndalama, Karonga, Ndege Makhaya and others continued to meet with Albright for Bible study.³⁹ They met at the Lilongwe Community Hall for a while and later moved into a rented grocery store that belonged to a Mr Kadango at Falls Estate, which is opposite to what is now the Baptist Theological Seminary (formerly the Baptist Bible School).⁴⁰ The classes were in session for several of hours a day twice a week to allow the participants to travel to the school and return to their homes before it was dark, because there was no accommodation prepared for them in town.

The first Baptist church organized by BMIM

It also gave the participants time to be with their families and to work on their fields. The students either walked or rode bicycles to and from the school. Sometimes Albright provided transport for the leadership team; he either drove them in his car, or gave them money for local bus fares. The date of the next meeting was agreed upon before the

---

39 Int Peturo Simoko, Phatha, 20.10.1998.
40 Int Yosofati Ndege, Chalendewa, 4.6.1998.

end of the last class of the week. Unfortunately no Achewa PIM pastor was ever sent to a theological seminary due to lack of a good working knowledge of English.[41]

Change of Name from APIM to Achewa Baptist Association

In October 1964 Achewa PIM began to be known as Achewa Baptist Association (ABA).[42] Albright did not want to be seen as working with a group that was associated with Chilembwe and Joseph Booth though he knew that this was a fact.

Probably he did probably not want other white people and missionaries to regard him as preserving the activities of APIM and PIM's founder.[43] Names were suggested but they settled for ABA, which took into account the two parties. The word "mission" was removed because Albright perceived BMIM rather than the local being the mission. The adjective "industrial" was also erased from the title because Albright understood BMIM as a faith mission.[44] Although ABA was the agreed name, in practice people continued to use "Providence" in the title and called themselves Achewa Providence Baptist Mission[45]. It should be noted that the cooperation was a local event.[46] Though Albright spoke as representing BMIM he did not make the decisions made between him and Achewa PIM binding. There was no formal agreement between the two organizations.[47] It is likely that Albright began to work with Achewa PIM because they were the first to respond to him. He started to work with them as friends.[48] Albright was trying to start a people's movement using an Independent African Church.[49] According to Achewa PIM and Albright, APIM was a Baptist church it was a Baptist they to come together in the first place without necessarily interfering with each other's church government.[50] Ache-

---

[41] Int Wiscot Thomasi, Nyanje, 31.8.1998.
[42] Saunders called it an "unexpected ministry". See "A History of Baptists", p. 129.
[43] Int Yosofati Ndege, Chalendewa, 4.6.1998.
[44] For possible definitions of faith missions, see Klaus Fiedler, *The Story of Faith Missions*, Oxford: Regnum; Sutherland: Alba-tross, 1994, pp. 11-13.
[45] Int Lositala Vizi, Phatha, 20.10.1998.
[46] Int Sam Upton, Lilongwe, 1.12.1998.
[47] See Buddy and Jean Albright, e-mail to Sam Upton, subject: Hany Longwe, 12.5.1999.
[48] See Rue Scott, "Answers to Hany Longwe's Questions Concerning the Achewa PIM", n.d.
[49] See Gene Kingsley's note to Hany Longwe.
[50] Scott agrees that Achewa PIM was Baptist until sometime in the 1970's. See "Answers to Hany Longwe", number 2.

wa PIM was happy to work with a Baptist expatriate without losing their autonomy in reaching people for Christ.

The Construction of the Baptist Bible School Buildings at Falls

Although Kamkalamba and others from rural Lilongwe were advanced in age, they were committed to the study of the Bible, which in turn resulted not only in their spiritual growth but in many converts. That was a big encouragement to BMIM, who responded by purchasing land opposite Kadango's grocery store. Albright often spent hours at a time in prayer with Kamkalamba and other Achewa PIM leaders on that wooded site.[51] By the end of 1965 the first permanent buildings for the Bible School were completed.[52] Since Malawi was largely rural and the people were found only in small centres, to teach the numerous villages the Word of God, BMIM opted for the training of lay pastors; and hence the construction of the Bible School. The School was geared to the needs of lay leaders, some of whom could barely read, and some whom were ready for more advanced study of the Bible.[53] After work had been started in a village, the group of believers there selected one or two leaders for training at the Bible school. Study sessions lasted only four to six weeks, allowing the men to not be away from their work at home for a long period at long stretches time. Each trainee was to attend one of the three sessions held each year.[54] Achewa PIM perceived the construction of the Bible School and the training it offered as a way of sharpening their skills in Bible reading and witnessing. Although they viewed it as their school and they encouraged their church members to take advantage of it, not as many members as was expected responded to the appeal.[55]

The facilities of the Baptist Bible School were dedicated in October 1966. Apart from containing offices for missionaries, the buildings housed two classrooms for Bible school sessions and for women's cooking and sewing lessons.[56] During the dedication ceremony the Achewa PIM leadership, which included Kamkalamba, Ndalama, Karonga and Ndege together with other leaders from BMIM's churches such as Galatiya and Makhaya, participated in planting three trees at

---

[51] Int Yosofati Ndege, Chalendewa, 4.6.1998.
[52] D.L. Saunders, "A History of Baptists", p. 128.
[53] Int LeRoy Albright, *The Commission*, Richmond: Foreign Mission Board, Southern Baptist Convention, (December 1966).
[54] Int Stephen Galatiya, Lilongwe, 3.6.1999. See also *The Commission*, December 1966.
[55] Int Wyson Mlamba, Mwase, 30.7.1998.
[56] *The Commission*, December 1966.

the roundabout in the middle of the facilities (See Plate 9). Two people would jointly plant a tree as a symbol of the unity of their churches.[57] In the same year courses of six to eight weeks duration were introduced. APIM leadership, which included, Kamkalamba, Ndalama, Kalonga, Ndege, Peturo Simoko, Nasoni Chalera and Makabisi Emasi, participated in some of the sessions of that school year.[58]

Introduction of Sunday Schools in Achewa PIM

Lay pastors began to teach their churches what they were learning or had learnt from the Bible School. They taught the Bible to other church leaders who in turn edified their congregations.[59] Southern Baptists rank Sunday School as the primary assimilation tool of the church. They believe that most of the church growth comes from the Sunday School. The teachers of the Sunday Schools are expected to organize the classes into pastoral care groups and to from guarding against unnoticed membership loss of the local church. The idea is for the churches to not lose people almost as fast as they gain them.[60] In addition, teaching is not optional in the church; it is a biblical imperative to be obeyed. Although missionary Sunday Schools are not biblically mandated, they are a cultural form established in the last two centuries to fulfil the mandate. How the church teaches is open to a variety of cultural expressions, but the Scriptures demand that the church educates its people for spiritual maturity.[61] In short, Southern Baptists encourage their local congregations to make full use of the Sunday School as the major outreach evangelism arm of the church.[62]

---

[57] Int W.A.C. Chisi, Lilongwe, 28.7.1998.
[58] See Plate 10 for a sample of a certificate issued after successfully completing training. Nasoni Chalera later became the pastor of Mphindo church in 1975 while Makabisi Emasi was a *mlaliki* at Chioza church.
[59] Int Enita Kamchedzera, Nsabwe, 25.10.1998.
[60] Thom Rainer, founding dean of the Billy Graham School of Missions, Evangelism and Church Growth at Southern Seminary, "Closing the back door of our churches", *Baptist Messenger*, (5 November 1998), p. 10.
[61] Perry G. Downs, *Teaching for Spiritual Growth: An Introduction to Christian Education*, Grand Rapids: Zondervan, 1994, p. 29.
[62] Harry Piland and Ernest Adams, *Breakthrough: Sunday School Work*, Nashville: Convention, 1990, p. 10. In a recent study of 567 effective evangelistic SBC churches, the researchers found the Sunday School to be one of the most important factors in the churches' success. When the survey was tested against nearly 200 non-SBC churches, there was little to no statistical differences except related to worship styles. See *Rainer, Thom, "Closing the Back Door of Our Churches", Baptist Messenger*, (5 November 1998), p. 10.

Albright had high expectations of Achewa PIM.[63] He supported the view that no single methodology is as effective in guarding against losing members as is the Sunday School.[64] By retaining as many converts as possible Achewa PIM congregations were expected to grow not only numerically, but also spiritually. BMIM organized training for Sunday School teachers. Although it was a new idea to them, a few APIM churches organized Sunday Schools (See Plate 11).[65]

Bible Way Correspondence School

Some members of Achewa PIM continued to study the Word of God at home through the Bible Way Correspondence School.[66] It was only in 1971 that Ndege received a certificate from Bible Way certifying that he had completed one of the courses that were being offered by the School (See Plate 12)[67].

Church Training

Achewa PIM realized that there was need for educating the whole church (See Plate 13). Every church leader needed some kind of training in order to effectively serve the Lord. Teachers for different age or class groups were a must for all APIM churches. They wanted to develop in all the areas of church ministry. Some of their own members were going to be the teachers, while they needed outside help for

---

[63] Int Yosofati Ndege, Chalendewa, 4.6.1998.

[64] In reference to the church, "back door" problem typically means loss of members or decreases in attendance. "Front door", then, refers to new members or gains in attendance.

[65] Most of the Baptist Convention churches in Malawi have taken Sunday School to be a special time during the Sunday service for the entire congregation to study the Bible in small groups based on age, gender or profession. In small congregations the entire church learns together. Some churches, because of the nature of their composition, have taken Sunday School to be for children only, and others, instead of having SS, they have Bible Study for adults during the week interest of Sunday School.

[66] Bible Way Correspondence School aimed at providing intensive Bible study for church leadership at local level as part of BMIM's literature program. See also D.L. Saunders, "A History of Baptists", p. 131. Bible Way was also used as an evangelistic tool of BMIM and its affiliates.

[67] It was difficult to get evidence from Bible Way of other APIM leaders who completed any of its courses. Two problems could be cited; 1) people used different names when they were being registered with Bible way, and 2) Bible Way's systems of filing are not easy to follow, not only for me, but also for its clerk who did most of the filing.

other ministries. By the participation of the expatriate in Achewa PIM, the desire to learn was rekindled.

Women: Training and Church Planting: Bible Study and Songs

Apart from participating in classes offered at the Bible School, training especially tailored for women was also started. Albright arranged courses for women, and wife Jean used Chichewa tracts together with the Bible. Not only did the women use the passages of Scripture from the Bible as evangelistic tools, they also utilized them to formulate songs and performed drama through which they encouraged, warned and taught each other.[68] At one such meeting, Nsabwe church won the first place, while Mgala, Chalendewa and Chinsamba came second, third and fourth. Nsabwe used the words of Genesis chapters 1 and 2 and sang a song entitled Chiyambi (The Beginning). From Matthew chapter 7:7-12, they composed a song called Pemphani (Ask). They also performed a play titled Ndichitenji? (What Must I Do?) from Acts 2:14-47. Enita received a Bible on behalf of the women of Nsabwe.[69]

Christian Women and the Home

Some Achewa PIM women also learned how to sew plain dresses and babies' clothes, home-care, how to live a Christian life and how a Christian woman could witness to her family. Some of the early women who had some training at the Bible School included Emele Ndalama and Kelita Kalonga, who were later joined by several other women such as Enita Kamchedzera.[70]

---

[68] Int Enita Kamchedzera, Nsabwe, 4.10.1998.
[69] Int Enita and Sandifolo Kamchedzera, and Yosofati Ndege, Nsabwe, 4.9.1999.
[70] Int Alexina Lenadi, Kachala, 4.10.1998.

ACHEWA PIM WORKING WITH FOREIGN MISSIONARIES   71

Some of the women who attended classes at the Baptist Bible School during the 1960s

Church Planting

Several women were instrumental in planting Achewa PIM churches in their villages. One such woman during that period was Siteliya Chakwela.[71] She organized a church at Mphanje. Chakwela and five others who included Simiyoni Chando and Edina Sitolo, used to walk almost 5 kilometres to Phatha for worship. These six persons asked for permission to start congregating in their village. By 1963 Chakwela was leading a small congregation in her village.[72] She enjoyed success as a leader and the support of both men and women.[73]

Nevertheless, Chakwela, like most Chewa women, never thought of herself becoming a pastor of a church one day although Chewa Traditional Religion accepted women in leadership positions. As in most churches in Malawi, subordination of women was thought to be divinely sanctioned. The Genesis account of creation was seen as the

---

[71] Int Simioni Kantevu, Mphanje, 21.10.1998.
[72] See Plate 14 for a list of names of members of Mphanje church in 1966.
[73] Int Edina Sitolo, Kakwere, 5.7.1998. Sitelia Chakwera died early in 1999.

biblical foundation for the domination of women by men.[74] Women in APIM never questioned their position in the church even though they formed the majority of the church membership and could have at least expressed themselves and won if they had the right vote as is the case in Baptist churches. In spite of that, church planting, plus *ulangizi* (counselling) and *chelamani* (deacon) positions provided scope for leadership talents to be developed among women. Lack of education, even very basic reading and writing, has prevented women from developing further their leadership skills in Achewa PIM.

Kamkalamba and the Leadership Team

Ordination of Kalonga, Zingano and Ndege as Pastors

Sometime during 1963 Ndalama, who was in some way second to Kamkalamba, had his movements and activities as a pastor reduced after he had fell from a moving ox-cart. He was bed-ridden for some time, which hampered his ministry. In 1963 Kamkalamba called Ndege to Ndalama's home. While standing by his bedside, Kamkalamba informed Ndege of their decision to ordain him as pastor to take over Ndalama's responsibilities. At first Ndege refused stating that he was not yet ready for that high post. Knowing Ndege's abilities, Kamkalamba and Ndalama told him to go home and think about the issue over. After several days of consultations with members of Chalendewa and other churches in the neighbourhood, Ndege went back and informed Kamkalamba that he was ready to take the offer.[75] There was however one problem Kalonga and Zingano had served in APIM much longer than Ndege, and they needed to be considered. Kamkalamba had deliberately sidetracked his brother-in-law, who was already his *mlaliki* at Nyanje. Both Kamkalamba and Ndalama knew Kalonga and Zingano's capabilities and that is why they chose Ndege. Nevertheless, others saw this as a problem. Kokha, who was a *mlaliki* but well advanced in age, suggested the ordination of the three as pastors.[76] Kalonga, Zingano and Ndege were ordained pastors on 23 November 1963.[77]

---

[74] For the opposite position see Janet Kholowa and Klaus Fiedler, *Pa Chiyambi Anawalenga Chimodzimodzi*, Blantyre: CLAIM, 1999, translated into English as: In the beginning God Created them Equal, Blantyre; CLAIM – Kachere, 2000.
[75] Int Yosofati Ndege, Gondwa, 11.10.1998.
[76] Int Numeri Kamunthu, Kalumbu, 26.10.1998.
[77] Int Lositala Vizi, Phatha, 20.10.1998.

Title Change: from Pastor to Bishop

With the ordination of three pastors at the same time and later three *alaliki*, Kamkalamba felt that his title needed to be changed to something that would express his seniority above the other pastors.[78] PIM had a president, a title that was very foreign to Kamkalamba and the people around him.[79] The title of chairman (*wapampando*), was common for anyone who was chairing a meeting of any kind and was thus not impressive. Kamkalamba was looking for a name above that of pastor. Soon he was convinced by the Zion Church leadership that the title of bishop was the highest as it was indicated in the Bible.[80] In 1964 Kamkalamba introduced the pastors to his title of bishop; later encouraged all their members to address him as such. The idea spread and no one stood up to challenge it. Kamkalamba became the first Bishop of APIM without formal arrangements and ordination by his church.[81]

Construction of APIM's Central Church Building at Nyanje

Kamkalamba led APIM's 14 member churches in the construction of the building at Nyanje for the central church designed to seat about 400 persons.[82] Bricks for the building were molded and burnt near the site of the church building. *Mudzi ndi mudzi* (village by village), people went to moulded the bricks. The women and girls brought in water from Nanjiri River or from nearby boreholes and springs. Men and boys prepared the mud and molded the bricks.[83] The value of bricks was estimated at US$ 1,000 at the time.[84] APIM membership raised the required funds although the cash income of the members was very small. The construction of the foundation which was quite deep and wide used a lot of stones. Some were picked from the Nanjiri river bed, while the bulk were moved from Chingombe Hill, north east of Nyanje church. All healthy members stood in a line, *kumapatsirana kuchokera ku phiri* (passing on the stones from person to another from

---

[78] Int Elenesi Wisikoti, Nyanje, 20.6.1998.
[79] The title of president was changed to that of chairman in 1966 when the MCP Convention that met in Kasungu asked Malikebu to change the title since there was only one President in Malawi, Kamuzu Banda. See Patrick Makondesa, "Muocha", p. 1.
[80] The NT *episkopoi* are overseers (plural) in a congregation, not overseers of the pastors of many congregations.
[81] Yosofati Ndege, Chalendewa, 4.6.1998.
[82] Int Lositala Vizi, Phatha, 20.10.1998.
[83] Int Yosofati Ndege, Chalendewa, 4.6.1998.
[84] "Adviser in Malawi".

the hill) without leaving the line. The only part of the body that was allowed to move was from the waist up as one turned left or right to receive and to pass on the stones. It took several days to move enough stones to do the work.[85] If the members had not donated labour for the construction work, the cost of the church building at Nyanje would have reached US $4,000.[86] The *mmisiri* (artisan/senior builder) was from Phatha.[87] By the time Kamkalamba died the church building at Nyanje had the rafters on, ready for the iron sheets.[88]

New Mount – Achewa PIM's central church at Nyanje

Albright's Strategy of Missions among the Chewa

The indigenuity of Christianity in Malawi, and among the Chewa in particular, was a crucial challenge to Albright. He had experienced the need for Christianity in an "at home atmosphere". Such a personal experience as one's own faith could not be thought of indefinitely as

---

[85] Int Lositala Vizi, Phatha, 20.10.1998.
[86] "Adviser in Malawi".
[87] Int Letiya Dooko, Msemanjira, 10.6.1999.
[88] Int David Tsokonombwe, Nyanje, 10.6.1999.

foreign or imported. The psychological and sociological needs of the Chewa of Lilongwe necessitated the involvement of their own people in the re-establishment of Christianity in Mangoni. Somehow Albright understood the Chewa beliefs. His eyes were open and he viewed the African people as capable of guiding themselves. He remembered and was aware that primitive Christianity had existed in North Africa long before it reached America. Many African church fathers had contributed to the formative years of Christianity. The challenge to use Chewa people in missions among their own people was a radical move in BMIM. It challenged the politics of the BMIM which, later brought some freedom to the new church that was to be known as BACOMA; and later the re-establishment of an independent Achewa PIM.

APIM's Contribution to Baptist Work

The Founding of Lilongwe Baptist Church

As a way of putting into practice what they had learnt and were learning from Albright, the Achewa PIM leadership and Albright himself spent much of their time witnessing to people in and around Lilongwe throughout 1963 and 1964. They shared tracts and invited them to for further discussions and for Bible study at Falls Estate.[89] In their witnessing, the Achewa PIM team and Albright did not talk about their churches but about Jesus Christ. As partners something new was being expected by both sides though neither side verbalized it. Converts won through the joint efforts of APIM and BMIM were for a new church. Of course it was a Baptist church since the witnessing was coming from Baptists and they wanted the converts to be like them. Though converts in rural Lilongwe chose to become Achewa PIM members, that did not threaten BMIM's existence. Nevertheless BMIM had more influence on those who joined the Bible study group at Falls. At first they met in Kadongo's building until the Baptist Bible School was built next door. They began meeting in a classroom and later in the dinning hall of the school. Albright was looking for a fully fledged church with regenerate membership that was affiliated to SBC through BMIM. He baptized the converts in Lilongwe River near the bridge. That in itself publicized the presence of the white missionaries working with Achewa PIM. As many more people were won to Christ, the decision was made to look for land in Kawale where a church building was to be constructed.

---

[89] Int Redson Mkaka Banda, Lilongwe, 10.8.1998.

A plot was acquired from the City Council in Kawale 2, and a building was erected. The new church moved to Kawale building under the name of Lilongwe Baptist Church. Converts in town chose to be called by the BMIM's name because they saw there is financial support and probably future links with the outside world. From another perspective here was a foreign mission that had money and other resources working with a local and relatively poor church to start a church that was going to form the foundation of BMIM's activities in Lilongwe, the Central and the Northern regions of the country. For Lilongwe, a church with a sociological composition very different from the APIM was needed.

Evangelism

APIM members, particularly their leaders, were involved in the evangelistic outreach BMIM initiated. In turn Albright attended and participated in the meetings Achewa PIM organized. On many occasions Albright provided transport mainly for APIM leadership to and from the meetings.[90] The first time Kamkalamba went to Njovu Village past Chiuzira, he was taken there by Albright. Several times after he had begun work there, Albright visited him. After the work was established Makhaya and others continued to minister to the people there. On account of Albright's support and occasional provision of transport, and because of Kamkalamba's spirit for evangelism, Kamkalamba probably preached to more people in the rural areas of Lilongwe East than any other Achewa PIM or Convention Baptist.[91] He was instrumental in the founding of churches at Njovu, Gumbi, Chingira, Serengo, Chidothi, Nkhoma and Mwinimudzi. Kamkalamba also participated in the laying of the foundation, for the Lilongwe Baptist Church which later became the mother church of several Convention churches in Lilongwe District which included Falls, Area 23 and Mtendere Baptist churches.[92]

The outside input awakened dormant possibilities in APIM. As they began to re-discover themselves, life-style of some began to rise higher. They began to do the best they could and did not feel guilty about witnessing. To make sure that they were in God's economy, APIM leaders kept their identity and accepted the way they were. God has a ministry and he had a plan for Achewa PIM, so they wanted to be faithful in the things they can do. They did not feel con-

---

[90] Int Elinasi Wisikoti, Nyanje, 20.6.1998.
[91] Int Chief Njovu, Njovu Village, 23.10.1998.
[92] Int S. Gedeya, Njovu, 23.10.1998.

demned by the standards of BMIM, instead they felt challenged. As they succeeded, they did it to the glory of God and not of people.

During the last half of 1969 a section of Achewa PIM congregations contributed some money towards an evangelistic meeting that was to be conducted in the following year. APIM church members did not just sit and wait for the American missionaries to provide for all the financial needs of the meetings, instead they contributed what they were able to share knowing that it was for God's glory.[93]

Laying the Foundation for a Church in Nkhotakota

In 1968, Ndalama, Kalonga, Ndege and other church leaders of Achewa PIM were in Nkhotakota as part of an evangelistic team whose aim was to lay the foundation of BMIM work there. The team preached at Linga and the surrounding villages for almost a week.[94] That was soon followed by the construction of a missionary residence which was occupied by Scott in 1969.[95] Another evangelistic meeting in Nkhotakota was conducted in 1970 in which Ndege also participated (See Plate 16). People who accepted the teaching were gathered into a Baptist church at Linga.[96]

The First Baptist National Crusade Organized by BMIM

While arrangements concerning visiting speakers, accommodation and other logistics, most of the Achewa PIM and BMIM members battled with the question, "1968 1969 1970 *chidzachitika nchiyani*" (what will happen)?, which was printed on posters as part of the campaign strategy (See Plate 17). No one for sure knew what was going to happen; only God knew. It was a powerful evangelistic tool because it

---

[93] Int Wisikoti Thomasi, Nyanje, 31.8.1998.
[94] The word *linga* means stockade, a protective fence of poles, while *mpanda* is the general word for a fence. The settlement that was established by Salim bin Abdullah that was under his control, was soon dabbed *linga* by the local people of Nkhota Kota because it had a protective fence against counter-inversions by local tribesmen under chiefs Malenga and Kanyenda he had overthrown. Though bin Abdullah's successors, also known as Jumbes of Nkhota Kota, were deposed by the British in 1895, the title *Linga* has since remained and it refers to the administrative centre of the District. See also a paper by David S Bone, "An Outline History of Islam in Malawi 1930", n.d., p.1
[95] Baker J. Cauthen, and Others, Advance: A History of Southern Baptist Foreign Missions, Nashville: Broadman, 1970, p. 168.
[96] Int Yosofati Ndege, Chalendwa, 4.6.1998.

kept everyone who read it in anticipation.[97] On 1 April 1970, Ndege, Kamchedzera, Simoko, Halisoni Kapatuka, and Kaligunde were among the many Achewa PIM members who left their homes for Blantyre to participate in the opening ceremony of the Crusade, which brought together local and international speakers.[98] On the morning of 2 April before the opening of the meeting, the team was taken on a tour of Malamulo SDA Mission. In the afternoon they were taken to the Nazarene Church. On 3 April, crusade participants were driven to Likhubula Bible School where they were met by Ronald Barrar, a Seventh Day Baptist missionary, and Chitonya, a pastor of Africa Evangelical Fellowship (See Plate 18a/b/c).

On the opening day of the crusade, Ndege led one of the opening prayers. Kapatuka and Kaligunde were among those who led the singing. They sang from *Nyimbo za Chigonjetso* (Hymns of Victory), a hymnbook had been printed year specifically for the crusade (See Plate 19). As a token of appreciation for Achewa PIM's contribution in evangelism, and in particular to the late Kamkalamba, Albright had a hymnbook printed with a picture of the face of "the Bishop" on its front cover.[99] Soon, it was branded "Kamkalamba Hymnbook". In the Achewa PIM congregations, They would say, "Turn to Kamkalamba number ....".[100] That did not go down well with Kingsley, and probably several other missionaries. He quickly printed a plain person on the front cover of the second edition of the hymnbook. In fact it was not a plain person; it was a picture of Gresham Alufandika, a member of Blantyre Baptist Church).[101]

The Establishment of BACOMA

Since 1962 BMIM had involved some of the Malawian leaders in much of the planning process. The funding for ministries carried out by BMIM in partnership with Achewa PIM came from America through the FMB. If anything, the Malawians provided the human resources. They walked long distances, witnessing with little or no BMIM financial support. By 1968 APIM and the leaders of the new church and BMIM had already begun discussions on the formation of their own *bungwe* (league or organization) which was later to be known as Baptist Convention of Malawi (BACOMA). The main reason for this was that the

---

[97] Int Sandifolo Kamchedzera, Nsabwe, 24.10.1998.
[98] Halisoni Kapatuka was one of the *alaliki* at Mphindo church.
[99] Beverly Kingsley, a note to Hany Longwe.
[100] Int Navisoni Simoko, Phatha, 24.10.1998.
[101] See also Beverley Kingsley, a note to Hany Longwe.

Malawian church leaders did not agree with the white missionaries on the interpretation of the indigenous church principle.[102] As far as they were concerned it was the responsibility of the missionaries to provide Malawian pastors with financial and moral support.[103]

Albright was then the chairman of the Literature and Music Committee, and he desired a rapid transfer of responsibility from missionaries to local leadership without having to remove the BMIM's financial assistance for the ministries. He then resigned from his position in the hope that Makhaya could serve as the chairperson. Unfortunately, it did not work out. BMIM could not allow Makhaya to serve as the head of the ministry; the best they could offer him was the vice chairmanship. That infuriated Albright because it meant that no local leader had the right to direct the use of funds from America though the money was destined for Malawi. His insistence on almost immediate devolution led to a conflict within the Mission.[104] This was not only a conflict between BMIM missionaries, but was also between BMIM and Malawian leadership. The only missionary APIM perceived as living a life of love for other believers was Albright. Albright honoured his desire to work in partnership with other Baptists without overshadowing them. He did not impose on them, instead Albright helped the local Baptists to work towards self-sufficiency through partnership. Albright saw no reason why he should hold on to some work that a Malawian was able to do just as well if not better than himself. On the other hand the Malawian leaders had been looking for that moment and nothing was going to stop them from fulfilling that desire. Achewa PIM

---

[102] Int Stephen Galatiya, Lilongwe, 13.6.1998. According to BMIM, the purpose of the International Mission Board of SBC is indigenous churches that reproduce themselves. An indigenous church is autonomous and independent. It does not depend on outside leadership and funds. The IMB accepts that it is not unusual for nationals to request help from the missionaries and for them to respond compassionately and emotionally. This practice is seen as having the potential of undermining the growth of strong indigenous national work. It is believed that when local Christians look to the Lord to provide for their needs through resources available in their context they are more likely to develop strong churches that reproduce themselves. Directs gifts or subsidy from the outside may undermine local priorities, erode local stewardship, create dependency, favour someone who is out of favour with national body, create jealousy, etc. See Baptist Mission in Malawi Primary Documents Manual 1995, pp. 1,2,5.

[103] The issue has persisted and, at various degrees, has strained the relationship between BACOMA and BMIM. all over the years.

[104] D.L. Saunders, "A History of Baptists", p. 139.

was an example of that freedom and determination. If they could do it, why not the new church?[105]

Achewa PIM remained an independent church despite the partnership with BMIM. They had their own leaders and their own congregations. They did not ask anyone to approve their work or one for financial support. Therefore they were free and nobody could hinder their plans and activities. APIM stood with the leaders of the new church because it was a Malawian cause, and they were a hundred per cent in support of Albright's vision and concept of a separate *bungwe*. Nonetheless, BMIM's agreement to the formation of a new organization was based on a different understanding. One reason was that it was thought of as a way of giving Malawians a means of co-operating with BMIM in winning the country for Christ. It was also seen as giving the local Baptists a means of making decisions in the work.[106] Another reason given was to provide an organization that would allow local churches to voluntarily cooperate in training, missions, and ministries.[107] BMIM interpreted it as a means of uniting Baptist churches affiliated to BMIM, and also as a way of giving them have a voice to speak in the Christian Council of Malawi and to the government.[108] But besides all this, it was a means of separating church and mission, and a way of continuing to tell the local churches to keep off the mission money. Whatever the reason, Achewa PIM was actively involved in the process of forming *bungwe la tsopano* (the new organization).[109]

Makhaya, Galatiya and Njolomole had worked with white people before. They, together with other Malawian Christians, expected BMIM missionaries to live differently from non-Christian whites though many of the Malawians thought that any white person they saw was a Christian. This was because it was difficult to separate the churches from the government since they had come together. The influence of Muslims also affected their definition of Christian. Muslims consider that anyone born in a Muslim country a Muslim. In the same way they say that anyone born in a country governed by Christians or a country that has a Christian majority, must be a Christian. Ndege was of the opinion that Malawians failed to realize that the missionaries were not experts in the Word of God nor more spiritual than them, but that they too were struggling in their walk with the Lord. When BMIM missionaries

---

[105] Int Yosofati Ndege, Chalendewa, 4.6.1998.
[106] Scott, "Answers to Hany"
[107] Swafford, an e-mail to Hany Longwe.
[108] Gene Kingsley, a note to Hany Longwe.
[109] Int Yosofati Ndege, Chalendewa, 4.6.1998.

failed to live by what they taught, the Malawians decided to form their own bungwe.[110]

Early in 1969 BMIM discovered that Albright had been meeting privately with the Malawians and had been encouraging them to fight for a fair share of American financial support which was being sent for ministry. Ndege and others were invited to attend a meeting at the Bible School to discuss the issue. On 5 August 1969 Ndege received a letter from Njolomole Phiri informing him of the decision by BMIM to relieve Albright of his duties in Lilongwe. On 14 August 1969 five Malawian leaders including Njolomole Phiri, Makhaya, Galatiya and Ndege; met with three missionaries: Davidson, Bickers and Swafford. Albright decided to move to Zambia instead of continuing to work in Malawi.[111]

The Albright/BMIM controversy may also have been part of a hardening of attitude in BMIM. In the beginning they were willing to cooperate. This was not a private matter because each missionary represented BMIM through his ministry in a given area. The beginning of the Bible School is enough evidence the attitude of cooperation with others shown by BMIM. They were willing to work with Zion Church, Achewa PIM and certain individuals and members of the "new" church that later came out of cooperative efforts between them. As more and more Malawians began to "see" and probably question certain policies, BMIM's cooperative position changed. The hardening of attitude seems to have continued to the present. If nationalization of BACOMA had been carried out as it was perceived, it may well have been the hardest of attitudes.[112]

Though the bungwe was subsequently constituted in 1972 and was incorporated the following year, BACOMA then operated under the mercy of BMIM with regards its financial support and institutional activ-

---

[110] Int Yosofati Ndege, Chalendewa, 4.6.1998.

[111] See D.L. Saunders, "A History of Baptists", p. 139.

[112] According to SBC International Mission Board Africa Region's understanding, nationalization meant handing over to nationals what the local SBC Mission perceived as belonging to the ministry and not to the missionary. This meant removing even curtains, tables, desks and chairs was seen as belonging to the Mission, and leaving empty buildings for the nationals to put in their own furniture and the like. Nationalization also meant removing all financial support and foreign personnel and expertise from the institutions and local congregations and letting the nationals run them on their own money and expertise. Instead of partnership, the IMB chose nationalization as if the church belonged to people and not to God. Nationalization has been a painful tension between a black church (BACOMA) and a white mission (BMIM).

ities.[113] On 26 May 1972 Ndege was appointed one of the first Trustees of BACOMA at a meeting held at the Bible School. The other Trustees were Njolomole Phiri, Christwick Gazamiala, Makhaya and Galatiya.[114] Ndege was also elected to the office of the vice-treasurer of the new *bungwe*. The rest of the officers were. Ndege and Gazamiala were in office for only a year because they lost their seats in August 1973 when the Convention held its second elections for office bearers.[115] Instead two much younger, more educated and energetic leaders from the "new church", B.P. Kanowa and J.B. Nyirenda, took their places. Neither Ndege nor Ndalama were able to attend the first meeting of BACOMA, which was held on 12 November of the same year after the elections. They were reported as being ill.[116]

Baptist Work in the Northern Region

On 8 April 1970 Achewa PIM leadership was involved in discussions on starting Baptist work in the Northern Region. Two teams were soon sent to survey the place and they reported back the same year. The discussions that followed led to Njolomole Phiri, who was then the Convention Chairman, being sent as the first BACOMA missionary to the Northern Region. He arrived in Mzuzu in April 1971, being financially supported almost entirely by BMIM. By the end of 1972 a church had been established in Mzuzu and a few other Bible study groups were meeting around the town. In 1973 BACOMA agreed at their meeting to assume a substantial part of Phiri's salary.[117] Nevertheless, BACOMA never met that goal; instead the BMIM continued to pay for Phiri for ten years and then stopped.

---

[113] Int Stephen Galatiya, Lilongwe, 29.8.1998.
[114] Christwick Gazamiala was a pastor of the "new church" at Jali in Zomba District. Ndege is still a Trustee for BACOMA, as are so are the other four men. In spite of the election of new Trustees after every two years, the names that appear in the records of the Registrar General in Blantyre are of the first five trustees. That shows of how little importance the office is.
[115] This also shows the sociological difference between APIM and BACOMA. In BACOMA, the leadership of the church was, and still is, not for life but for a set period.
[116] See also BACOMA minutes of 12 November 1973.
[117] See D.L. Saunders, "A History of Baptists", pp. 141-142.

Material Support for Church Leaders: the Case of Ndalama and Baduya in Harare

On 5 October 1973 Ndalama and Baduya went to Harare in search of material help.[118] A certain Christian from Zimbabwe had visited Malawi and met with BACOMA and Achewa PIM leaders at which time the Malawians talked to him about their plight. The Zimbabwean invited them to visit him in his country an offer taken up by Ndalama and Baduya. The Malawians were looking for *makomo otseguka* (opened doors) through which, they hoped; some of their problems would be solved. The BMIM had so much material wealth yet would not share it with their co-workers, since BMIM perceived that the best way to accomplish transition was through holding back the Mission's material resources to Malawians.[119] Although Ndalama and Baduya came back with some things, these were not enough and their effect was short lived. Ndalama and Baduya had hoped to return to Zimbabwe, but for some reason, they never did.[120] The visit to Zimbabwe by Ndalama was the only time Achewa PIM had contact with the outside world in their search for material support. Through various missionaries BMIM several times promised them financial assistance and suits for pastors that were to come from the USA, but that never materialized.[121]

Adoption of CCAP's Concept of Alangizi by APIM and BACOMA

Courses that were geared for *alangizi* were later developed.[122] Mission agencies working among the Chewa (and also Yao) responded differently to some cultural practices that affected the women of that society. The first Protestant church in DRCM the areas of chiefs Mazengera, Kalumbu and Chadza's banned *chinamwali* because some of the things in the ritual conflicted with the demands of Christianity.[123] Banning *chinamwali* made it difficult for Chewa women to join the Church, so a way to attract then had to be found In the 1930s *chinamwali* was Christianized and accepted by DRCM. All female child-

---

[118] Baduya was a Convention pastor stationed at Dedza *Boma*.
[119] D.L. Saunders, "A History of Baptists", p. 310.
[120] Int Yosofati Ndege, Chalendewa, 4.6.1998.
[121] Int Sandifolo Kamchedzera, Yosofati Ndege, Navisoni Simoko, and Wisikoti Thomasi, Chalendewa, 13.6.1998.
[122] Int Enita Kamchedzera, Nsabwe, 25.10.1998.
[123] *Chinamwali* is the first initiation ceremony which marks the end of childhood and the beginning of womanhood.

ren of church members were required to go through the Christian initiation rites which were called *chilangizo*. The obvious similarities were the stages of the rite: puberty, marriage and pregnancy, while the major change was the replacement of *anankungwi* with *alangizi*.[124] These were Christian women chosen by the church itself.

The concept of *alangizi* as it was understood in Nkhoma Synod was introduced in Achewa PIM and BACOMA in the early 1970s.[125] From the beginning of the partnership, one of the major concerns of APIM and BACOMA was to have an *alangizi* program similar to DRCM. Elizabeth Phiri and Carolyn Swafford, who were serving on BMIM/BACOMA Women's Joint Committee, got some information on *alangizi* when they interviewed Mrs Hofmeyr at Nkhoma. After they had organized the information into a booklet, Achewa PIM used the program in the training of *alangizi*. To make sure that elements that the missionaries felt were incompatible with Christian teaching were not taught to the girls or young women, women who were chosen to be *alangizi* had to receive training before they could be called *alangizi*.[126] *Alangizi*-to-be were taught by Malawian women who had received the training from Phiri or Swafford, and later the new *alangizi* taught other *alangizi*-to-be. It was only in the late 1970s that the training of *alangizi* became the responsibility of pastors in the Achewa PIM. They emphasized Christian family life and values; but nothing on *chilangizo*, which was left to the women themselves. That meant the women had to teach what *anankungwi* taught during *chinamwali*, and not as in *chilangizo* although they included some elements of Christianity in their instruction.[127]

APIM, BACOMA and Expansion

The Baptist Mission in Malawi used Achewa PIM as a stepping stone to start its work in Lilongwe that later spread to all district of the Central Region. Although BMIM used some of the leaders in evangelistic meetings outside Lilongwe, Achewa PIM did not expand its mission field beyond the Chewa people. However, Achewa PIM's belief that it was a Baptist church was further authenticated. The first BMIM missionary initiated the partnership view of Achewa PIM as Baptist, but his view was later challenged by those who came after him. From the

---

[124] See Isabel A. Phiri, "Women", pp. 57-58.
[125] See a copy of the e-mail from Gary and Carolyn Swafford, "Questioneer for Hany H. Longwe", 18 March 1999, p. 1
[126] Int Yosofati Ndege, Chalendewa, 4.6.1998.
[127] Int Enita Kamchedzera, Nsabwe, 25.10.1998.

time they separated from PIM (Mbombwe) to the time they went into partnership with BMIM, Achewa PIM had gained some characteristics that were not Baptist. For example, Achewa PIM introduced the office of a bishop with several pastors immediately below him. At first this was not questioned that. The idea of a central church was a direct copy of New Jerusalem Church at Mbombwe: neither was this questioned. Through the introduction of Sunday School, women's groups (which later resulted in the formation of Umodzi wa Amayi a Baptist ku Malawi, a replica of WMU in America), and Achewa PIM involvement in crusades and training programmes, BMIM tried to impose its understanding and interpretation of Baptist beliefs on a church that was steeped in traditional modes of operation. The establishment of BACOMA was a result of the partnership between Achewa PIM and BMIM. Right from the beginning of their relationship BMIM did not specify its real intention: on the other hand, Achewa PIM did not claim ownership of the new congregations. The other reason was that members of the new churches wanted to be associated with the expatriates because BMIM was viewed to be by far superior to Achewa PIM in terms of education and funding. The artificial break between BACOMA and BMIM was mainly due to BMIM's refusal to be equally responsible the SBS's financial support for ministry in the country.

Chapter 4
Independent Again

Build-up to the Separation

Pastors' Support

When concerns are not addressed and dealt with fully, they are bound to resurface in the future and may do more harm than if they had been resolved. That is exactly what happened with the issue that led to the separation of Achewa PIM on the one hand, and BACOMA and BMIM on the other hand. One of the issues was that of pastor support. This issue started sometime in 1965 just before Galatiya returned from Gweru Seminary, and became a thorn in the flesh for both missionaries and the local churches. BMIM did not want to support the church leaders financially because of the experience their fellow missionaries had had with the Convention Baptists in Zimbabwe.[1] When the SBC established work in that country and its ministries were growing, national evangelists and later pastors were employed and most of the Baptist Convention of Zimbabwe's (BCZ) budget was paid for by the Baptist Mission of Central Africa (BMCA). In 1963 the BMCA voted to reduce the church subsidy at a rate of 10% per year with the hope that the new churches indigenous according to their interpretation of the New Testament indigenous church principles. That was of course met with resistance, which led to strained relationships especially between 1965 and 1967. Although the situation improved, the churches never became totally self supporting.[2]

When the leaders of the new church in Malawi asked for a similar set-up, the events in Zimbabwe were still fresh in the minds of the missionaries, who were quick to refuse the idea. BMIM expected the local churches to support their own pastors.[3] The straining of relationship between BACOMA and Achewa PIM was because the latter was not pushing hard enough on the issue. Achewa PIM saw that they were just being drawn into a conflict with which they were not comfortable.

---

[1] D.L. Saunders, "A History of Baptists", pp. 127-129.
[2] Baptist Convention of Zimbabwe, Programme Base Design, Bulawayo: BCZ, 1984, p. 17.
[3] Int Yosofati Ndege, Chalendewa, 4.6.1998. See also D.L. Saunders, "A History of Baptists", p. 127.

From its founding, Achewa PIM never paid its pastors, and since the formation of the partnership with BMIM, APIM had never asked BMIM to financially support its pastors or any other church worker. What the new church was asking for was not compatible with APIM's concept of church government. BACOMA did not accept the stand taken by Achewa PIM, and therefore a way had to be found to dissociate themselves from APIM if BACOMA were to get what they wanted from BMIM.[4]

Resentment of APIM Pastors by BACOMA Leadership

Another issue that contributed towards the separation was resentment or rivalry. BACOMA leadership had not been happy by the way Albright talked about Achewa PIM leadership's commitment to ministry. The new church leadership forgot that it was through the Achewa PIM that Albright was able to reach many people in Lilongwe with the Word of God, and the formation of the first BACOMA church in Lilongwe which later gave birth to several other churches in the Central Region and the development of several of their leaders.[5] Albright had every right to be proud of the partnership with Achewa PIM that had resulted in the new church. Although Achewa PIM leaders were not as schooled as BACOMA pastors, they did a better job of reaching people of Lilongwe with the Word, than did BACOMA leaders during the years of working together with BMIM. The white missionaries had high regards for APIM and their participation in ministry in high in spite of their lack of formal education. Maybe, or maybe not, that BMIM was taking advantage of their lack of formal education. It could have been that it was just a way of buying time; delaying the training of Malawians to take over the responsibility of the denomination from the missionaries.[6] Whatever the reason the white missionaries talked highly of Achewa PIM's leadership, and that was not pleasant to BACOMA pastors. Separation between the two was the ultimate solution.

---

[4] Int David Tsokonombwe, Nyanje, 20.6.1998.
[5] Lilongwe Baptist Church, situated in Kawale 2, was the first BACOMA congregation which started Falls, Area 23 and Area 25 churches. Lilongwe Baptist Church produced leaders such as W.A.C. Chisi, Emmanuel Chinkwita Phiri, and Fletcher Kaiya, and others who have been instrumental in the growth and development of BACOMA.
[6] Int Stephen Galatiya, Lilongwe, 9.12.1998.

Achewa PIM Accused by BMIM and BACOMA of False Doctrine and Sexual Immorality

The final blow that brought about the separation of APIM from BACOMA and BMIM came as a result of accusations filed against the APIM leadership at the time when Scott was the area missionary for Lilongwe. Sometime in 1974 as Scott was visiting with Achewa PIM churches he heard them teach about baptismal regeneration and keeping the Ten Commandments for security of one's salvation. Scott claimed that there was a lot of preaching about works and very little about grace.[7] He felt compelled to challenge them about their doctrine.[8] In spite of repeated challenges from Scott, Achewa PIM leaders are said to have not changed their teaching. Therefore, Scott concluded, first, that people could not find Jesus as their Lord and Saviour by listening to the preaching of Achewa PIM, and second, that Achewa PIM were not Baptists in teaching.[9]

Scott later learned from a certain lady that Achewa PIM were celebrating John Chilembwe Day on the 15th of the month, and on that day it was alleged that Achewa PIM leaders could choose any woman to be their companion for that day and night.[10] Scott spoke to either Ndalama or Ndege who defended the practice by quoting 1 Corinthians 9:5 from the Chichewa Bible, "*Kodi tiribe ulamuliro wakuyenda naye mkazi, ndiye mbale, monganso atumwi ena, ndi abale a Ambuye, ndi Kefa?*"[11] Neither doctrine nor ethical practice of Achewa PIM proved to be biblical, Scott concluded, they were not Baptists. The Achewa PIM leadership did not use the verse to defend sexual immorality but the meeting of men and women together. Achewa PIM knew themselves as Baptists in spite of what Scott or anybody else thought. They could trace their roots to Chilembwe who

---

[7] Scott, "Answers to Hany Longwe".
[8] It was Scott's habit to stop anyone from preaching if he thought that the teacher was not proclaiming the truth.
[9] Scott, "Answers to Hany Longwe".
[10] Int Rue Scott, Oklahoma City, 6.11.1998. Scott could not remember who this lady was. See also Scott, "Answers to Hany Longwe".
[11] *Buku Lopatulika ndilo Mau a Mulungu*, Blantyre: Bible Society of Malawi, 1997 edition. APIM leaders certainly interpreted the verse as they understood it in their mother language. The mistake came because *mkazi* can mean a wife or a woman. The Chichewa version does not state whether it is one's own wife or somebody's wife. It is only when one reads it in English that the meaning is clearer though there is still some debate as to who the women were.

was a Baptist. The BMIM had to decide what to do next since Achewa PIM leadership could not change their position.[12]

Scott discussed the issue with the chairman of BACOMA, Njolomole Phiri, and they agreed to teach Baptist doctrines of salvation, security of the believer[13] and the life of a true Christian. Invitations were sent not only to Achewa PIM leaders but also to chiefs; T/A Chadza, who was a member of the CCAP.[14] The chiefs were invited because they represented the people and the government. They were regarded as *maso a boma ndi makutu a anthu* (the eyes of the government and the ears of the people). In the invitation Scott pledged to reimburse transport costs for those who would attend the meeting, and also provide meals for them at the Bible School.[15] The instruction was conducted in what was (classroom Number 1, just left of the then open courtyard. As Njolomole Phiri was teaching, chief Chadza pointed his finger at Scott and said, "*Inu ndinu mbala*" (You're a thief).[16] According to the Chief, it was wrong and unacceptable for BMIM to have stolen the Achewa PIM and made them part of BACOMA. Scott insisted that they repent and be baptized again or go their separate ways.[17] There was agreement between those who were teaching and several of members of Achewa PIM.[18]

Nevertheless, Ndalama, Kalonga and Ndege did not agree to the demand. Three words were written on the chalk board, and these were, *umodzi*, *ubale* and *ubwenzi*.[19] The Achewa leadership was asked to choose the one that best described their relationship to BACOMA and BMIM. For Achewa PIM, it was like *kuchita maere* (casting lots).[20] They were divided in their choice. Ndalama and Ndege chose *ubale*, while Kalonga chose *umodzi*. Seeing that they were not agreeing on the choice of the kind of relationship they perceived existed between them and BACOMA and BMIM, the Achewa leadership suggested that another meeting be convened in due course to allow

---

[12] Scott, "Answers to Hany Longwe".
[13] This is a typical American Baptist doctrine, definitely not shared by all Baptists.
[14] Scott, "Answers to Hany Longwe".
[15] Int Rue Scott, Oklahoma City, 6.11.1998.
[16] Scott, "Answers to Hany Longwe"
[17] Int Levi Mitsinje, Lilongwe, 25.9.1998.
[18] Scott, "Answers to Hany Longwe".
[19] *Umodzi* means unity or fellowship. It also has the idea of strength: *mutu umodzi susenza denga* (one head cannot not carry the roof), meaning that two heads are better than one. *Ubale* means relationship between members of the same family, while *ubwenzi* is relationship between friends.
[20] Int Yosofati Ndege, Chalendewa, 4.6.1998.

them to straighten out their differences before a final decision was made. Njolomole Phiri and Scott encouraged those who had chosen *umodzi* to be one with them by repenting and being baptized again.[21] After the meeting, only two leaders, Gumbi Banda of Mphindo and L.K. Sandalamu of Dziwe churches invited Njolomole Phiri and Scott to visit their churches and teach the members about salvation and Baptist beliefs and practice, which they did several days later.[22]

Achewa PIM Fighting against Suspicion: Competing for the Souls

Right from the beginning, APIM: and of course PIM: was described as *Mpingo wa Mpatuko*: a church that sold people, a church in which the female members hid knives under their headscarfs, a church of people who were involved in promiscuous sexual intercourse, and a church that advocated abortion and birth control. Achewa PIM had been swimming up-stream, as it were. Like many others, Kamchedzera discovered that there was nothing wrong with what APIM was offering. In fact it was like every other church of Jesus Christ that was aiming at transforming lives in Jesus' name. The church was different because it brought the Good News of Jesus Christ in a different package to the community. Despite being the message delivered in an unconventional wrapping, the emphasis was on a personal relationship with Jesus. Jesus was being presented as the truth, the way and the life. That threw off any dirt that was being smeared on APIM.[23]

The worst and the most popular accusation against APIM conduct—from the time of Kalemba to today—has been on promiscuous sexual intercourse amongst its members. Achewa PIM was accused of encouraging free sex especially between married men and women members.[24] Kalemba was alleged to have been deliberately promoting this as he sent *alangizi* and *alaliki* who were not husband and wife on church errands that in many cases necessitated them sleeping outside their homes. The Achewa PIM members were accused of promiscuity, and the fact that no signs of it were there (children, paternity disputes, maternal confessions in difficult child birth, etc.), was explained by the next accusation that they advocated birth control. They were accused of teaching their members about birth control in

---

[21] Int Nasoni Chalera, Mphindo, 24.10.1998.
[22] Int L.K. Sandalamu, Lilongwe, 9.12.1998. Sandalamu was a *mlaliki* at Dziwe at the time, the highest office at that church.
[23] Int Sandifolo Kamchedzera, Gondwa, 10.10.1998.
[24] Several Lilongwe-based BACOMA pastors and members perceive Achewa PIM as being a church for people who want their sexual desires met.

order for them to enjoy sex.²⁵ Many children have been born ever since then, many of whom are members of Achewa PIM. There are no records of members who are barren: in fact most families have more than five children.

These accusations say nothing about historical facts, but a lot about the opinions of the people. It is said that there is no smoke without fire, but the accusation that Kalemba, and subsequently Achewa PIM, sold people, cannot be taken as "smoke that proves that there is a fire", since the people who disappeared regularly came back alive from Bible School or conferences. But the rumour can be interpreted as a reaction to a new religious and social entity disturbing the status quo; or it can be seen as a conscious attempt to discredit the new force that was coming in. The accusation that women hid knives in their headscarfs means that these women were perceived as different, and as such, perhaps as dangerous. All these accusations are examples of rumours that do not relate to facts.

Kamchedzera delayed joining Achewa PIM because of these accusations. Though he was from a CCAP background, Kamchedzera had been fellowshipping with APIM for several years; and he too had been convinced that that was the right church for him.²⁶ He later went to Zimbabwe in 1954. For almost a year Kamchedzera was a regular attender of a PIM church at Magaba in Harare. In 1955, Kamchedzera was back at his home. In the same year, after proving for himself that the allegations against APIM were false, Kamchedzera was baptized by Ndalama at Mphindo. Kamchedzera became a member of Msendere church when Chimowa was its chairman.²⁷ He vowed that if ever he found out that his wife had sexual intercourse with any men in the church, he would immediately leave Achewa PIM.²⁸

Church Planting in the Midst of Confusion

While people were discussing separation, new churches were being planted. One of them was at Chioza on the way to Thete from Linthipe. In 1973 Chalosi, then a young person and a primary school leaver, moved with his sister from Kaphuka to join their mother at Mwala near Chief Tambala's court. It was also a centre of *Gule wam-*

---

²⁵ Int Yosofati Ndege, Chalendewa, 12.10.1998.
²⁶ Int Sandifolo Kamchedzera, Nsabwe, 25.10.1998.
²⁷ Int Yosofati Ndege, Nyanje, 1.8.1998.
²⁸ Int Sandifolo Kamchedzera, Nsabwe, 11.10.1998. Before marrying him his wife had been with Nkhoma Mission.

kulu.[29] Chalosi tried to start a congregation at Mwala but it did not work. When his mother died and they had noone to depend on as a guardian in that village, Chalosi and his sister decided to move back to Kaphuka where they lived with their grandmother. There he was able to organize a church as a result of a revival meeting. Immediately after the meeting Chalosi was picked up by the MCP Youth League for questioning because they suspected him of being *wa Mboni* (a member of the Jehovah's Witnesses). He was soon released, and together with some early converts there, he erected a church building which was dedicated on 14 September 1975.[30]

Continued Dialogue: APIM's Support for the Continuation of the Partnership

On 31 December of the same year, Kalonga, Ndege, Kingsley, and Gumbi discussed the issue of separation. Another round of talks followed later which resulted in the Achewa PIM calling for a meeting at the central church for its members. The members met on 3 January 1975 and they unanimously agreed to continue meeting with BMIM and BACOMA in order to save the partnership which they viewed as beneficial to the people of the area. Nevertheless, about five days later, Achewa PIM received a letter informing them that BMIM and BACOMA had terminated the partnership. In spite of that the leadership of Achewa PIM continued to work to save the partnership. On 8 September 1975 the Achewa leadership met for the last time to discuss the partnership issue and the decisions that had been taken by the Lilongwe Baptist Association which had met at the Bible School.

Conflicting Ideas about what is Baptist and what is not

Some BMIM missionaries argue that Achewa PIM was never a Baptist church.[31] In spite of that BACOMA recognized APIM as Baptist from the very beginning of its existence as a new church and from the beginning of the partnership between APIM and BMIM. By 1973, several Achewa PIM churches were registered as BACOMA churches, and these included Nyanje, Mphindo, Mwase, Mwinimudzi and Dziwe.[32] These churches were listed under Lilongwe Baptist Association Urban, and not under Achewa PIM. BMIM and BACOMA used different criteria for identifying what was and what was not Baptist. Accepting all or

---

[29] Int Shadreck Chinsera, Nyanje, 20.6.1998.
[30] Int Chalosi, Nyanje, 30.7.1998.
[31] Gene Kingsley, a note to Hany Longwe.
[32] BACOMA Meeting Minutes, item 14/8/73, and minutes of 15 January 1975.

some of Achewa PIM congregations as Baptist depended on BACOMA as a growing organisation responding to the diverse conditions and tensions of the communities in which the churches were being planted. The first BACOMA churches owe their beginning to Achewa PIM despite BMIM saying that APIM had never been Baptist by 1974-75. BMIM claimed that during the partnership, baptism was done by APIM leadership and all the converts became part of Achewa PIM and not of the new church, and that there were no new churches even after the revivals.[33] The truth is that after the National Crusade in which Dr. W.A. Criswell preached, the people who were baptized lived in the villages where the only church was Achewa PIM. BMIM did not start other Baptist congregations in the same villages where there were Achewa PIM churches.[34] In fact BMIM did not start any new church in any village in Lilongwe District. That proves that Achewa PIM was recognized by BMIM as Baptist, and that BACOMA started as a rural church, which it has remained until till very recently. Including Yosofati Ndege in the Board of Trustees for BACOMA meant that Achewa PIM was accepted as Baptist. If by wrong teaching a church ceases to be Baptist, many BACOMA congregations and individuals would not qualify to be called Baptist. Many of those who have come from other denominations hold on to certain teachings from those denominations, such as children's baptism as a means of cleansing the child from sin, and different forms of church government.

The argument may have been a result of Achewa PIM's failure to change to a system that BMIM was advocating. Someone told Albright, that Scott had all of those that wanted to work with BMIM baptized again, but he did not believe them.[35] Though it is estimated that a total of 200 people were baptized at Dziwe and Mphindo churches, the figures may not be a true reflection of the movement then.[36] There has never been a total of 200 members at one given time between the two churches from their founding until the separation. If they were, it would have meant the whole churches turned to BACOMA. It is more likely that individuals from other congregations were rebaptized as well.

---

[33] Gene Kingsley, a note to Hany Longwe.
[34] Scott, "Answers to Hany Longwe".
[35] Albright, e-mail, 12 May 1999.
[36] Scott, "Answers to Hany Longwe".

Schism: Some Congregations Leave APIM for BACOMA

From Nazalete Achewa to Mphindo Baptist Church

Through the invitation of Gumbi and some of the church leaders, Njolomole Phiri and Makhaya made several visits to Mphindo where they taught Baptist beliefs and practice. They insisted that what Achewa PIM was teaching and practicing was not compatible with Baptist beliefs and practice. The BACOMA leadership invited those who wanted to be part of the new church, which was working together with the white missionaries to be rebaptized or baptized for the first time by them. Decisions were made, and on 27 June 1976, forty of the sixty one members at Mphindo church were rebaptized in the Nanjiri river by Njolomole Phiri and became members of BACOMA . The remaining twenty-one, who were led by Chalera and Halisoni Kapatuka, refused because they saw no theological justification for rebaptism . Baptists do not teach that every time one sins, one has to be baptized again. Baptism does not remove sins

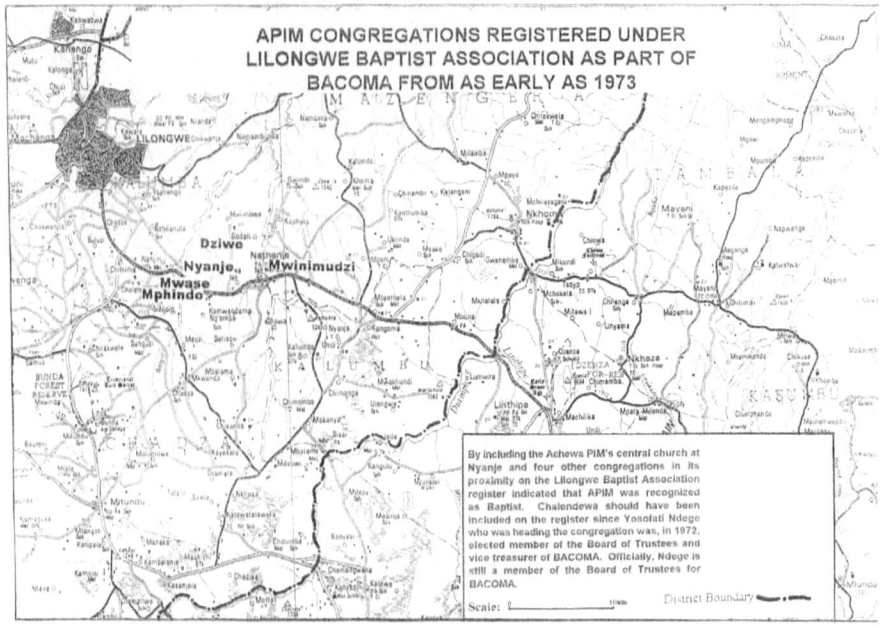

instead it is a one-time event that identifies one with the new life in Christ.[37] Only those who had not been baptized by immersion needed

---

[37] Int Nasoni Chalera, Mphindo, 24.10.1998.

to be baptized if they wanted to join BACOMA. Albright accepted Achewa PIM's baptism. BMIM did the same throughout the early 1970s, but all of a sudden refused to recognize Achewa PIM's baptism. Though BMIM taught that baptism does not save, by rebaptizing they contradicted themselves.[38]

After Njolomole had taught, the word "Achewa" was erased from the title "Achewa Baptist Church" that was written on the inside wall behind the pulpit of Mphindo church.[39] The church at Mphindo did this in order to identify itself with BACOMA and BMIM. Achewa PIM as a whole, however, refused to drop its identity.[40] It was impossible for APIM to accept this, because it was like removing *ubatizo wa John Chilembwe* and replacing it with that of the "foreigners". Partnership or no partnership, that was not the way to foster cooperation. When Albright talked with APIM leadership about partnership, one thing that brought them together was the "Jordan".[41] They were all baptized by immersion. Both had Baptist roots and called themselves by that name. No baptism was superior to the other.

The anti-rebaptism group was forced out of Mphindo church. There was no way that two differing groups could meet in the same building. Chalera and others moved to a new site south east of the village, and began meeting in the shade of a tree. A year later they erected a grass thatched church building. The building was renamed Nazalete (Nazareth), the original name of the building then occupied by BACOMA. Chalera, who had participated in some of the instruction that had been offered at the Baptist Bible School, became its pastor. Since then the two churches have co-existed. Whenever some Achewa PIM congregations such as Mphindo had a meeting, they invited BACOMA to send a preacher or representatives to participate not just observe. At no time did BACOMA give Achewa PIM leadership opportunity to preach at their meetings at Mphindo. Nevertheless, Achewa PIM still regarded themselves as one with BACOMA.[42]

---

[38] Int Jese Mnjolo and Halisoni Kapatuka, Mphindo, 24.10.1998.
[39] Int Lemia Yohane, Mphindo, 7.6.1999.
[40] Int David Tsokonombwe, Nyanje, 20.6.1998.
[41] Int Yosofati Ndege, Chalendewa, 4.6.1998.
[42] Int Yulita Mgala, Mphindo, 2410.1998.

Changing Churches. Rebaptism at Mphindo

Out of Dziwe Came Kafumbula Baptist Church

Another church that came out of Achewa PIM is Kafumbula Baptist Church. In 1975, the Achewa PIM church building at Dziwe was destroyed by fire.[43] The BMIM came to their rescue. They bought iron sheets and repaired the roof. Dziwe was one of the churches that the Convention registered as part of Lilongwe Urban Baptist Association, even though this was never discussed with APIM. In addition, Dziwe is nowhere near the town of Lilongwe to be entered as under urban; it is actually outside the current municipality of Lilongwe boundary. By then a group led by Sandalamu had already identified itself with BMIM and BACOMA.[44] Seeing that the majority of the members at Dziwe, unlike those at Mphindo, did not want to have anything to do with re-baptism, the group moved out of Dziwe church and started meeting at Kafumbula which is less than two kilometres away. Sandalamu and his group were in the process of building a church and were in need of roofing materials iron sheets.[45] When Dziwe refused to dance to the tune of Scott and Njolomole Phiri, Sandalamu pressured

---

[43] Int Navisoni Simoko, Chalendewa, 25.9.1998.
[44] Gene Kingsley, a note to Hany Longwe.
[45] Int L.K. Sandalamu, Lilongwe, 9.12.1998.

Scott to remove the iron sheets from Dziwe church and give them to Kafumbula.[46] Scott planned to do just that, but before he could do so it, the matter was reported to Chief Kanduna II. BMIM had bypassed Achewa PIM because Baptists believe in the autonomy of the local church, but when the pastor of Dziwe, Kamchiliko, could not stand the pressure from Scott and BACOMA leadership, he reported the matter to the Achewa PIM leadership who in turn took the matter to the chief.[47] Kanduna summoned the two sides to his court, and the issue was discussed on 13 December 1976 (See Plate 30).

Representing the government was the MCP delegation in the area as was common in those days. The chairperson for the MCP area office asked Scott why he wanted to remove the iron sheets from Dziwe church building. Scott told the court that Dziwe church was not living according to Baptist beliefs and practice.[48] The Chairman reminded Scott and his colleagues that the Government, and in particular the people of the area, viewed the roofing of Dziwe church building as the missionaries' contribution to the development program of Malawi. Now that they were contemplating destroying what they had built, the church felt that their motive was much more than trying to teach Dziwe a lesson. He concluded that the iron sheets that they had given to Dziwe as a gift had become the property of Dziwe, and not of the giver.[49]

The Women's League of the MCP was very vocal against BMIM. As Kamuzu's *mbumba*, they emphasized that their concern was the President's business, and BMIM knew that very well.[50] The women warned BMIM of the consequences of forcing people to do what the missionaries wanted. Malawi was no longer under any colonial power, and therefore the people had the right to choose their destiny. The best way was for the missionaries to leave Dziwe alone and start anew. If they removed the iron sheets at any time, that signalled that they were anti-Kamuzu, anti-MCP and against the people of Malawi. It also meant that the missionaries had lost the vision of their mission, and deserved to be deported as prohibited immigrants.[51]

---

[46] Int W.A.C Chisi, Lilongwe, 4.10.1998.
[47] Int Yosofati Ndege, 4.6.1998.
[48] Int Oliva Masalaza, Mphanje, 26.9.1998.
[49] Int Shadreck Chinsera, Nyanje, 20.6.1998.
[50] Int Velina Khama, Mphindo, 7.6.1999. *Mbumba* means kindred, those sustained by one, thus one's female relations; it also means descendants.
[51] Int Wisikoti Thomasi, Mwase, 14.5.1999.

Ndege gave an illustration on relationship from a Malawian perspective.[52] He said that if a man was struggling to finish the roof of his house and a friend gave him some grass with which to thatch the house, the owner of the house would gladly accept the gift. Supposing some time in the future the two disagreed on a certain matter, would the one who gave the grass demand that the roof be robbed of the grass because they had disagreed? What had the disagreement to do with the roof? Gifts or services were not given in order to manipulate the ones who had received the donation. The recipients were free to choose their own destiny with or without the contribution. Immediately Ndege said this, Scott chose to not remove the iron sheets from the church building.[53] This also applied to the central churches at Nyanje and Chalendewa, which had iron sheets given to them through BMIM. The only difference was that these two church buildings had received their assistance during the time of Albright: probably that is why there was no immediate threat on them although Nyanje was listed as a Convention church. The world would have known if iron sheets were removed from Nyanje because it is a big church in terms of size, and a very important one in the history of Achewa PIM.[54]

Kafumbula church building had a tin roof within a fortnight from the day of the meeting.[55] The members there did not go through the process of applying for assistance through the Church Development Committee (CDC), as was the practice of the day if a Convention Baptist church wanted to get help from the BMIM for the construction of a church building.[56]

---

[52] Int W.A.C. Chisi, Lilongwe, 4.10.1998.
[53] Int L.K. Sandalamu, Lilongwe, 9.12.1998.
[54] Int Yosofati Ndege, Gondwa, 10.10.1998.
[55] Int L.K. Sandalamu, Lilongwe, 9.12.1998.
[56] The church building policy was that the local church built its building and BMIM would provide for the roof, though there were slight variations that depended mostly on the character of the missionary in the area. The village church had to build the wall to roof height and then the BMIM would put on the roof up to a certain size. For anything bigger than what BMIM stipulated as standard, the members had to look elsewhere for iron sheets and timber. That was recorded as the congregations contribution of about 20% since most of the walls were of mud. The most expensive part has always been the roof. At one time town churches had to have 50 members and a budget to pay the pastor. Whether the church would actually pay the pastor or not was another matter; what was required was to show it in their budget. That being the case, BMIM would finance the whole building. Later where town planning required more expensive buildings, some additional funds were provided, but

From Mwinimudzi to Nathenje

A third Achewa PIM congregation that became at least partly a Convention church was Mwinimudzi, which was at a village by the same name, several kilometres across Nathenje on the left hand side of the M1 from Lilongwe.[57] It was led by village headman Mwinimudzi. Almost the whole village had followed the chief in joining Achewa PIM through the preaching of Kamkalamba. In 1976 the members again followed the chief when he made the decision to join BACOMA.[58] Mwinimudzi existed as a Convention Baptist church for just over a year. Due to the demand for more farming land, the chief decided to move to Mchinji District where land was available. Many people moved with him but a few remained in the area. Since the key person had moved away most of the remaining few either moved to other churches or stopped worshipping altogether, but one or two continued as Convention Baptists.[59] The church building had a tin roof; something that was not easy to get unless the church had money or received outside help. Since there was no church meeting, there anymore and chances were against it growing again due to the movement of people from that area, the Convention decided to relocate the church to Nathenje TC where there were a few Convention Baptists meeting in the open. Possibilities were that the church would grow since people were moving to Nathenje and that it would be a springboard for evangelistic crusades into the surrounding villages. The church building at Mwinimudzi was replaced with a new one at Nathenje in 1977.[60]

The Differing Positions of Albright and Scott

Albright had gifts of giving and of mercy. The major reason behind his choice to work with Achewa PIM instead of any other churches in the area was not because APIM was a Baptist church, but that he realized a dynamic of great importance in tribal churches: and that was a mass or people movement.[61] This means that people become Christians in groups. Chewa people, like other strong group-oriented tribes,

---

local congregations were asked to contribute about 20% of the total cost (See Gene Kingsley, Scott and Swafford).
[57] Gene Kingsley, a note to Hany Longwe.
[58] Int B. Kapalamula Banda, Lilongwe, 26.1.1999.
[59] Int Yosofati Ndege, Gondwa, 10.10.1998.
[60] Int W.A.C. Chisi, Lilongwe, 18.3.1999.
[61] Gene Kingsley, a note to Hany Longwe.

make decisions on issues such as marriage, migration and use of land as a family or group acting as a whole.[62]

Albright emphasized on people and not their cultures for he realized that Jesus came into the world not to save cultures but people, and he came to change them into his likeness. Albright did not talk about Southern Baptists as the version of the church that most closely represented the system that included particular kinds of behaviour, institutions and personality traits called for in Scripture though he might have had that at the back of his mind. As APIM's life and social relationships were being changed, so were his.[63] Albright quietly threw away what he saw as not Christian in APIM and spent much time on publicizing things that contributed to the expansion of God's Kingdom. Almost 28 years after his departure from Lilongwe, memories of Albright were still vivid in the minds and hearts of the Achewa PIM, who described him as a disciple of Jesus Christ, one who could easily say with Paul, "Imitate me".[64]

Although Scott had known about Achewa PIM since 1968, he was directly engaged with Achewa PIM only after Albright's departure in 1970. Unlike Albright, Scott was a teacher.[65] Such being the case, he was motivated by making sure that facts were accurate so that decisions that were made upon them could also be correct. He was very alert to what he considered false teachers and their teaching. When he heard that the Achewa PIM leaders teach that a person had to be baptized and keep the Ten Commandments in order to be saved, he saw no choice but to condemn them though he tried to correct them although courses of instruction he and Njolomole Phiri led at the Bible School. The instruction by these two men became the credentials by which APIM members were to be approved as Baptists. That yardstick was also applied in BACOMA congregations. The practical wisdom of

---

[62] Hiebert, Paul G. and Eloise Hiebert Meneses, *Incarnational Ministry: Planting Churches in Band, Tribal, Peasant, and Urban Societies*, Grand Rapids: Baker, 1995, pp. 159-161.

[63] Cf. Sherwood Lingenfelter, *Transforming Culture: A Challenge for Christian Mission*, Grand Rapids: baker, 1992, pp. 17-19.

[64] Int Julius Mbalame, Sitoliya Chakwala and Oliva Masalaza, Chalendewa, 26.9.1998. Cf. 1 Corinthians 11:1.

[65] I knew Scott personally. He was my TEE (Theological Education by Extension) class teacher and area missionary for Nkhota Kota at the time when I was working under the engineering department at Dwangwa Sugar Corporation. It was when I was studying under him that I decided to quit working in the secular field and go into Christian ministry of some kind. He always wanted to confirm that the statements one made were true and accurate, and that they would bring salvation.

these unschooled people was minimized. Scott and Njolomole Phiri made the mistake of concentrating on intellectual knowledge rather than spiritual enlightenment.[66]

Though BMIM had hoped to transform APIM into an unquestionably Baptist denomination through a people movement, and though there was a deliberate attempt to transfer a particular Baptist system from the USA to Mangoni, it did not work. BMIM was in a rush to win people without giving them time to digest what they heard and what was expected of them. A couple of months to decide to change from whatever they were to "Baptist" was too short a time. As a result, APIM chose to remain independent, free from outside domination.[67] Their theology also remained shallow. In a way, Achewa PIM saw the work of BMIM more as a reflection of American social life; they were imposing their culture on Achewa people. BMIM was not a reflection of the interests of Christ on the Achewa people. It was in the best interest of Achewa PIM to part company with BMIM and maintain their identity as an indigenous African church.[68]

BMIM has argued that APIM remained independent because they wanted to maintain the offices of the bishop, "big" pastors and "lesser" pastors.[69] The office of bishop was established during the early years of the partnership between Achewa PIM and BMIM. To because Achewa PIM to change because of those offices does not do justice to the autonomy of Achewa PIM. From the teaching of Kalemba they knew that they were a Baptist church among many Baptists in the world. That was confirmed when Albright began working with them. Albright did not start new churches for Achewa PIM, instead they were instrumental in the founding of Convention Baptist churches in Lilongwe and other districts in Malawi through the preaching of the so called bishop and "bigger" and "lesser" pastors.[70] Convention leadership followed in areas where these men had already pioneered.

---

[66] Njolomole Phiri was removed from BACOMA's chairmanship in 1980, and membership in 1981 after a struggle. In March 1979 he had borrowed MK2,000 in the name of the church.
[67] Gene Kingsley, a note to Hany Longwe.
[68] Int Yosofati Ndege, Navisoni Simoko, Wisikoti Thomasi, Sandifolo Kamchedzera, and others, Chalendewa, 20.6.1998.
[69] Gene Kingsley, a note to Hany Longwe.
[70] Gumbi, Chingira, Serengo, Chidothi, Lilongwe, Nkhota Kota Baptist churches, and several in Chikwawa and Phalombe districts, to mention a few.

Church Structure after Kamkalamba's Death

Kamkalamba died on 22 June 1967 and was buried on 24 of the same month. Since he had been the leader of Achewa PIM, his death was reported to the *boma* (in this case to the District Commissioner and the MCP) by the APIM leadership, which was led by Ndalama, Kalonga and Ndege.[71] A burial site was chosen close to the central church and it was approved by chiefs Mazengera and Chadza. Even after Kamkalamba's death the relationship between APIM and BMIM remained strong. Sometime in 1968 Albright contributed a lot to the construction of Kamkalamba's *chiriza* (memorial pillar over the grave). He did this in order to acknowledge Kamkalamba's Christian fellowship, to affirm Kamkalamba's missionary cause, which Albright had helped cultivate among the Achewa PIM members.[72] Furthermore Kamkalamba was a man of vision. He directed Achewa PIM to reach new heights in their history. Though he was a man of small stature, Kamkalamba was very energetic in all he did, be it in missions or in the construction of a church building. He was also admired for his firm stand on what he believed and practiced.

Aaron Kamkalamba's Chiriza

---

[71] Int Yosofati Ndege, Kakwere, 4.7.1998.
[72] Int Peturo Simoko, Phatha, 20.6.1998.

Kamkalamba's *chiriza* (memorial pillar) has no equivalent.[73] It is truly *chiriza cha munthu wamkulu* (for an important person), but there is nothing else like it in the area. It is a design that was brought to the people by Albright. In fact he brought a couple of designs to the leaders of APIM, and suggested the design of the *chiriza* that is there today. [74] The bricks required for the erection of the *chiriza* were molded near the site by church members, who also brought some of the stones that were required for the foundation. Albright paid for the purchase of construction steel and bags of cement. He also paid the builder and his assistants.[75]

Kamkalamba's *chiriza* reminds me of the *machila* (hammocks) that were used as a means of transport by early missionaries and other white travellers in Africa. Though at first the use of *machila* was confined to ladies and invalids, its use gradually became universal by all white travellers, men and women alike. From a hammock slung on the shoulders of two strong and faithful *machila* men, came two-poled hammocks that enabled two men to walk or run abreast.[76] Kamkalamba's *chiriza* seems to me to be a further improvement from the 4-men *machila* to a 6-men *machila*. It has six sturdy pillars, three on each side, built on a concrete base. The pillars support a concrete platform on which is built a large chair. Instead of representing the person being carried as lying down on a *machila*, Kamkalamba's *chiriza* portrays him as seated on a chair, a sign of authority, placed on a firm foundation, Jesus Christ. Kamkalamba was thought of as having the key to the success of Achewa PIM since the death of Kalemba. The chair on the *chiriza* was also meant to show that Kamkalamba had left with his chair and it was going to be difficult to find his replacement.[77] Even the current leadership and members attest to Kamkalamba's contribution to the success of APIM as second to none. *Sitidzampeza wina monga madala* (We will never find another one like the old man).[78] In an attempt to justify their actions of about 30 years previously, BMIM missionaries have interpreted the chair on the *chiriza* as a deliberate attempt on the part of Albright to put an

---

[73] Int Yosofati Ndege, Chalendewa, 13.6.1998.
[74] Int Elenesi Wisikoti, Nyanje, 20.6.1998.
[75] Int Letiya Dooko, Msemanjira, 10.6.1999.
[76] Barbara Lamport-Stokes, *Blantyre: Glimpses of the Early Days*, Blantyre: The Society of Malawi, 1989, p. 134.
[77] Int Elenesi Wisikoti, Nyanje, 20.6.1998.
[78] Int Yulita Mgala, Oliva Masalaza, Yosofati Ndege and Navisoni Simoko, Chalendewa, 24.10.1998.

end to the office of "bishop" since Baptists in general do not talk of denomination leaders as bishops.[79]

When Kamkalamba's wife, Alesi, also died, the chiefs requested that she be buried on the same site as her late husband. When his sister died, her remains were buried by Kamkalamba's grave, on the other side[80] It is cultural practice that a family is buried together. The burial site, which is also called *mudzi* (village), is seen as a continuation of the family's fellowship and unity beyond the grave. This reminds me of what Joseph asked for from his brothers in Egypt: when he saw that the time was near for him to die he asked that they take his remains back to their homeland the moment God delivered them from Egypt.[81] In the case of Kamkalamba, Alesi and his sister, they were given a special place for their contribution and the impact they made on Mpingo wa Mpatuko and the community as a whole. The three graves are a symbol of hard work, dedication, unity and fellowship within the church, the home and the community.[82]

Pastoral Leadership of APIM's Central Church

After the death of Kamkalamba, Kalonga became the pastor at Nyanje. Dooko was ordained *mlaliki* while Tsokonombwe became *mkulu wa mpingo*. Tsokonombwe had been to South Africa once, before he made several trips to and from Zimbabwe between 1962 and 1974. For two years he worked in Almond Shaft No. 2, part of a gold mine in Johannesburg. For just over 4 years Tsokonombwe worked at Clifton Estate, a tobacco farm in the Sinoia area. During one of his trips back to Malawi, Tsokonombwe had met with Mary from Chimpeni near Chiuzira, and they had become friends. On his final trip back home Tsokonombwe found out that, like his mother Kelita, Mary had met with and had been abandoned by another man who had also left for South Africa when she was already pregnant. Though she was pregnant by another man, he was still attracted to Mary and he married her and he married her.[83] It was during the same year that Kamkalamba died that Nyanje gave permission to some of its members to start a church at Chakwawa south of Nathenje TC.[84]

---

[79] Gene Kingsley, a note to Hany Longwe.
[80] Int Elenesi Wisikoti, Nyanje, 20.6.1998.
[81] Genesis 50:25.
[82] Int Letiya Dooko, Msemanjira, 10.6.1999.
[83] Int David Tsokonombwe, Nyanje, 10.6.1999.
[84] Int Letiya Dooko, Msemanjira, 10.6.1999.

It was Mary who was instrumental in the establishment of a church at her home, Chakwawa.[85] She owed her stand in the community to her late father, who had prepared her for a challenging life. People in the area thought of her as having a man's heart in a woman's body. She was courageous and hard working. Mary lived on the farmland her late father had bought. After joining Achewa PIM and walking to and from Nyanje for worship, Mary and three other families decided to ask Nyanje to grant them permission to start a church at her home. When permission was given, Mary gave part of her land on which the congregation met and later erected a church building. Not only did she give the land, she also contributed materials for the construction and maintenance of the church building. Each time there was a section meeting being held at Chakwawa, Mary provided much of the food, including milk from her cattle, to feed people attending the fellowship. People just loved to be close to her. Mary's life was a testimony of Christian character.[86]

An Interim Leadership Team: Fulfilling the Role of a Bishop

The death of Kamkalamba left a vacuum in the Achewa PIM that needed to be filled. The three "big" pastors took the place of Kamkalamba's office. Achewa PIM was not divided into three small groups of churches each with its own leader as suggested by because of a power struggle as was suggested by Saunders.[87] What he did not understand is that APIM, like PIM (Chiradzulu), was divided into sections, and each division was headed by a pastor. Although Ndalama lived at Kumisu, he was responsible for all the churches in Nkhoma and Dedza areas, while Kalonga was responsible for all the churches near to Nanjiri and Nathenje Rivers including Chiuzira and Nambuma. Ndege was left with churches from Katunga and Chinsamba in the south to Mpindo in the north. One could easily get to these churches from Chalendewa via Chadza or Bunda Loop routes. There is no record of these men ever fighting for power, instead they are known to have acted as one person despite disagreeing at times over certain issues.

In Chewa culture, the next head of the tribe or clan can only be installed after at least a year since the last chief was buried. The interim head is known as *kalinde* (attendant). In the case of the Achewa PIM, Ndalama, Kalonga and Ndege acted together as *kalinde*. It is during

---

[85] Int Shadreck Chinsera, Nyanje, 20.6.1998.
[86] Int David Tsokonombwe, Msemanjira, 10.6.1999.
[87] D.L. Saunders, "A History of Baptists", p.130.

mpalo (ritual shaving of the hair on the mourners' heads ritual) that the next chief is chosen and initiated.[88] That also applies to families. A year or so was to elapse before a widow or widower could marry again. The Achewa PIM was not in a hurry to choose a bishop. The three-in-one *kalinde* provided the leadership APIM needed. From 1978 after the death of Ndalama, Kalonga and Ndege guided Achewa PIM until 1985 when Kalonga died and Ndege became the sole *kalinde* until 1986.

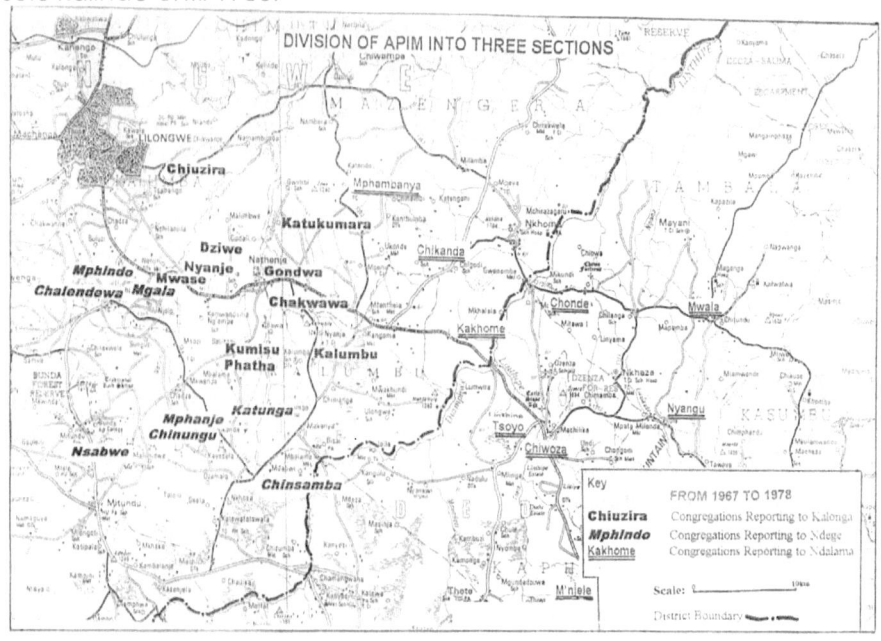

Division of APIM into three sections

The Second Achewa PIM Bishop and his Vice

Soon after the death of Kalonga, APIM membership began talking about finding someone to fill the office of the bishop.[89] At a meeting which was held at Gondwa, a nominating committee of five women and four men, Kamchedzera, Vizi, Nkhalamba, Akim Ndege, Bezina Folomana, Enita Kamchedzera, Mrs Nkhalamba, Chakwela and Mrs Marudo met in Sopo's house and agreed to present Ndege as the on-

---

[88] Int Kasinja Nyengere, a Chewa, and a cook at the Baptist Theological Seminary, Lilongwe, 26.7.1999.
[89] Int Seliasi Kantigiri Sopo, vice bishop of APIM, Nyanje, 31.8.1998.

ly candidate for the office of bishop of APIM.[90] During their deliberations, Sopo appeared in the room and asked the committee members whom they had nominated. When they told him their choice, he replied, "*osaiwala vaisi*" (don't forget the vice), and he quickly left the room. Achewa PIM members present unanimously chose Ndege to be the next bishop of Achewa PIM though some participants were not in favour of him because *anali wamasiye* (widower)[91].

Mwambo wodzodza bishopi (The ordination of the Bishop) was done during the Annual Meeting in August at Nyanje. Ndege was seated between two female *aphungu* (councillors) in front of the congregation, which numbered over two thousand adults. His head and shoulders were covered with a white cloth. *Ulaliki wa odzodza* (the message on ordination) was delivered by Chief Chadza, who preached from Psalms 47:1-2; Proverbs 25:2; Isaya 28:9; and Titus 1:15.[92] After the preaching, a song was sung, and then came *kuika manja* (laying of hands). Chief Chadza of Zion Church at Matapila, Ndalama and two other members of APIM laid hands on Ndege's head.[93] Each participant laid his right hand first, and then the left on top of the previous person's right hand. They all prayed softly while the congregation sang. After the congregation had been seated, it was time for *chilangizo* (giving counsel or instruction) to the newly elected bishop. Those who had the opportunity to instruct repeated what others had already said, which is known as *kuthira ndemanga*. They encouraged Ndege to work with and to take care of the members. At the end of the ceremony, the cloth over Ndege's head was removed by one of the counsellors amidst *nthungululu* (shrill trill), clapping of hands and dancing and singing from the congregation. A closing prayer came from one of the members of APIM, and the service was handed over to the congregation. Members went past where Ndege was seated and shook his hand in turn and said a few

---

[90] Nkhalamba and his wife were members of Gondwa church where he was a deacon. Bezina Foloma and *amayi* Marudo were *alangizi* from Phatha and Katunga, respectively, while Akim Ndege, a deacon at Chalendewa, was Ndege's young brother.

[91] Int Seliasi Kantigiri Sopo, Falls Estate, 11.8.1999.

[92] Int Sandifolo Kamchedzera, Nsabwe, 4.9.1999. Chief Chadza was at the time a member of APIM, but when he was *anagwidwa ufumu* (he was initiated as a chief), he immediately left the church.

[93] Two of the people who had been invited to participate in the ordination but did not make it were Jawati from Nyangu in Dedza and Kachiko from Kumisu. Both men were PIM pastors. Kachiko failed to attend because one of his children had died and his burial was on that very day. No apology was received from Jawati.

words of congratulation or encouragement. Immediately, Ndege ceased to be *Kalinde* and was now the Bishop of APIM.[94] Though Baptists rarely have bishops, the ordination followed the common Baptist practice, as the authority to ordain is with the churches, not with a higher authority. A Baptist ordination is usually done by lay and ordained church members together, while in the Presbyterian tradition the power to ordain rests only with the ordained. Ndege did not move to the central church but remained at Chalendewa. In 1985, Dooko had become the pastor of Nyanje church and was being assisted by Tsokonombwe as *mlaliki*.[95]

Sopo became the vice bishop, but he was not ordained. Two weeks after the ordination of Ndege, Kamchedzera and the nominating committee held a meeting with representatives from APIM congregations at Gondwa where they confirmed Sopo's position.[96] The choice of the vice bishop gave the people of Nkhoma to Dedza area someone to act as a connection between them and the bishop.[97] Travel in these areas where APIM churches are located is not easy, not only for the aging bishop but for everyone. Many churches are not connected to good roads, but to footpaths. Since there are many marshy areas and streams to cross, one often has to follow long and winding footpaths. Even if there were good roads and public transport in the area, most of APIM members would not be able to afford the fares. They either walk or ride bicycles or ox-carts. The presence of the vice bishop, for the majority of the APIM members, helps also cut the cost of attending g -every meeting with the bishop. He is centrally situated at Nathenje so that he can get to Chalendewa and to Nkhoma relatively easily.

APIM History: an Interpretation

The emergence of PIM in Mangoni was met with suspicion by the Government, by other missionary churches and by local people. The members were forced to bind themselves together in defence of their newly won religious identity. PIM grew even stronger in Mangoni when it was forced to go underground. In spite of the threats of isolation and even death, Kalemba built men and women who stood for what they believed was their right. Kalemba was identified as one among the Chewa sages. He was a Chewa leader amongst Chewa follow-

---

[94] Int Enita Kamchedzera, Nsabwe, 4.9.1999.
[95] Int Letiya Dooko, Msemanjira, 10.6.1999.
[96] Int Sandifolo Kamchedzera, Nsabwe, 4.6.1999.
[97] Int Sandifolo Kamchedzera, Gondwa, 10.1.1998.

ers. He was the undisputed founder of the Church in Mangoni, and received full support from the members. In 1934, almost the entire PIM joined Kalemba to form Achewa PIM. That gave Anderson Nyangu an opportunity to lead the few PIM (Mbombwe) loyalists, who later multiplied also. Still PIM membership has not been high in the areas where Achewa PIM has existed.

Achewa PIM would not have been organized if it were not for Malikebu's attitude to his subordinates, especially Kalemba. Malikebu's dictatorial attitudes were shown in his monopoly of the Church offerings, in the performing of all baptisms and celebration of all marriages. In spite of Kalemba's agreement to operate under his leadership, Malikebu should not have forgotten that it was Kalemba who had begun PIM and had kept it alive in Mangoni.

His treatment of Kalemba was a departure from Chilembwe's method of treating co-workers. The movement of almost all PIM members in Mangoni to form APIM was an indication of their resentment of Malikebu's leadership. Malikebu showed no respect for Kalemba. He should have treated Kalemba differently from other subordinates because Kalemba had been carrying out orders for Chilembwe in order to keep the Church alive. Malikebu's attitudes toward Kalemba and others distracted from for what Chilembwe had stood, to lift Africans from degradation and make them decent members of the larger human race. There was no way people in Mangoni would modernize themselves under the dictatorial rule of Malikebu. PIM members in Mangoni wanted freedom and independence and as a result they agreed to dissociate themselves from Mbombwe.

They were unable though to widen their mission field beyond the Chewa people. One reason could be the tribal boundaries that existed in those days and that the members of Achewa PIM did not want to incite tribal quarrels. On the point of theology, the Achewa PIM had not really thought of the Great Commission. They needed to do the same thing that Chilembwe did to drop "Ajawa" from the title of his church when he realized that the church was designed to make followers from all ethnic groups. Culturally, the Achewa PIM were proud to be identified as a people concerned about reaching their own people with ideas which worked for other Africans in the country. Kalemba was a living testimony of that.

It was Kamkalamba who led APIM into partnership with BMIM, a relationship that benefited BMIM more than Achewa PIM. During the partnership, Achewa PIM membership was introduced to a wider mission field for the benefit of the expatriates. Regardless of that exposure and the nature of the partnership, Achewa PIM's mission field remained the Chewa people. The results of their labour outside their area throughout the Central and the Southern Regions went to the expatriates. They got the credit. During the partnership, BMIM tried to change APIM by imposing SBC's interpretation of Baptist beliefs and practice. Achewa PIM resisted the changes that BMIM was imposing on it, instead it continued to operate in its traditional manner. The leadership style, church fellowship, men and women relationships, the church singing and sharing of the gospel suited well the Chewa people. Everything was done in a Chewa package, so to speak. The expatriates wanted it to be presented in an SBC package, which was not acceptable. The partnership was severed because of the demands imposed on Achewa PIM by BMIM and the fruit of their joint efforts, BACOMA. There is no big difference between an Achewa PIM and a BACOMA congregation in the same neighbourhood in the way they worship. The only major difference is in the uniform and the predominance of women in the leadership teams. They all have the same difficulties in interpreting the Bible and living what they teach. The other major difference is the complete absence of any hope of a white missionary visiting with them.

Apart from missing the occasional white missionary's visits, free Bibles, and so on, Achewa PIM has survived as a Christian church, a Baptist one for that matter, within the Chewa people, although it has through the years acquired some AIC characteristics. Achewa PIM, from Kalemba's time, has since been a home for many apart from the Chewa people. Geographically, Achewa PIM is still confined to Lilongwe and Dedza.

Chapter 5
The Present State of Achewa PIM

Local Church Leadership

Central Church: Nyanje

Dooko died in 1996 and Nyanje was without a pastor until 1998 when Tsokonombwe was ordained to pastor the church. Up until the time of writing Nyanje church had no *mlaliki*, but *mkulu wa mpingo*.[1]

Sections

Since the ordination of the bishop and his deputy Achewa PIM began to show two sections or groupings of stations (churches). Stations from Gondwa and Kalumbu in Lilongwe to Mwala and (Chambray) in Dedza District area started meeting as one section under the leadership of Sopo and several other pastors like Alison Gilbert (Mafia to find the right word) of Mauna. Stations from Chakwawa at Nathenje and Chinsamba in the east to Chiuzira and (Cochlea) in the west are identified as one section. This section has been under the bishop who is helped by several pastors who include Kamchedzera, Chalera, Thomasi and Simoko. Chakwawa station was supposed to be under Sopo but it chose not to. Much of the work in their section is done through the other pastor who is very dedicated to their ministries.

Kamchedzera has in most cases been acting on behalf of the aging bishop. He has been acting as the head of the section and on behalf of the bishop on matters pertaining to the entire Achewa PIM. Kamchedzera has not interfered with the other section when it comes to day to day running of church affairs in the section. The only time he has been involved in the other section is when he was mandated by the bishop to act on his behalf and indeed on behalf of Achewa PIM. One such case was when he had to represent the bishop and Achewa PIM in Dedza during the 1999 elections registration exercise. Though the vice bishop was there, the bishop chose Kamchedzera to go to Dedza to meet with the authorities there because he is articulate and a diplomat more than Sopo. Kamchedzera is able to negoti-

---

[1] Int Letiya Dooko, Msemanjira, 10.6.1999.

ate and bargain constructively. He is also charming and pleasant to talk with on any issue.

Leadership Training

By 1974 one *mlaliki* and two pastors had been recognized as teachers of APIM leadership, and these were Eliah Marumo and Petro Simoko.[2] The bishop has been responsible for issuing certificates to candidates who had successfully completed their course of training, either as *alaliki* or *abusa*. If for some reason the student was not successful, it is the duty of the bishop to re-examine him in order to verify whether that the candidate had actually failed. If in his opinion the candidate had failed, he would give the candidate a second chance to undergo the same training at another time.[3]

Church Meetings

Apart from the usual Sunday meetings, Achewa PIM meets on the first Sunday of every month for fellowship of churches in a section. The January meeting is a time of celebrating the end of a stage and welcoming each other into a new period. It is seen as a transitional meeting. Another annual meeting is called the August Meeting which is normally four days long with its climax on the first Sunday of August. The August meeting draws members from all the stations throughout Mangoni to the central church. At all the meetings the Lord's Supper and baptism are administered, only the dedication of buildings is done during the monthly fellowship meetings. All members take care of their transport costs to and from the venue of the meeting. In most cases people walk or ride bicycles. In some cases donkey or cattle-pulled carts are used as means of transport.

Monthly Fellowship Meetings

The congregations meet at a station, a venue which has been chosen and agreed upon at the previous monthly meeting. The meetings begin on Saturday evening, and most of the members arrive at the venue before it is dark. Some people get to the meetings early on Sunday morning. Almost every age group, both male and female, is represented. Since the members walk long distances, normally the

---

[2] Int Yosofati Ndege, Chalendewa, 4.6.1998.
[3] Int Yosofati Ndege, Chalendewa, 4.6.1998.

meetings are scheduled to end on Sunday afternoon, preferably around three, in order to allow people to get home while it is still day.[4]

Food and Accommodation

The hosting church is responsible for providing food and accommodation to the visiting members. Since the meetings are held in the villages, homes of members and of their relatives are normally used to accommodate those who sleep there on Saturday night.

Church leaders, especially the bishop and the pastors, and other special guests, are treated to traditional meals for visitors, that is, *nsima* (staple food cooked from maize flour) with meat or fish and vegetables for *ndiwo* (relish). In most cases the meat is either beef or goat meat. It is impossible for the hosts to provide the traditional food to every one who is attending the meeting. Instead, loose *phala* (porridge) has been found to be the most practical way to feed multitudes of people at any one time because the ingredients for *phala* are readily available in practically every village. To prepare *phala la chimera*, first, maize grain is immersed under water for several days in drums or any other containers available such as large clay pots, until it germinates.[5] Second, the sprouting maize is dried and pounded into flour. In most cases it is mixed with other granules, pounded together and cooked into *phala*. This may include a little bit of millet if it is maize *phala*, and vice versa. At some meetings as big as 210 litre drums are used. People are served straight from these containers all day long. Any time one feels a need for a drink, it is there. *Phala* is served mostly in cups, but sometimes on plates. No spoons of any kind are used since not many people have such utensils or even dream of owning them one time. Any left-over *phala* is usually given away to people in that village some of whom let it leave long enough to ferment into beer. Some APIM members feel it is not right while others have no problem with that since those who receive the left-over *phala* are not members of APIM and they are free to drink beer. Others see it as APIM encouraging people to drink beer.[6] There has been no record of Achewa PIM calling someone to answer charges of beer drinking.[7]

---

[4] Int Seliasi Kantigiri Sopo, Falls Estate, 2.7.1998.
[5] *Chimera* comes from *kumera*, to germinate or sprout. It means malt made out of maize, millet, and so on. For example, *chimanga* (maize) *chimera* means maize that germinated. Therefore, *phala la chimera* means porridge made out of maize that has germinated.
[6] Int David Tsokonombwe, Nyanje, 20.6.1998.
[7] Int Yosofati Ndege, Chalendewa, 5.7.1998

Achewa PIM celebrates two annual meetings, one in January and the other in August at the central church, New Mount. Such gatherings are commonly known by most churches in Malawi as "*misonkhano ya misasa.*"[8] Each congregation is expected to erect its own shelters way before the meeting dates to be used as boarding by its members. Since the month of August is mostly dry, the shelters need not have roofs.

Women preparing food for a meeting

Annual Meetings

Unlike those used in August, shelters erected for the January assembly have to have some kind of roof because it is during the rainy season. A few shelters are elaborate with hinged doors and complete roofs. Each congregation identifies its shelter by putting a name on it. The names are made out of the soft core of maize stalks.

---

[8] *Misonkhano* means meetings, while *misasa* means temporal shelters. The shelters are made out of sticks or maize stalks and grass, either dry or green, depending on the time of the year. Most *misonkhano ya misasa* are held during the dry season.

Shelters can spread right around the central church. Somewhere away from the shelters temporal toilets are erected over existing pits that were dug for the purpose years back. Once they are full new ones are dug. Since the congregations meet twice a year, digging of new pit latrines is done after many years. Normally the bishop and some of the pastors and alaliki sleep in the vestry which can easily accommodate twenty people. Alangizi who may be part of his "entourage" sleep with other women. Some members, especially the youth, sleep in the auditorium because they sing almost throughout the night. There are several choirs which want to outshine each other.

Regional meeting at Nyanje

The only time they think they can do that, is during the evening when most of the old folks have gone to sleep. Others end sleeping in the noisy auditorium because they did not erect their misasa in advance. While the January meeting is held to thank God for the past year and to ask him to see them through the new year, the August assembly is mainly for fellowship and edification of the body of Christ. The August gathering follows the pattern that was set in 1930 by Malikebu. Provision for the annual assembly was made in the Constitution of PIM which was adopted in 1945.⁹ Not only has the annual assembly been a unifying force of PIM congregations, but also for Achewa PIM

At every annual meeting, each church prepares food for its own members unlike during the monthly fellowship meetings. The only exception is that the central church includes all invited guests in its budget. Some assistance comes from a central fund which is raised specifically for that purpose.¹⁰

The leadership at a regional meeting

The alaliki call people to gather together for worship. They begin by singing a couple of hymns. Although they call out hymn numbers, hardly any member has a hymnbook apart from a handful of church leaders. They are the ones who lead in the singing. Most of the songs are sung from memory. When people have assembled they stand and sing what they call an opening hymn, after which a prayer is voiced and then all are asked to sit down. APIM congregations do not sing choruses as they are known in most Christian churches. After the singing one or two alaliki preach, followed by the vice bishop or the bishop himself, who then declares that the meeting is opened. People then retire for the night. Some do not actually sleep, but dose off now

---

⁹ See Patrick Makondesa, "Muocha", p. 10
¹⁰ Int David Tsokonombwe, Nyanje, 20.6.1998

and again amidst discussions and laughter that go on throughout the night.

Faith is Oral: the Role of the Bible in APIM

Although in every worship service the Scripture is read and preached, very few people have Bibles with them either during the services or in their homes.

Many do not know how to read or have lost the ability to read, while others do not exercise it, and some do not buy Bibles or Bible portions. Faith comes by hearing.[11] APIM feels that a few persons are chosen and sent with the message and the majority listens and responds to what they hear.

Meeting: Misasa

What they hear and learn they effectively and faithfully transmit to others around them. This oral instruction is alive and surprisingly intact despite urbanization of the society. Oral culture has been as effective as teaching methods and using books. In addition, the oral use of songs and so forth has been a uniting factor for a non-reading society. When an APIM congregation begins to sing, one can quickly sense their` togetherness as they express their faith in God. It is through oral tradition that APIM members learn God's Word Sunday after Sunday, and week after week.

---

[11] Romans 10:17.

Learning how to read does not deprive one of the oral tradition, in fact it enhances it. One who can read is expected to memorize larger chunks of information and is able to share with others on demand. In many cases APIM members who can read never open their Bibles and read for themselves. They expect two or three people each worship service to read to them and they memorize and sometimes share with others. In many instances, Bibles are used as ornaments on mud shelves in their homes

Having a Bible is seen as a step to qualification as a church leader. During the partnership, BMIM encouraged church members to own Bibles. Whenever a convert joined a local church, he/she was given an opportunity to own a Bible free of charge. They were asked to memorize certain Scripture verses and say them in the presence of the congregation. Those who were determined to have Bibles memorized the verses. It did not matter whether one could or not. Most Bibles were used only on Sunday or during other church meetings.

Misasa

A few people who could not read at all at first, were able to do so after working hard on reading the Bible.

Preaching

Preaching has remained central in the worship services of Achewa PIM. The presiding *mlaliki* introduces the speaker who is usually another *mlaliki* or a pastor. The presider reads the Scripture before the preacher expounds it for the audience. Their messages are relatively short, 5 to 10 minutes.[12] If there is more than one speaker, the messages are interspersed with some music. The pastor, senior pastor or the bishop speaks last. In most cases the preaching is a fragmentation of texts which are used out of context. The preaching is not systematic and thought-out, but a calling of God's people to enjoy him by repenting of their sins and living according to God's commandments.

APIM leadership, excluding women unfortunately, takes every regular and special gathering of its members as an opportunity to preach the Word of God. Since all APIM pastors and *alaliki* have not been trained in the modes of reading (like the three forms of biblical criticism), they read the Bible pre-critically. That is also true for the members who are non-literate.[13] It is a hard task for the preachers to earnestly study so that they can correctly analyze and accurately interpret what they read from the Bible. Some spend more time in Bible reading than others, but the bulk of the exercise is for personal growth and not for preaching.

Almost all the messages preached have one passage read. Rarely do sermons have more than one passage read. The choice of passages from which to preach is not limited to either the Old or New Testament. Virtually every sermon ends with the preacher asking the audience to apply the message to their own lives if they are to remain true to God. APIM preaching is very simple in structure and style and is mostly delivered in the imperative mood. The Achewa people use short statements but to the point. Many times the statements are in the form of similes or idioms. Hardly ever did the Achewa PIM preachers spent time speaking about their church or ask the hearers to join Achewa PIM. Instead they stress repentance in order for one to truly belong to Christ. He is seen as God, Lord and Saviour, and through his death on the cross, people are saved.

Though storytelling is cherished by many Africans, and has been promoted for use in preaching in Africa by Western scholars, stories are told sparingly in sermons delivered in APIM gatherings probably because stories are usually told to younger people or children by senior adults.[14] Since there are more seniors in Achewa PIM congregations and the preachers are in no way much older, stories hardly find their way into their preaching. Re-telling or repeating what they have read is very common and popular. Stories are retold because the majority of the readers struggle as they read that it would be difficult for

---

[12] This is also reflected in H. Mijoga, *Separate but same Message*, Blantyre, CLAIM, 2000.
[13] For a fuller discussion see H. Mijoga, *Separate but same Message*, p.14f.
[14] Ibid.

the audience to follow the story. Above all, it has been a way of reinforcing what has been heard and that involves a lot of paraphrasing, additions and omissions in order to make the passage suit their worldview.

Achewa PIM preachers and membership alike do not use exclamations such as "hallelujah-amen", and so on, in their meetings or anywhere else in their daily life though these are very popular and are commonly used in most evangelical and Protestant churches in Malawi. BMIM never used such language until very recently though BACOMA has been using that for many years now because of the influence from other evangelical and Pentecostal churches surrounding them, and the desire to go with the flow of things. Achewa PIM have stuck with what they have known from the days of Kalemba and time will tell they will be moved to use the language other churches are employing. Since they are not involved in contemporary Christian evangelistic rallies, and as they do not use that language in their churches, they will remain free from the contagious usage of "hallelujah-amen" and other clichés.

Songs form part of the preaching and a large contribution to worship of Achewa PIM. Almost all the songs are from the hymnbook, either of Nkhoma or BACOMA. The tunes do not resemble the original Western tunes in any way, but they are well known. The choice of songs is governed by the popularity of the songs amongst the members, and by how many members know them. Hymns were not necessarily chosen for their appropriateness to the messages. In many instances the preacher starts a hymn as he comes to preach and the presider or worship leader takes over and then leads the congregation in singing the song. Hymns are sung to mark the beginning and the end of a segment or the entire service. They are not used as commentaries on the messages. Congregational singing involves the audience. APIM worship leadership involves the audience in the entire service and not just as a way to facilitate involvement in the sermon. Though Africans are said to love singing so that they use it for admonition and instruction for example, no APIM preacher ever used singing in place of a sermon.

Baptism Class and Service

Baptism brings one into membership of Achewa PIM. Anyone who is baptized by an Achewa PIM minister automatically becomes a member of that church. Candidates for baptism attend a *Baibulo kalasi* (Bible Class) immediately before they are taken to the Yorodani early one Sunday morning. Bible Class was instituted during the time of Chilembwe and has continued till today.[15] In some cases there are as many as four teachers for a Bible Class. At Kakwere, for example, the teachers were Chisomba Mositafa from Mgala, Leonard Levinara of Kachala, Harison Saidi from Ching'oma and Frank Njoka of Kumisu.

Candidates for baptism have their names written on individual pieces of paper whose size depends on the availability of stationery. The day's date is also written on each piece of paper.[16] Each candidate was asked to pay MK 2.00 in 1998. Some names are not accepted once the teacher(s) think(s) it is not Christian or that the name is for the opposite sex. For example, a woman whose first name was Hawa, from Nsabwe, was told to change her name because the senior teacher thought that it was a man's name.[17] Before she could chose a new name for herself, Mositafa had already given her the name "Esitere" (for Ester). Since she wanted to be baptized and be a member of APIM, Hawa respected the decision and accepted her new name. It did not matter much to her since in Chewa culture, women are never called by their first names anyway, but by their clan names.[18] Two other candidates at that baptism had their names changed because the names were as if someone was talking back or revenging. Such names like *Tilekeni* (leave us alone), *Tsokandiwe* (you're the misfortune or bad luck), *Dzikambani* (go on talking), are not approved as names for any one to call himself or herself by especially if he/she desires to be a member of Achewa PIM.

As soon as all the names of the baptism candidates have been written and the fees have been collected, one of the teachers gives instruction on baptism, what it is and what it means, who can be baptized and how. Since what is taught is not written down, the teachers remind each other what needs to be taught or what has been left out of the teaching and must be included. All female candidates are required from now on *kuika mpango ku mutu* (to cover their heads with a scarfs). During the lesson on baptism, one of the things taught to new members-to-be is that Achewa PIM does not allow its members to drink alcohol.

The journey to the Yorodani begins after the lesson and a prayer. All the members present at the assembly are encouraged to witness

---

[15] Patrick Makondesa, "Muocha", p. 3
[16] See Plate 32 for sample copies.
[17] In fact, Hawa is the Yao and Swahili version of Eve. One must also remember that in Malawi names such as Chisomo (Grace), Chikondi (Love), Yankho (Answer), and so on are given to both girls and boys.
[18] Int Hawa Solomoni, Kakwere, 5.7.1999.

the baptism. Each candidate is given a flower that will be left in the Yorodani

Bible Class in Session

Bible Class in Session

Baptism represents death and burial of the old person. The flowers represent wreaths that are placed on the grave after burial.[19] Therefore, each candidate carries his/her own wreath. From the village to the pond or river, people sing joyous and happy hymns. At the pool, church leaders and members line up around the edge of the pool or stand along the banks of the river.

The candidates are lined up one after the other facing the pool. The officiating pastor and his assistant search for a place where they can hide and change their clothes; once they have done so they walk into the water, and another pastor delivers a short message. Someone amongst the church leaders is asked to pray. After this and between each task, music fills the gap. The officiating pastor and his assistant survey the pond and agree on the spot which they are going go use for baptism, depending on the level of water. They normally look for a place where at least the candidate is able to kneel down and still keep his/her head above the water. They use a stick which is pushed onto the ground and is left on the spot. Once that has been done, baptism can begin, and the first candidate is called in.

One of the pastors or *alaliki* receives the little paper on which the candidate's name is written, and he reads the name aloud, then the candidate is ushered into the water. According to Chewa culture, men first. As the candidate walks or is carried into the water, in case of a child, the congregation sings. Once the candidate has been received in the pond, the candidate drops his/her flower into the water, and the officiating pastor raises his hand, the singing stops only to resume again after the candidate has been immersed in and emerges from under the water. With one hand raised, the officer calls out the name of the candidate and declares that he is going to baptize him or her `the Father, the Son and the Holy Spirit. With his hand at the back of the candidate's neck, he pushes the candidate's body forward into the water until the whole body is immersed, and quickly pulls him/her out using the same hand, while the other hand is wiping away the water from the candidate's face. The assistant helps the candidate to steadily walk out of the water amidst applause and singing. At the end of the baptism, the officer, his helper and candidates all go and change clothes while the congregation waits for them. Once everybody has changed, the people walk back to the village amidst messages of encouragement and appreciation. Others discuss what went on during the baptism. But all in all, people are happy that some have been baptized into the Body of Christ. In the village food is served and people rest until the next event which is, in

---

[19] Int Yosofati Ndege, Kakwere, 5.7.1999.

most cases, worship followed by the Lord's Supper. It is during the Lord's Supper that new members are welcomed into the church. They are asked to stand in the front row and the church leaders file by passing them as they greet and congratulate candidates for the move they have made.

On the way to baptism

At the baptismal pond

The Present State of Achewa PIM

Membership cards are issued to the new members through their respective congregations.

The Lowering of Initiation Age

After Kalemba had died and time went on, Achewa PIM began to baptize children and not just adults as before. Some of the baptism candidates are too young to know what is going on although it is against APIM's teaching to baptize anyone who can not verbally profess Christ.[20] Nevertheless, I have witnessed some children as young as five years old being baptized most of whom cried before they could be baptized just because they were afraid of the water. For a time BACOMA has refused baptism of children under the age of 12 arguing that at that age and below, the child was not capable of knowing what it meant to be saved. Nevertheless, the age of conversion and baptism has since gone down in BACOMA as it is with APIM. My daughter, Grace, is among many examples of a challenge to traditional belief about the age of baptism.

Lining up for Baptism, the youngest at the rear

Together with three other eight-year olds, Grace accepted Jesus Christ as Lord and Saviour of her life after my wife, Molly, had taught them in a *Sunday School* for children at Twin Palm Baptist Church in Lusa-

---

[20] Int Yosofati Ndege, Kakwere, 5.7.1998.

ka.[21] Several BACOMA pastors have baptized children as young as five years old, nevertheless, some have felt that anywhere between ten and twelve years old acceptable minimum age for believers' baptism.[22]

Chewa culture strongly emphasized the period of transition from childhood to adulthood. The rite of passage took much time and resources to prepare and carry out. Through the years people have felt traditional initiation as too much of a strain on both time and resources. That has led to the reduction in the length of time taken for the initiation process. The biggest challenge has been towards the age at which one can be initiated into adulthood. Nowadays *Gule wamkulu* has lowered the age requirement to include children.[23] Also among the Yao circumcision which is supposed to introduce one to adulthood is now being administered to children as young as six years old. The lowering of the initiation age is seen as an African phenomenon, be it traditional, Muslim or Christian.[24] Achewa PIM, like all other Christian churches, cannot ignore African initiation if they are to compete against African Traditional Religion (ATR) and survive in the next century. Achewa PIM may be reacting to ATR when it baptizes children. It is also seen as a way of protecting them.

From the Bible Class teaching, a few things need to be noted here. First, APIM emphasizes adult candidates for baptism though children are accepted. It is because the teachers constantly called upon adults to pay attention because they were able to make decisions. This means that teachers of Bible Class did not see the children making decisions for themselves to be baptized. This is in line with regenerate membership as generally taught by Baptists. Second, no one should be forced into baptism. Those who believe in Christ and sense that is what God wants them to do are the ones who should be baptized. Third, by emphasizing "Yorodani" and the preaching of John the Baptist in the desert, APIM recognizes baptism by immersion even if it

---

[21] Int Molly Longwe, Lusaka, 11.8.1995.
[22] Int Misinde Phiri and S. Gunya, Lilongwe, 22.11.1998. See also Klaus Fiedler, *Faith Missions*, pp. 341-342.
[23] Orison Chaponda, "*Gule wamkulu* in Catholic Lilongwe Rural: Its Cultural Phenomenon and a Personal Problem", a paper presented at the colloquium, University of Malawi, 1998.
[24] See Klaus Fiedler, "Bishop Lucas' Christianization of traditional rites, the Kikuyu female circumcision controversy and the 'cultural approach' of conservative German missionaries in Tanzania", a seminar paper, and Patrick Makondesa, "Christian Initiation rites in Southern Malawi", MA module 1, Department of Theology and Religious Studies, University of Malawi, 1999.

means walking long distances to where there is enough water for one to be immersed. They have sympathy for those who have any other form of baptism such as is done in CCAP and RC churches. Fourth, for one to be baptized, one must know Jesus as a personal Saviour and Lord. Though Nicodemus was a religious person, a Jewish Rabbi for that matter, he had no personal relationship with God through Jesus. That is being born again. Fifth, the teaching on baptism emphasizes newness of and everlasting life. Baptism symbolizes dying to self and rising into new life which is eternal. APIM also teaches that everyone who believes in Jesus Christ even if he dies, will live forever in glory. Fundamentally, APIM's teaching touches all areas that are generally accepted by Baptists.

Dedication and Naming of Church Buildings

Once a new church building is built, it is given a name from the Bible during its dedication ceremony. A name is chosen and agreed upon by both the bishop and the congregation. No two church buildings are supposed to have the same name. Unfortunately, that happened. As I compiled the list of churches and the names of the buildings, I was the first to discover that three sets of two churches used three similar names. Buildings at Kakhome and Chilanga are both called Yerusalemu, while those at Nsabwe and Mphambanya are both named Beteli, and Chonde and M'mbalo buildings are called Galileya. The matter was reported to the Bishop who blamed Ndalama and also Sopo for not consulting other leaders when names of the buildings were suggested. Chilanga, Mphambanya and M'mbalo were under Ndalama and are now under Sopo. He refused to be blamed for the first two, but agreed that he overlooked the name of M'mbalo.[25] In addition to two church buildings sharing one name, I also discovered that one name for sure did not come from the Bible, and that is Geneva, for the church at Phatha.[26] The other name I am not sure of is Tilinati.

---

[25] Int Seliasi Kantigiri Sopo and Sandifolo Kamchedzera, Nathenje, 11.9.1999.
[26] At first I thought that they might have named the building, *Genizah*, hiding, storehouse, and the name changed over the years due to pronunciation, but the word does not appear in the Bible either. Genizah is a place in the synagogue set aside for the storage of unwanted written and printed material of a religious nature. It also means a cemetery in which these materials are buried when they are removed from the synagogue. See Merrill C. Tenney, *The Zondervan Pictorial Encyclopedia of the Bible*, Grand Rapids: Zondervan, 1977, p. 695.

After going round the building, the congregation enters and they take their seats. The name of the building is unveiled and there is jubilation. That is followed by Bible reading and preaching. At the end of the ceremony, either the bishop or his representative exhorts the members meeting in the new building and the entire Achewa PIM membership to remain faithful and live exemplary lives among believers and non-believers.

Procession at the Dedication of Kakwere Church Building

The Respect the Bishop Enjoys

At his home, the bishop is just like every other man in the village. If one arrives at his home, one can not know that he is the physical head of Achewa PIM, unless one is introduced to him by that title. He wears no special clothes or puts on an insignia such as the ones worn by bishops of other denominations, such as RC and Anglican. He is normally in a long-sleeved shirt and a tie, and on occasions, in a jacket. He normally puts on a jacket if it is cold or when people come to visit with him, or when he is going places away from his home. The tie and jacket are not of a particular colour; it is anything that he can find as long as it is of dark colours.

It is only when one attends Achewa PIM meetings that one realizes that this very simple looking man is the head of a church that respects him very much. In his early life as bishop, Ndege used to ride a bicycle or walk to the meeting place. He was normally accompanied by a couple of *alangizi* and deacons from Chalendewa. Since 1996 Ndege has been waiting on his nephew to carry him on a bicycle or some Good Samaritan to drive him to and from the venue of the meeting.

Pastors prepare well for his arrival at the venue of the meeting. A house in which he will stay for the duration of the meeting is identified and cleaned. The house is normally one of the better houses in the village hosting the meeting. The church building is swept clean and some repairs are done to it if need be. They are not major repairs, but some kind of reconditioning so that one feels welcomed and at home. If there is no church building, a temporary shelter is erected. Where the people are unable to build one that will cover everybody, they construct a large enough shelter that will accommodate the bishop, pastors and their wives, *alangizi*, and other church leaders. The structure is usually made out of wooden poles and thatched with grass; depending on the season, it is either green or dry.

Some senior pastors and their wives and *alangizi* are assigned to welcome the bishop and usher him into the designated house. They keep watch of the bishop's appearance at the venue. As soon he arrives close to the venue, the appointed ones walk towards the bishop, greet him and usher him into that village and take him straight into the house allocated to him. The door is closed and the leaders salute him while all are seated. The address is very brief since they want him to rest a little before anything else is to be done. Usually the bishop waits in the house with an "entourage" of one *mlangizi* or two *alangizi* to serve him with a drink or just to keep him company. Sometimes *amayi busa* (pastor's wife) serve him since they are also *alangizi*. Outside the house, a couple of steps away from the front entrance, a couple of *alaliki* and/or chairmen stand as if on guard, but casual, just to alert the people that someone important is in the house. The door to the house is kept closed. It is only opened when one enters or leaves the house. Keeping the door closed is a sign of respect for the one who is in there. In most African cultures south of the Sahara, older children desist from entering their parents' bedrooms. If for any reason they want something from the room, the youths send little children in after permission is granted by the parents. In fact little children who are related to the bishop are not stopped from walking straight into the house to meet with and even eat with him.

After the bishop has rested, pastors and other church leaders call on him individually or in groups. Whenever they reach by the door and before they can actually turn the door handle or open the door, they say "chuzi".[27] Either the bishop or the *alangizi* or someone who

---

[27] Int Eliamu Mlongoti Chijere Nyangu, Mchinji, 19.9.1999. "*Chuzi*" is a transliteration of "excuse", and when they say "*chuzi*", it actually means "excuse me,

might be with him, replies, "eeh" (yes), sometimes with *"lowani"* (come in), and they come in. As they walk in, they are very careful not to make wrong moves, and gently they come before the bishop and kneel down before they can lift their hands to give him a handshake. Both men and women look at his face as they shake his hand and greet him, *Muli bwanji abambo?* (How are you father/sir?). They rarely say, *"Abishopi muli bwanji?"* ("How are you Bishop?") Bishop is a title that seems to keep the members at a distance from the man, while *"bambo"* (father), characterizes a unique relationship between the members and the church leader. The bishop is in a way *tate wa mpingo* (the father of the church) in the sense that, by virtue of being the head of the church, he is responsible for the welfare of all the members. All are to blossom under his protection, love and guidance.

Bishop Ndege Accompanied by Pastors and their Eives, Church Chairman, Alaliki and Alangizi, Proceeding from the house where the Bishop is putting up to the Meeting Place, at Kakwere Station.

When everything is ready for the meeting, the officiating pastor followed by other leaders including *alangizi*, of course, call on the bishop and brief him on the meeting, the programme and what they

---

please". This was learnt from Kalemba and Nyangu. You can hear this whenever a member of PIM, APIM and IBACOMA is approaching senior members or if they want to show respect to the one they are encountering.

The Present State of Achewa Pim 131

intend to achieve. During their deliberations all are seated, some on chairs and others on mats. It does not matter who is seating on what.

They behave like children of the same age before a grandparent who is waiting for them to sit before he begins to teach them through a story. Instead of the bishop talking first, it is a normal practice for the meeting to start with a word of prayer from one of the church leaders. The bishop is then officially briefed about the meeting.

Meetings Means of Transport (Nyaje, August 1998)

During the briefing, the bishop gives short comments and words of encouragement, or asks questions, or corrects some ideas, and then authorizes that the meeting be started. After a closing prayer all stand up, the bishop last, and, one by one, walk out of, and line up outside the temporal residence of the bishop. One of the members in that group leads in singing a song as they all walk together to the church or the shelter. The bishop is always in the front line with senior pastors and *alangizi*, followed by the rest of the leadership team members. As the bishop and his entourage approach the congregation, all the members are asked to stand while singing, and allow the bishop to sit followed by those accompanying him. The bishop is usually flanked by *alangizi*. All the leaders sit on chairs or something of that nature. Men are interspersed by several women since there are more *alangizi* and pastors combined, than there are men.

At all the meetings, the *alaliki* play the role of master of ceremony. Whenever they stand up to speak, or someone is asked to do something, they turn, face the bishop, and bow, and turn to the congregation and do what is expected of them. When they finish, they bow again and sit. At the end of the meeting, the spokesman asks the congregation to stand while the bishop and church leaders leave for the bishop's temporary residence. The leaders bid the bishop farewell, and he does the same to them. Everyone finds their way home. In most cases they stand around in groups for a while, before they actually disperse on foot, on bicycles, and sometimes, on ox-carts.

Original Quest for Education: What Happened?

The Achewa PIM, a church which has a very low education rate, started in the quest for higher education. That original quest for higher education can also be interpreted as a quest for African independence. Though APIM never achieved much education, it still achieved African independence. The arrival and leadership of Kalemba was a mark of increased social status and independence for the Africans of Mangoni. The people were made to feel independent of the colonial masters who included the white mission church, and of their own tribal traditions. Achewa PIM membership became free to decide the fate of their faith and life.

Gule Wamkulu: Kamchedzera's Case

One of the largest problems that has affected the growth of education and Christian growth in Mangoni is *Gule wamkulu*. Conflict with Gule is confrontation with Chewa society. Therefore, a Chewa person fighting against Gule is like fighting oneself, and that is not easy. Achewa PIM is very sensitive to the impact Gule has on the Chewa people, and so, love and sympathy is shown to the converts and their extended families. Since Christian churches have emphasized a complete break between Gule and Christian faith, almost all Chewa chiefs have kept their *zirombo* (translated, beasts, the performers in the Gule dance) away from church buildings and functions, but they have not been able to keep *zirombo* from harassing people. The case of Kamchedzera is an example.

Mwana akabadwa, akalandire mwambo (When a child is born, it must receive instruction).[28] Not all instruction is good training. *Osametedwa* (those who have not been shaved, meaning, those who have

---

[28] Int Seliyasi Sopo, Gondwa, 11.10.1998.

not received the instruction), have to learn to live with those who have received the instruction. Kamchedzera had always wanted to go to school but did not make it because of Gule.[29] He attended a few classes that helped him to barely read and write. Kamchedzera since improved his skills in reading and writing because the modern world requires people to read and fill in forms and the like. It has not been easy for him. He has had difficulties to get the employment he desired. As a result he tried to increase his financial base by going to Zimbabwe, but it was short lived.

Kamchedzera was determined that his children remain *osametedwa*, but instead, go to school. That is what he perceived as the answer to independence. He made sure that his children were going to live a better and fulfilling life. In 1974 it happened that Crispin, his eldest son, was kicked by one of the *zirombo* because he was not able to respond to them as he was one who was *osametedwa*.[30] When Kamchedzera heard about this he was very upset and quick to act. He followed the *zirombo*, and when he caught up with them, he beat the one that had kicked Crispin. When the people heard about the incident, Kamchedzera was accused of *kufula dziko* (expose the nakedness of the land, which in this case, meant the people). The case was brought before the traditional court and after the hearing, T/A Chadza asked among his sub-chiefs who had authorized the *zirombo* to come out, that is, to perform outside their court called *mzinda*, and why. When he got no proper response, T/A Chadza charged the chief from whose *mzinda* these *zirombo* came to pay Kamchedzera. Instead of taking the money, Kamchedzera gave it to T/A Chadza stating his refusal to associate himself with *zirombo*.[31]

Immediately after the court case Kamchedzera decided to leave Nsabwe, and settle in Kasungu District where he thought his children would not be molested by *zirombo* and would be able to continue with education. When he asked for *chilolezo* (permission) from the T/A, he was refused. Instead the chief wrote a note to the sub-chief requesting him to give Kamchedzera a piece of land of his choice outside the village. In 1975 Kamchedzera moved his family to where their home is today.[32] Over the years other families have since moved close to the Kamchedzeras for different reasons. By protecting his

---

[29] Int Sandifolo Kamchedzera, Nsabwe, 4.9.1999.
[30] *Osametedwa* need *kugula njira* (buy the way), which means that if one who is not instructed, is able to respond when one encounters *zirombo*. That gives one the right of way.
[31] Int Sandifolo Kamchedzera, Nsabwe, 4.9.1999.
[32] Int Sandifolo Kamchedzera, Nsabwe, 4.9.1999.

children from *zirombo*, he has set a record in APIM and probably the surrounding area. This family has produced college graduates who include Garton, a law lecturer with Chancellor College of the University of Malawi.

The Role of Women in Achewa PIM

The tremendous potential of women to do meaningful ministry in the church was recognized by Kalemba early in his ministry. Women possess tremendous strength of character as required for the development of an independent church's enterprise.[33] Though they do not hold positions of power, they have the power to decide the direction the church is to take. In addition, women have the power to chose and support the leader and those who work with him. Without the women's spiritual and physical support, and their services such as the logistics for feeding the multitude that attends the monthly fellowship and annual meetings, APIM would not have survived till today. Women form the bond of friendship and love amongst the members. Though no man ever thanked or praised them openly, women continue to labour tirelessly for the survival of Achewa PIM, just as it is not characteristic of typical African husbands to say to their wives, "I love you", and yet the wives continue to serve them. Probably the last time an African woman heard the husband say that was when they were dating. This does not mean that he has stopped loving her; it is just that African men have other ways of expressing their love to their wives. Women are not neglected; they are appreciated inwardly by the male membership.[34]

Since the Albrights' departure, APIM women stopped meeting for fellowship and study as it is done in other churches. They do not have an officially recognized group like that of *Umodzi wa Amayi* (women's guild) as found in BACOMA, for example. Nevertheless, they have some consolations due to them being in the majority in Achewa PIM. The first relief is that they constitute a larger portion of APIM leadership and can easily endorse, reject or change a proposal. Though their ministry assignments include organizing church meetings and being part of representative teams of local congregation leadership at section meetings, their role has been counselling young girls and newly weds and participating in wedding ceremonies. Counselling has been left particularly to *alangizi*, while participation in weddings is expected

---

[33] Int Elenesi Wisikoti, Nyanje, 20.6.1998.
[34] Int Sitoliya Chakwala, Mphanje, 21.10.1998.

of all women maybe with some special assignments to particular women.

The training of *alangizi* has been an on-going exercise. Every time new *alangizi* are chosen, they are requested to attend some training to equip them for their special ministry. Once the *alangizi* have completed their training, the pastors report to the Bungwe la pa 15. It is the responsibility of the Bungwe to announce to the churches at the monthly fellowship meetings that certain *alangizi* have qualified and can start serving in that capacity in their local congregations as well as is the entire APIM. Certificates are given to successful candidates officially recognizing them as *alangizi*. The certificate is signed by the pastor of the local church responsible for the training. Whenever Achewa PIM is concerned with the behaviour of some of its *alangizi*, or any other leader for that matter, a special joint meeting is called to discuss the issue.[35]

APIM and Children

Although most families bring their children or grandchildren to church, APIM made no effort to have a children's ministry within the church. It is the responsibility of each household to bring its children to church. Though it is the wish of every parent or guardian to educate their children in the things of God, there is no coordinated effort towards that goal. There are no ministries such as Sunday School,[36] Bible Study, or Bible clubs in APIM, let alone for children. Adults and children learn God's truth through the preaching of the Gospel during weekly and monthly worship services. Children are supposed to learn through shared living. Belief systems and practices are more caught than formally taught. Since they can not concentrate for long periods, children spend much of their time playing outside or, if they are tired, sleeping in the hands of their guardians or on the floor. What becomes of the children after they grow up and leave their parents' homes is anybody's guess. Some remain in APIM while others join different churches, and the rest go their own way and leave the church altogether.[37] Almost all the children are baptized when they are still young, not at their own request, but at that of their parents. Even if

---

[35] See Plate 36 for an example containing a list of names of *alangizi* called to such a meeting in 1970.
[36] No Sunday School has survived from BMIM times.
[37] Int Dumbanya, Katunga, 20.10.1998.

they leave APIM they are still recognized as members and if one day they come back, they are welcomed and not baptized again.[38]

Some have left APIM not because they wanted to, but because they were far from an established APIM congregation. An example is that of Garton Kamchedzera. It was in 1985, after receiving his degree in law and being offered a job that Garton had to decide with which church to worship since there were no Achewa PIM congregations near Chancellor College.[39] The closest church, he thought, that was similar to his home church, was PIM at Chiradzulu.[40] Though he had known of the Baptist Convention church next to Chancellor College it had not registered that it was the closest, until he inquired with his farther who also consulted Ndege. The result was that Garton was directed to Zomba Baptist Church because it was one with APIM in theological convictions.[41] When he met with Elizabeth, Garton's father was worried that he would leave and marry in a CCAP congregation. Sandifolo did not want his son to join any church that was not Baptist.[42] His worry was not justified for Garton married Elizabeth in the Baptist church there in Zomba. The two have been active members of Zomba Baptist Church ever since.[43]

Training children together with adults is not how the African culture does it. Most of the day parents work either in the fields or on some tasks around the home except for the elderly and the young who keep watch of the homes. It is typical of African honours for elderly to care for and teach the small children. Storytelling is a lively and popular cultural vehicle in the instructional task the African society has used and still uses today. Children gather together around and listen to the elderly. Much interest is generated by audience participation. They learn the values of the society in such a communicative way which is a mixture of music, narratives, poetry, drama, dancing and drumming. Interaction with the performers was and is desirable because the whole experience is characterized by great enjoyment and expression of feelings. I am not so sure why APIM, and of course most African churches, have not used this effective instructional vehicle which has been acclaimed even by the Western world as being successful. Maybe it is because people are placing massive emphasis on formal education, reading and writing in place of oral tradition.

---

[38] Int Kamuikeni Kasamu, Chinungu, 20,10.1998.
[39] Int Sandifolo Kamchedzera, Kakwere, 4.7.1998.
[40] Int Garton Kamchedzera, Lilongwe, 7.2.1999.
[41] Int Yosofati Ndege, Kakwere, 4.7.1998.
[42] Int Sandifolo Kamchedzera, Kakwere, 4.7.1998.
[43] Int Yosofati Ndege, Kakwere, 4.7.1998, Klaus Fiedler, 2004.

Chapter 6
Conclusion

I trust that my attempt to construct a comprehensive history and to describe the current everyday reality of Achewa PIM mostly from oral sources and testimonies that were made available to me during the research, has been accomplished. I am also aware that my association and experiences with certain individual members and congregations of APIM suggested the possibility of biases in interpretation. It was impossible for me to come to this study without some form of inclination, nevertheless, a conscious effort was made to achieve historical objectivity in arriving at the conclusions that are cited below.

Evangelism and Church Growth

Though its local congregations are soundly organized they are not mushrooming as is the standard expectations for AICs. In spite of being introverted and rather static without expanding across tribal or even national boundaries, APIM shows no sign of dwindling. Achewa PIM normally count all baptized persons as members. That includes those who have been put on discipline for a period which does not exceed three months. Membership is also counted in terms of those who attend the worship services. In this case the numbers are given as averages. A total community count is taken at all meetings. That takes into account all persons present, and that includes babies and casual attenders. All three methods are all right at different points.

In terms of the number of congregations, there were more churches planted after almost all PIM congregations in Mangoni decided to go with Kalemba as its leader than before that period. In about 11 years there were 8 new congregations established. The reason was that there was much input from men who had had some training under the DRCM and later under PIM from which they had received formal and theological education, respectively. Achewa PIM was on full steam ahead to reach more people for Christ. For a while they had new information and input to share though they had decided to live in isolation from PIM.

From 1945 to 1962 Achewa PIM had virtually lost its power to grow in terms of churches. Only four churches were started in a 17-year period. Achewa PIM was folding in because they were in complete isolation from any outside influence. Those who were then in position of leadership had very little or no formal education and no theological input from outside Achewa PIM. Theological changes and emotional choices caused them to wander in a foreign land apart from the fellowship they so desired and possibly stray from the will of God.

Between 1963 and 1975, the period of partnership between Achewa PIM and BMIM, nine churches were begun in about 13 years. It was like the 1934-1945 period in which the influence of outside sources inspired numerical growth within APIM. They worked side-by-side with foreign missionaries who were also their teachers. Men and women who had had no previous formal and theological education found themselves rubbing shoulders while doing evangelism with foreign university graduates who were attempting to put into practice what they had learnt about planting churches cross-culturally. That made Achewa PIM to witness with power. They were revitalized; they became alive again to reach others for Christ Jesus.

Since 1976 Achewa PIM has gone back into an isolation that has led to stagnation. Only eight churches have been started in a 24-year period. Life is no longer simple. Not long ago life's issues revolved around existence - whether or not there was a roof over our heads or food on the table. Today's technologies have created a new wave of expectations. The world is now bent on success and when we do not achieve it we fall into isolation mode which leads to stagnation, and no growth. Achewa PIM is waiting for someone to come by and crank them to progress forward. There is so much going on around them so that they do not know what to do in order for new life to flow within them for growth.

By the end of 1998 there were 37 Achewa PIM congregations as opposed to 14 by the time Kalemba died, and 23 churches at the close of Kamkalamba's era. In almost 62 years, Achewa PIM began 22 new churches in Mangoni which is a poor performance in terms of church growth. Currently the population of Malawi is estimated to be 9.8 million.[1] In 1987 it was just under 8 million, out of which 12 per cent lived in Lilongwe District. It was also estimated in that year that population growth was 3.2 per cent per year.[2] Therefore, using estimates for both years, Achewa PIM membership is between 0.13 and 0.18 per cent of the Lilongwe District population.

Statistics concerning church affiliation are always confusing. APIM being a minority institution, but of long standing, it has worked out some way of living whereby its interests are protected in exchange for

---

[1] The count is most likely too low since the census figures are unreliable, so that 11 million may be a good guess.
[2] National Statistical Office, *Malawi Population and Housing Census 1987: Summary of Final Results Vol. 1*, Zomba: Government Printer, July 1991, p. 17.

Conclusion

a willingness to remain relatively static. In some way, APIM has constituted a closed ranks, with new members almost entirely restricted to those born into the church. That has limited the church's evangelistic zeal, for growth would induce suspicion. The reason that the operation of the Holy Spirit cannot be subjected to directed observation or to statistical indices of success and failure, keeps me from undue generalization about APIM's church growth from statistical evidence alone.

Achewa PIM Churches

Location	Name of the Church	Year founded	Founder(s)	Mother Church	Current Leaders	Members
Kalumbu	Gologota	1914	Peter Kalemba	New Jerusalem	Ezara Chikalema	44
Nyangu	Yeriko	1923	Elina Sasitoni	Kalumbu	Biniwelo Chatuluka	53
Nyanje	New Mount	1929	Aaron Kamkalamba	Kalumbu	David Tsokonombwe	34
Chikhanda	Kalivale	1929	J. Kokha and Eleni Chijere	Nyangu	N. Binda	69
Mphindo	Nazalete	1932	Gilisoni Gumbi and Yosiya Chalimba	Nyanje	Nasoni Chalera	76
Chinungu	Esitele	1932	Nadoni Wisikoti			57
Chiuzira	Samaliya	1933	Kenani Kumanda	Nyanje	Nelson Sikatero	78
Kalumbu	Gologota	1935	Peter Kalemba	Nyangu	Ezala S. Chikalema	80
Chonde	Galileya	1935	Hoseteni Biyuzi		Henele Mafiyo	21
Phatha	Geneva 1935	1935	Andreya Chiwoza Lositala and Esitele Vizi		Peturo Simoko	129
Dziwe	Antokia	1935	Kamchiliko Chingowe, Matthew and Mary Ndalama	Nyanje	Yesaya Changata	157

Katunga	Tilinali	1935	Bobo Jesitala	Kalumbu	Laimoni Kadumbanya	102
Mwachilolo	Getsemani	1935	Dziyele and Fane Dzakata	Kalumbu	Pilato Stazio	171
Msendeli(Nsa-bwe)	Beteli	1941	Jamisoni and Falesi Chiwona	Phatha	Kamchedzera	127
Chituwi	Yerusalem-mu	1949	Sikefa Kaphala	Kalumbu	Adisoni Mafuta	189
Chalendewa	Makedonia	1951	Yohane Chikadula	Mphindo	Yosofati Ndege	50
Chiwoza	Sidoni	1956	Kadzibwa	Nyangu	Chinzimu	85
Mgala	Alabiya	1962	Abele and Yulita	Mphindo	Peturo and Kilinesi	95
Mphanje	Tibeliya	1963	Simiyoni Chando, Siteliya Chakwela and Edna	Phatha	Peturo Mazanga	217
Chinsamba	Yudeya	1965	Damalekani	Katungu	Marko Langwani	103
Mnjele	Keseleya	1966	Izeki Wachi	Nyangui	Chimayimba	147
Chakwawa		1967		Nyanje	J. Mofati Phiri	52
Gondwa	Damasiko	1967	Seliyasi Sopo and Frakisoni Chinkhalamba	Dziwe	Seliyasi K. Sopo	110
Mphambanya	Beteli	1968	Hezekiya Chidama	Mwachilolo	Jesta Khombe	93
Tsoyo	Azitona	1971	Lumwila	Nyangu	Jonase Makombe	32
Mwala	Samaliya	1972	Chonde H. Mafio	W.C. Maliketi		272
Mwase	Sekemu	1973	Wisikoti Thomasi, Lefiyasi Mnyongo, Lemitala Jayira	Nyanje	Wisikoti	51
Mbewa 2	Rute	1986	M'nyangale	Phatha	Lamiyoni Kaputeni	37
Ching'o-	Sinayi	1991	Saidi	Mphanj	Juliyasi	52

Conclusion

ma					e	Mbalame	
Kachala	Kidesi	1992	Feliyasi and Elizabeth		Chale-ndewa	Feliyasi and Elizabeth	105
M'mbalo	Galileya	1994	Falesi Chimayi-Mba		Nyangu	D.N. Msuzi Manjer	42
Chilonga	Yerusalemu	1994	Harry Tembo and Aida Numele		Nyangu	Harry Tembo	57
Chaponda		1997	Abrahamu and Maria Ndalama		Dziwe Ndalama	Abrahamu and Maria	30
Kakwere	Kanani	1997	Laveke Layisoni		Mphanje	Abel Mangani, Kalebu Gwaza	106
Kamunga		1998	Mose Nefitale and Nekisoni		Mphanje	Mose Nefitale	43

Note: Under membership, the top figure represents baptized members in the year shown while the bottom number is the current membership. Be reminded that the dates of when these churches began may vary slightly especially for those that were started under "Mpingo wa Mpatuko" between 1915 and 1937.

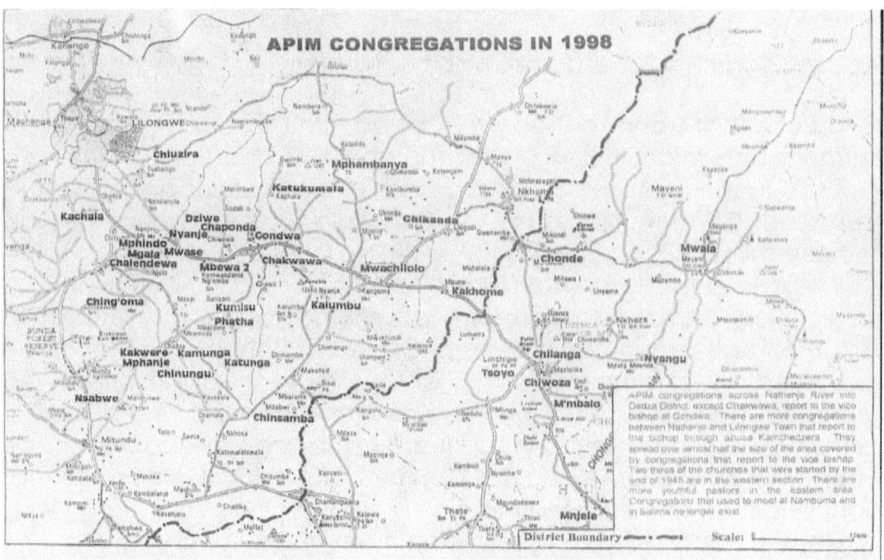

Theological Education

The Achewa PIM membership tends to consist of poorly schooled people. It is very rural and it is composed of people, the majority of whom can barely read and write. While theological education has probably been the main focus of many of the churches in Africa, it is not so with APIM. The church is led by relatively uneducated pastors. As a result of that, Achewa PIM is ignored by the educated minority in Mangoni. For APIM this is an upset which needs sincere attention. There are no records of educated people or even of those whose parents are members or pastors of APIM joining the Achewa PIM. For the church to grow and survive into the next century, Achewa PIM needs to attract people of all classes of the society who live both in the rural and urban areas. To do that the Achewa PIM needs to encourage its young people to aim high in education and take up positions of leadership both in secular and religious circles. Very few members of Achewa PIM have come to a realization that they have missed on theological education, not only for the church leadership, but also for every church member. In order for APIM membership to exercise their particular skills to the glory of God, they need the support of trained ministers and professional theologians. Semi-educated pastors can not hope to have much influence especially amongst the fast growing numbers of the elite.

Accepted Doctrine against what is Practiced

One thing that stands out about Achewa PIM's theology is their commitment and faithfulness to what they believe and value. They hold monthly meetings at which all churches in the sections are expected to attend. Children, adults and senior adults walk long distances just to have fellowship one with another. At no one time did I hear of BACOMA coming together for fellowship in such large numbers on foot or bicycles. They would complain about the means of transport to and the frequency of the meetings. Once the date and venue of the next meeting is announced, no letters are sent as reminders. The members themselves are the letters and reminders. No one person or church complains of not having heard or having been told late as it happens with BACOMA churches. In the case of BACOMA, once that happens, the turnout for the meeting is small.

Despite receiving almost nothing from their congregations, the leadership is very dedicated and faithful throughout. They walk to fellowship and special meetings with their members, and serve them and God with all their hearts. The focus is not on the congregations for their survival, but on God. They believe that God can use anybody to help them in every area of their lives.

Personal or Private Mixture (Syncretism)

Christianity has often found itself modified and even altered to some extent by the environments into which it entered. The first form of mixture (syncretism) is in which some traditional elements are absorbed and are to some extent accepted and are officially approved. It is true that Christianity has caused fewer significant changes in the basic culture than is commonly assumed. African Christians are still culturally African, showing immediate traditional African responses to life's major crises. Some educated Africans may return to traditional rituals and remedies in illness and go back to the village for the festivals. In Achewa PIM some elements are publicly acknowledged while others are not. *Kumeta* (shaving of the hair on the head) of bereaved person(s) after the dead has been buried, is accepted without question, but washing the face and hands in water that has been treated with herbs as protection against the spirit of the dead from haunting the bereaved, is not permitted.

The second form of mixture is the retention of traditional practices by individual members in their own particular religious experience, such as attending *Gule wamkulu*, in the case of APIM members, despite the official disapproval by the church. *Gule wamkulu* still plays a significant part in the life of Christian churches even though Christianity has been around in the country for over a hundred years. Some have mixed the teaching, tradition and customs of Christianity and Gule because they were perceived as complementary and probably, as one and the same thing. This is so because both are seen as teaching people a better and fulfilling life. Nevertheless, there is a big difference between Christianity and Traditional Religion. Gule has stopped many and delayed some Chewa people from being educated. That is seen in the educational level of Achewa PIM membership, for example. In the entire APIM, the only family that has produced college graduates was that of Sandifolo Kamchedzera, who strongly opposed *Gule wamkulu*.

Common Way of Understanding

From a socio-economic point of view Achewa PIM appears generally to be below most mission churches because they don't have access to donations from outside the country. Nevertheless, APIM offers some privileges to its members. Achewa PIM tries to make Christianity more real and more meaningful in its social context. One advantage that APIM has above mission churches is that its leaders share a common way of understanding and coping with joys and sorrows in the lives of their members. APIM approaches Christianity more in tune with a culture that wants to see the relevance (*phindu*) of beliefs to everyday life. The Achewa PIM is also able to provide, both symbolically and practically, a step into the wider world beyond the realm of the traditional family because its leadership comes from the same cultural environment as their followers, and they are able to cater for the way followers understand their lives.

It is common amongst the membership to report to the church problems they are facing in their homes. Achewa PIM encourages its members to seek help from the traditional healers because they do not see it as being inconsistent with the Bible. They base their argument on Matthew 9:12 saying that "*zinalembedwa kuti wodwala ndi amene afuna sing'anga*" (it is written that it is the sick who need a doctor). Nevertheless, Achewa PIM is against a member who indulges in consulting mystical powers, instead one should just get the medicines as it is done in the hospitals. Any member of Achewa PIM who consults other powers apart from God is seen as not a true believer and therefore, deserves some punishment. The traditional healer that APIM recommends to its membership is one who, like all doctors, after hearing from the patient, examines the patient and prescribes the medicines. If a member of APIM goes to a government hospital and does not get well, or the hospital tells him/her to see a traditional doctor, which Achewa PIM leadership says is common, APIM encourages its members to report to the leadership of his/her intention to visit the medicine person. If he/she has been to a government or private hospital, the church needs to see the ticket of discharge before the member goes to the traditional doctor. Supposing soon the member dies after consulting with the medicine person, Achewa PIM is prepared to give the member a decent burial because they would have been following the case. The church understands what their members are going through and identifies with them.

Expression of Pain, Frustrations and Desires

Although it is generally felt that many of the African initiated church leaders had previously been members of mission churches and became frustrated in their ambitions for leadership within the churches, it was not so with Achewa PIM. There is no trace of protest against white-run denominations in their sermons. Generally, members of Achewa PIM are very proud to be associated with Chilembwe and not with Malikebu. From their little knowledge of history, they conclude that Malikebu sold the church to the white people when he married an American woman and when he retired in America.[3] Achewa PIM is not aware that Flora was an African from the Congo who was taken to America by an Afro-American woman missionary. Their desire, though, is to be identified, first, as Christians, and second, as Baptists, and not as an African Independent Church. The term "African" is perceived as derogatory when used as a description of the church.[4]

Polygamy as a Means of Attracting Adherents

Polygamy has been used by some AICs as a means of attracting adherents, but that has not been the case with Achewa PIM though its first leader, Kalemba, divorced a couple of times. As far back as APIM can remember it was not acceptable for a man to have more than one wife, or to have a wife and a concubine/mistress or a female companion. Any person who wants to have more than one woman friend or man friend is directed to churches that allow that. The moment an APIM member unites to another man or woman apart from the one known and accepted by the church, he/she is excommunicated from the church. If he/she holds any office in the church, he/she is relieved of that position. If a polygamist heard the Word and wants to be a member of APIM, the candidate is asked to divorce the second wife or any other additional wives on top of the first one. It is the woman who is accused of adultery and not the man. The men are free to take care of the children but not of their divorced mothers. Although Achewa PIM is situated in agricultural areas and a number of wives for each male member would provide cheap labour, polygamy is never condoned. In fact APIM encourages and supports its members to have a complete break with the past.

Social Demand

One must recognize that the church is influenced to a large extent by the society and culture of which it may be a part. At the same time one must be aware of the fact that the church is a supernatural institution. For this reason when one has evaluated some of the human

---

[3] From the text of one song sung by a youth choir on Chilembwe at Kakwere on 4.7.1998.
[4] Part of a speech made by Sandifolo Kamchedzera as he introduced me to the congregation at Kakwere.

factors involved in church growth, one cannot presume to have said all that there is to say.

A Family and Tribal Church

Achewa PIM is a minority institution although it is of long standing in Mangoni. Despite being labelled Mpingo wa Mpatuko, Achewa PIM was allowed to exist but its membership never increased proportionally to the population growth. APIM constitutes a closed group with new members almost completely restricted to those coming from families of their members. That costs the church its evangelistic zeal. Like all churches growing on family lines, APIM tends to grow quickly to the size of 40-60 members, but almost immediately thereafter growth stops. For many years there has been little or no increase. I many cases the local congregations grew to include virtually all the members of certain families. These family connections have become not only bridges for growth but also barriers to further growth. Achewa PIM did not have any significant growth during certain periods in its history because it was so much tied to is ethnic origins both in culture and language, that it could only absorb those who had grown up within the framework of Chewa lifestyle. It has failed to grow largely because it has little or no concern for evangelization of people from outside Mangoni. Achewa PIM is largely self-contained and happy to be counted as one among the Christian churches.

Social Organization and the Structure of Achewa PIM

Though Achewa PIM calls itself "Baptist", it tends to function like most Chewa social institutions, that is to say, under paternalistic control of a leader. Its form of church government fits the local social structure so closely that it does not allow for new creative leadership from within or outside itself. Since APIM placed broad control in the hands of the "elders", the bishop, pastors, *alaliki*, and *alangizi*, it almost overlooks young pastors and other leaders' contributions.

As an indigenous church, it has grown with very little foreign leadership and guidance. Although APIM is one generation removed from the missionary cause in the sense that its founding leadership was led to the Lord by Chilembwe who was converted through missionary enterprise, it is for that reason entirely indigenous. The leadership is very close to the people. The church structure, therefore, has a good deal of local authority and considerable vagueness about statistics. The leaders cannot provide adequate information about the very organization they head because the leadership is dependent far more on their personalities than upon the organization of the local congregations, and of cause, Achewa PIM itself.

One would ask why APIM is so highly centralized if it is a Baptist church. The highly centralized form of government was fitting during Chilembwe's era, but it should have changed after more people had been trained to take up responsibility in the church. At the beginning of PIM, Chilembwe's role was that of a father to the new and young church. He died before the church had reached maturity in which case he would have worked side by side with the church as co-labourers or partners, with the church assuming more responsibility. NBC Inc, on the other hand, remained extremely centralized, first, because some of the boards to the Convention antedate the Convention, and the boards have sought to act independently of the convention or assert control over its own property.[5] Second, NBC Inc has a history of strong presidents who have consolidated their power during their tenure of office. Nevertheless, Achewa PIM would have by now reached a stage where the leadership and membership were partners according to the generally accepted Baptist church polity. In the congregational form of church government, the denominational leaders really depend on the people for their power. In times of emergency, dependence on the people for their power may be a weakening because nothing can be done in time to save the situation. The leader has to have time to consult the churches before acting. That is not so with Achewa PIM. The bishop or his representative acts on behalf of the church with or without the consent of the church or Chififitini. The church does not question his power to act on behalf of the church. The strong relationship to the chiefs and to Chewa culture may also have strengthened these conservative tendencies.

Working together with Chiefs

Since the time of Kalemba, chiefs were consulted on issues that affected the life and ministry of Achewa PIM, from its registration to everyday relationships with people in whose areas APIM introduced congregations. Every major decision Achewa PIM makes, is done in consultation with the chiefs or their representatives. The chiefs are constantly made aware of what the churches are going through. Achewa PIM appreciates the role the chiefs play in the life of their subjects. The chiefs are responsible for the land on which churches are built,

---

[5] H. Leon McBeth, *The Baptist Heritage: Four Centuries of Baptist Witness*, Nash-ville: Broadman, 1987, p. 786.

and in turn, APIM invites them to dedication ceremonies of churches, ordination of ministers, baptism and wedding ceremonies of its members. That makes Achewa PIM a church of the local people.

Nevertheless, APIM separates the role of the church from that of the chiefs and the state. Since Chewa chiefs are installed under the banner of *Gule wamkulu*,[6] Achewa PIM does not accept them into church membership. The chiefs themselves cannot even apply for church membership because they know that Gule and Christianity do not go hand in hand. In spite of that, Achewa PIM encourages chiefs to fear God and govern their people with fairness. The church is not to interfere in the administration of the villages, just as the chiefs are not to meddle in the affairs of the church. The two respect each other's roles and are able to work side by side. Achewa PIM appeals to the chiefs on issues of land and politics, while the chiefs appeal to APIM for spiritual and moral direction of the people. Achewa PIM sets an example for the people to follow which in turn cements mutual relationships between APIM and the chiefs.

Relationship to other Churches

Achewa PIM does not have close links with either PIM or BACOMA churches in the area though they claim to be one with PIM through Chilembwe, and with BACOMA through the American Baptists. Achewa PIM does not want to be lumped together with AICs, especially African Abraham and Zion churches. Surprising enough, the African Abraham, African Emanuel and Independent Baptist congregations in the area have on occasions attended APIM's monthly fellowship meetings. Sometimes local Churches of Christ and Seventh-day Adventist church leaders have made their presence known at such meetings. Since monthly meetings are festive in nature, people in the local areas want to be part of such gatherings even if they have nothing to do with their churches. In spite of their presence, one would hear Achewa PIM leaders presiding over the meeting saying that they are not an African Abraham church.

Gender issue

Though APIM is a male dominated church that accommodates women folk strictly on its terms, there is agreement among male members that the church needs not only look to men for leadership, but to women as well. The prominence of women in APIM is a sure

---

[6] Molly Longwe, *From Chinamwali to Chilangizo*, Zomba: Kachere, 2007.

challenge to the gender issue most Malawians are struggling with. If a Westerner came and experienced the relationship that existed between men and women in Achewa PIM, they would wonder why Malawians are looking to the West on gender issues. The Achewa PIM is a typical answer to the issue. Despite that women are not looked upon as pastors (an issue that is still challenging the modern Church), they play a major role as advisors or counsellors, not only to women and girls, but also to the church and its male dominated leadership. Nowhere did APIM gather without the presence of its women folk. It does not matter who sits where and on what in any gathering. If there are not enough seats, it is not strange to see a woman sitting on a chair and a man sitting on a mat. Women have a different role from that of men, but that does not make them in any way inferior to their counterparts.

A woman is as responsible for herself and others as is the man. They look at each others as partners in advancing the kingdom of God. I have never been to a church were African women were so proud of being who they were before men and God. While our schools are plagued with the gender issue, the Achewa PIM created an environment in which girls and women experience the unity of purpose with men and boys. Instead of Malawians looking to other nations for examples and answers to the gender issue, Achewa PIM is an able contributor to the search for an ideal relationship between men and women. The Achewa PIM members are conscious of how they differ on the gender issue with other churches. They are very proud of their relationship which they view as biblical from the standpoint of brotherly love.

The gospel of Jesus Christ revolutionized the place of women in Jewish society. For sure something like that would take some time to work through particularly against the backgrounds of deep prejudice. Jesus did not treat women like chattels, but as equals of men. The *imago dei* lay in the harmonious interrelationship between man and woman in God's creation, and not in domination of one by the other. Women had a role in the church of the first century. The value of this is immense especially in a culture which requires a high degree of segregation between men and women.[7] In Achewa PIM women are engaged in the ministry of teaching. In addition, women hold the office of deacons.

---

[7] For further treatment on women and ministry see Michael Green, *Freed to Serve: Training and Equipping for Ministry*, London: Hodder and Stoughton, 1988, pp. 82ff. See also Willard M. Swartley, *Slavery, Sabbath, War and Women: Case Issues in Biblical Interpretation*, Scottdale: Herald, 1983, pp. 152ff.

It has not been difficult for Achewa PIM to accept women as equals because women traditionally play a major role in the society, from the selection of a chief to choosing where to make a home for the family. Women are present in the chiefs' courts and at all discussions that affect the community of which they are part. Sitting and discussing, working and sharing with men is not strange in the Chewa culture, therefore, the teaching of the gospel of Jesus Christ finds fertile ground on which women also have a lot to contribute in the life of the society and the church. It is also clear that in the family it is the task of the man, not the woman, to lead. It is differentiation of function and there is nothing derogatory about that. The harmonious inter-relationships between men and women did not come about because of the presence of missionaries among the Achewa PIM. The Achewa PIM makes one think again that some of the sections of the Christian church which was in the forefront of women's liberation in the first century do remain some of the last organizations in the world today to respect women as equal to men, and allow them to a significant place in leadership.

Practical Theology

Liturgy is the form in which the believers dress their prayers, praises and their confession of faith at the same time. The worship leader in the Achewa PIM has authority over everything that goes on during the service. He speaks with a very authoritative voice like an army commander and everyone does as he says. As a call to worship, the leader reminds the members that they are in the presence of God, therefore, the Lord deserved their total being. The whole congregation becomes silent, and thereafter, he prays or asks someone else to pray. Their prayers are very short. They don't use flowery language or the Christian clichés which are very common in BACOMA for example.

Almost all of the pastors are old men with little schooling, but try very hard to read audibly the Bible. Most of the time, they are quite steady in their reading. The congregation has great respect for their leaders such that the moment the leader stands to read the Word, all eyes are glued on him. That in itself signals respect for God's Word and his servant. In other churches I have seen members greeting each other or sorting themselves, their attire or hair, instead of paying attention to the Word. Here is a group of people who are thought of as being low in everything, and yet who are high in the value of listening to God's Word. There is very little in the way of distraction from the congregation during worship, instead the congregation uplifts the reader and gives him the support to explain the Word in the way that people would understand and appreciate.

The Achewa PIM worship service is a time when members are free from daily drudgery. It is a must for all male members to wear jackets and ties. Normally they put on dark colours and no fancy dress. They do that, especially the leaders, not to attract the audience to themselves. Men do not wear robes, or pin badges or emblems on themselves as an indication of their position in the church. One cannot tell the bishop from the rest of the male members by looking at the dress alone. Nevertheless, it is different with women. Pastors' wives wear long black dresses with white headscarfs, while *alangizi*'s attire is long white dresses and white headscarfs. At no one meeting will one find women, young and old, without headscarfs. All the members of Achewa PIM endeavour to dress well for worship. Of course some do wear torn clothes, but it is the better ones that they wear for church.

Church Music

Evangelical Christianity is characterized among other things by its emphasis on singing, for wherever the gospel has been taken, people express their joy in singing. APIM is no exception to this. Its music cannot be well defined. The music is redirected and modified so as to cause it to be Christ-centred and God-glorifying. APIM Christians chose which part of the musical system can be best retained and what part is unsuitable because of associations. For example, some music in the Chewa culture is definitely tied to *Gule wamkulu*. Achewa PIM church choirs whose members are mostly young people use hand-made drums and cymbals as accompaniment, otherwise the church uses vocal music accompanied by hand clapping and some dancing. Though Achewa PIM has adapted some Western hymns to suit their indigenous styles, many of the songs are simple repetitious melodies. Those indigenous songs and a few Western hymns that have been adapted rather than translated are a great blessing to Achewa PIM. That is evident from the enthusiasm with which APIM members sing them in their meetings. Often a leader sings a line, then the entire congregation takes up the refrain. Sometimes two different melodies are sung simultaneously to produce a beautiful effect. A leader may also have an associate who sings more or less on a tangent or in support of the leader while the rest of the group sings its own part.

Like in many other Christian churches I have visited, music in APIM is used in several ways. Sometimes it is used to call the congregation together and to get the service started. The moment the leader starts singing and a few people join him, it signals the beginning of the meeting. Music is also used to fill time. Achewa PIM is not comfortable with silence, and so they sing. Music is also used to bring a stronger feeling of participation with other members in a common religious expression. It also serves as a living expression of worship. Sometimes music is an exercise of personal virtuosity. Achewa PIM uses music also as an effective and inspiring statement of personal and corporate Christian experience. All in all, Achewa PIM singing comes from the heart.

Nothing seems to stir most Baptists' passions like a discussion of the way they worship. Baptists seem to get more anxious about worship music than anything else. While some elderly and others who despise modern worship music and the young innovators are ready to go to war in some Baptist congregations, Achewa PIM works on win-win solution for both. The adults allow the youth to sing what they enjoy. Time is set aside for as many youth choirs as possible to sing. This in itself strengthens the young people and encourages them to participate in the life of their church. On the other hand, the young seem to hold back from forcing absolute change on their elders. There is a sense of blending that allows both groups work together to build the kingdom of God and fortify Achewa PIM.

Ministry: Local Responsibility

Like many churches in Africa, much of the financial problem in APIM is due, not so much to poverty, but to that fact that the members have not been educated adequately with regard to giving to God through the church and the careful use of the resources by the church. Pastors are not financially supported by the churches. Many of their church buildings are in very poor condition. The central church building is in dire need of maintenance or else they will soon loose this beautiful historical monument. What the churches contribute is not enough to cover the cost of maintenance of these church buildings. Nevertheless, they are responsible and they do not ask for any outside help since they don't have any established foreign contacts.

Without external funding and assistance, Achewa PIM congregations are unable to construct permanent structures. Almost all their church buildings are built of mud and have grass-thatched roofs. With grass becoming more and more scarce and as a result expensive with the growth of the population and the destruction of forests, it is also becoming hard to put on and to maintain such type of roofs on church buildings. As a result, every year several buildings fall because the roofs leak and the mud walls become soaked and wet so that they fall. By the end of 1998, several Achewa PIM's church buildings had either fallen or had no roofs.[8] Despite that, APIM did not loose members to churches that had permanent buildings, but it contributed to slow or nil numerical growth of local congregations. It was the same with those that were using their homes as meeting places due to lack of church buildings. Gone are the days when people could joyfully congregate and multiply their membership while meeting under a tree. Although the Achewa PIM leadership agrees that lack of church buildings is a contributing factor for lack of growth, without outside help, there is nothing they can do to reverse the situation. There is no way they can raise enough money to construct one church building even if they molded the bricks, hauled sand and stones, and provided part of the labour force in the current economic environment in which Malawi finds itself.

The Role of Chilembwe in the Contemporary Achewa PIM

Though most adult members of Achewa PIM do not talk much about Chilembwe, the youths do. Achewa PIM is very proud to be associated with Chilembwe, but it is not something that they talk about in their normal day-to-day gatherings. In spite of that, both adults and youths talk and sing about Chilembwe as their hero and liberator of African people of Malawi and Africa as a whole.[9] According to some members of APIM, Chilembwe still lives and is ready to participate in their daily struggles for freedom and unity of Africans, especially of those who follow him. Majority of the members do not call Chilembwe "Saviour" because of the teaching the church has had since its founding about who Jesus Christ is to them, and what it means to be a Christian. Nevertheless, APIM members always feel a sense of pride at the mention of Chilembwe.

Despite the fact that they do not fellowship openly, both PIM and APIM claim Chilembwe as being their founder. Just as we Christians do not worship Abraham but love to be associated with him because of his faith and success, some Achewa PIM members desire that, too, with Chilembwe as people talk about his role as a nationalist and educationist. Since life in the areas where they live is not easy, young people in Achewa PIM feel strong and are encouraged by the life and ministry of John Chilembwe to cope, largely on their own, with a

---

[8] The churches included Chinungu, Nsabwe, Mgala, Gondwa, Chakwawa and Kumisu. Nsabwe has since had a new building.
[9] See for part of a message preached at Kakwere in praise of John Chilembwe.

variety of situations in their villages without outside help. They work hard in order to survive.

Achewa PIM: AIC or Baptist?

AICs are generally regarded as social groups that are apparently not progressive. The term depicts a society whose lifestyle is non-literate and primitive yet in their variety of facets and practices, they depict "the church of God", be it in Corinth, London, Philadelphia, Johannesburg, or South of Lilongwe. The term AICs has been applied to a very large extent by white Africans and Europeans who have had some interest in the churches in Africa. The writers came to the subject with preconceived conclusions which were mostly negative to anything African including the church.[10] They have used the word "church" as an ornament for the groups they did not accept as identical to churches in the West. Just as churches in the West have their own history and culture, so too the churches in Africa. The term AIC is foreign, Western, and not theological but sociological. It is not theological because wherever the church meets, it was and it is called the church of God. One would like to know which are European Indigenous Churches (EICs), American Independent Churches (AICs), or Asian Instituted Church (AICs). African churches are so called probably because of the absence of *azungu* (white people) in these churches. The so called AICs are Christian churches in Africa although they are different in their organization from the so-called mainline or mission churches.

AICs are mainly called breakaways. Barrett suggested that a number of factors combined to produce the tribal "*zeitgeist*" (spirit of the times), with its tendencies toward independence. Independence is the more likely the more these factors are present in the tribal unit.[11] That suggestion has no reference to the Anglican, Presbyterian, Baptist and Methodist churches, to mention a few which broke away from the Roman Catholic Church which also broke away from the Catholic Church. Why should a break-away church in Africa be described as and be called African when no break-away church in Europe or America is called European Independent or American Initiated? I contend to call churches in Africa as either Christian or non-Christian or pagan.

---

[10] See B.G.M. Sundkler, *Bantu Prophets in South Africa*, 2nd ed., London: Oxford, 1961, p. 302.

[11] Barrett, DEB., *Schism and Renewal in Africa: An Analysis of Thousand Contemporary Religious Movements*: Nairobi: Oxford, 1968, pp. 109ff.

CONCLUSION

If they are Christian churches, one would find theological weaknesses just as one would experience in churches in Europe, America and elsewhere. They may be different in type and depth and so on, but there would be some weaknesses that need to be addressed in either church. The churches in the West have brought the message of Jesus Christ in Western packages, and found it difficult to accept the same message in African packaging. While churches in Africa are being accused of not openly condemning the practice of Traditional Religions in their congregations, some of the Western churches are watching individual freedom and human rights steer them to condone homosexuality to the extent of allowing them to be pastors and to marry in church. Achewa PIM are independent or autonomous not because they are African, but because they have chosen to follow the Baptist form of church government (with some modifications). It is important to note that throughout the history of the Church, new groups have been forming and will continue to do so as the spirit of renewal is manifested.

If a church is a Christian gathering, it must be called Christian. Christian churches which were started by Africans for Africans are not just movements, but churches in their own right. Achewa PIM is a church in its own right. Barrett also suggested that the root cause common to the entire AICs is the missions' failure to demonstrate considerably the biblical concept of love in the African context. One may ask: has that changed? If so, are there no more churches breaking away? If not, then one would expect to see more and more churches breaking away. Achewa PIM is not a breakaway from the "mission", that is, mainline church, and therefore, its existence is not as a result of a failure on the part of white missionaries to demonstrate love towards APIM. PIM is a church started by a Malawian for Africans. Therefore, Achewa PIM and of course, PIM, are lumped together with churches that broke away from white mission churches for lack of a better term.

Be reminded that there are no African Church Fathers, but Church Fathers. Missions are as much the result and undertaking of Christians from the world over. Again describing some churches as "missionary" and others as African does not do justice to the teaching and command of Christ to go. Westerners have deliberately divided the Christian church in Africa into the one brought by Westerners and the other that was started by Africans themselves.[12] Calling other churches "AICs" is a way of perpetuating segregation in the church of God.

---

[12] See Hilary Mijoga, Separate but Same Message, Blantyre: CLAIM, p. 1.

Some attribute the rise and development of AICs to the need for fellowship and security.[13] That is not so with Achewa PIM. They started as a church and not as a "fellowship" group.[14] People gather for fellowship in their churches, but the type of fellowship depends on the group needs. Every Christian and every person looks for fellowship and security and that cannot be only for AICs.

Here in Malawi the so-called AICs are looked upon as schismatic and syncretistic by the Christian Council of Malawi (CCM). AICs stimuli have been misinterpreted. CCM has considered division and segregation as a denial of the unity of the body of Christ.[15] AICs cannot be admitted into the CCM as they are not considered truly Christian churches. For them to be admitted into the national organization it seems the AICs have to justify their existence to the gatekeepers and meet their criteria before they can have the right of admission. AICs are thought of as having no idea whatsoever about what theology is all about because they are led by unschooled pastors. As a result the mainline clergy refuse to be in the same meeting where AICs are in the majority. Such churches as Achewa PIM are viewed by mission church ministers as being inferior. They don't see themselves as equal before the God they both serve.[16]

Achewa PIM has maintained the centrality of Jesus Christ as Lord and Saviour. They do praise John Chilembwe as an earthly leader who founded the church, but he is not regarded as Lord and Saviour of their lives. Just like in other mainline churches, the knowledge of the Christian faith of some of the members is limited. As a result, some discrepancy exists between the doctrine accepted by the church and the practice of some of its believers. Despite that, Achewa PIM affirms faith in Jesus Christ in African traditional forms just as it is in many BACOMA congregations. The celebration of the Lord's Supper and believer's baptism are seen as symbolic of the death, burial and res-

---

[13] Ibid., p. 34.

[14] The term "fellowship", came to mean those Christian groups that were formed specifically around the 1970s and 1980s by Christians who were not happy with their churches such as CCAP and Assemblies of God which did not involve their laity more in the ministry of the churches. In recent years BACOMA members are more and more getting involved in fellowship groups, especially in the towns and cities, for several reasons. One reason is of association, and the other is of piety and recognition as spiritual by the outside world.

[15] Peter Falk, *The Growth of the Church in Africa*, Grand Rapids: Zondervan, 1979, p. 460.

[16] James Tengatenga, "Religious Pluralism in Malawi: A Challenge to the Church", *Religion in Malawi*, No. 8, April 1998.

urrection of Jesus, and each believer's identification, by faith, with Jesus, in both dying to sin and rising to new life with him. This christo-centric gospel is preached from Achewa PIM pulpits Sunday after Sunday, for its proclamation retains the central place in Baptist worship.

Achewa PIM is conscious of its obligation toward BACOMA and BMIM and is willing to re-establish fraternal relations with them. Its leadership team accepts that there is need to engage BACOMA's Bible teachers to instruct pastors and other church leaders if the church is to survive as a Christian church in the 21st century. APIM has not been like Baptist churches in the area of evangelism. Baptists take pride in evangelism because they are committed to sharing their faith, to the extension of the kingdom of God, both at home and afar. Despite that, Achewa PIM's radiant joy and assurance of conviction that testifies to their relationship with Jesus Christ is convincing evidence of their Christian faith.

One other area that Achewa PIM has not matched other Baptists is prayer. The demands for Christian witness and discipleship necessitate prayer. Baptists encourage corporate prayer and a pattern of individual spirituality that requires each member to engage in regular prayer and Bible study. Nevertheless, Achewa PIM are very much aware of the freedom of opinion and religious practice, not only for themselves, but for all people, including non-believers. Each individual needs to be free to make choices about faith and commitment undisturbed by outside agency. Such freedom has led Baptists to be diverse people with no overarching rule demanding common thought or practice among all Baptists.

Achewa PIM is definitely different from mainline churches. It is also different from individual BACOMA congregations especially those that are in the towns and cities and have been led by a pastor or church leaders who has had theological education from a seminary or college. If one visited some BACOMA churches in the rural areas and later visited with Achewa PIM congregations, one would probably find it hard to differentiate between the two. The only difference noticed easily is the women with their uniforms. Some of the Achewa PIM churches that have had close contact with BMIM in the 1970s are much more organized than some BACOMA churches in terms of worship services. The preaching may not be very different from most BACOMA churches either in towns or in the rural area. The interesting thing is that Achewa PIM is part of the whole God-fearing Christian family.

A Religious Island

In this dissertation I have tried to show that the periods Achewa PIM stayed without meaningful interaction with other Christian groups, were times of retardation. The use of "Achewa" in the title of the church meant that it was a local church which became an umbrella for religious individualism and separation. The people of Mangoni felt that they were just as good, if not better, than the people across the Shire River, and were capable of living in isolation from PIM with its headquarters at Mbombwe. PIM grew considerably from about 1924 until 1934, but even more so for just over ten years when the "Chewa" people worshipped in isolation from PIM, despite being labelled "Mpingo wa Mpatuko". The Christianization of many Achewa people was more evident because of a strong group identity and good communication channels. Face-to-face relationship and homogeneity were the underlying factors to the conversion of many households to APIM. This linguistic and cultural group became a religious island though most of its leadership at the time had had some influence from PIM and DRCM in terms of secular and religious education. The decision taken by Malikebu to excommunicate Kalemba also contributed to Achewa's development in isolation from the world of their day. Instead of thinking of the world at large, or to be more practical, to think of all ethnic groups in Malawi, as their goal for evangelism, APIM limited themselves to their own cultural group, Achewa.

It was not long that some of the stalwarts of APIM began to question the viability of APIM in the face of increased culture contact. Already Mangoni, and not to mention the whole country, was becoming a small village with the arrival and ministry or work of people from within and from outside the country. Trading Centres were being flooded with people from other tribes who were looking for work or education. Missionaries from Europe and South Africa were increasing their activities in both rural and urban areas. There was increased culture contact within that ten year period, and it was going to increase even further. A few of those who had had some contact with PIM and DRCM took a rather serious look at their responsibility and their ministry as a church in the light of rapidly increasing culture contact. That was not questioning the validity of the indigenous church philosophy, because they knew very well that in every cultural environment those who feared God were acceptable to him since God is no respecter of language or culture. They quickly realized that culture contact and integration of Achewa PIM into the larger PIM group was inevitable and desirable. In that case, some of the men attempted to serve as mediators between APIM and PIM, a child and parent so to speak, respectively. In 1945 a good number of families moved back to PIM.

Between 1945 and 1962 Achewa PIM slowly ran out of steam. They were isolated from the information that had stimulated growth during the period before 1945. People cannot survive on the good old days theory. Since no more new information was being infused into the life of the church, Achewa PIM soon lost power to win more converts, and power to develop as a whole. From the time of PIM through the formation of Achewa PIM to the time when others went back to PIM, the training of church leadership insured the introduction and diffusion of new information which was needed for the survival of the church. The re-establishment of ties with PIM brought hope and momentum to PIM in Mangoni under Kalemba. PIM (Mbombwe) introduced training programmes for church leaders, especially in the pastoral ministry, and secular education with schools in and around Chiradzulu district. Several individuals and groups from the Mangoni section of PIM had some training there. They in turn, introduced what they had learnt to the rest in Mangoni. That in itself acted as fuel for PIM congregations. Those who had received some education in PIM schools brought new ideas and impetus to the church that kept rekindling their fires to do more for the church. The church had a vision, to reach the people with the Word. It was not limited to the people of Mangoni. They wanted to apply what they had learnt to the communities they came into contact with. Lack of continued renewal of information through education blurred that vision, and was then restricted to "Achewa" as the target people.

The little bit of information they had soon became so familiar that it did not challenge Achewa PIM members enough to do more for the church. No more members were receiving education anywhere apart from what I would term 'in service training' provided by Kalemba and later by Kamkalamba. That remained so until the period of partnership with BMIM. After Achewa PIM was separated from BMIM in 1976 the situation returned to an 'in service training' period in which the church just dragged its feet and sort of folded in. Even if they had wanted to receive training from outside, it was not going to be easy for them. Limitations of both finances and personnel restricted their educational possibilities. As village people their financial resources were too meager to pay for the education. When they were part of PIM and later of BMIM, Achewa PIM overcame the limitation because the mission met the cost, in part or in full, of the training some of their members received. Since most of those who had received some education from PIM had separated themselves from Achewa PIM and had since returned to PIM, APIM was left without enough personnel of that ability.

Even if they had been found, they needed to be sent outside the Achewa environment to acquire the needed education. Unfortunately, Achewa PIM has not produced eligible candidates for further training amongst its membership. Generally education has not been one of the major thrusts of Achewa PIM such that very few families have children who have finished secondary school education, and only one family had produced at least one college graduate. Supposing a person of ability had been found who had gone through school and had finally acquired theological education, he would not be able to find a meaningful niche in his society. It would be very difficult for that individual to come back into the tribal setting of Achewa PIM or any other church in a constructive way. School leavers and college graduates leave Achewa PIM and, either join churches of other denominations, or stop going to church altogether. Lack of people of ability greatly retarded the speed at which Achewa PIM could minister to the modern world and thereby slowed down its own development as a church.

There was a realization amongst some of the members that they were missing out by keeping the church "Achewa". Christianization by means of a group movement was by no means the perfect answer to the evangelization of the people. It reinforced existing tribal ethnocentrism. The "Achewa" did not only separate themselves from PIM, they also separated from people who were different from them. To be part of Achewa PIM became something to be proud of: *"Ife ndife Achewa"* (We are Achewa). As a result of isolation from people who are different, Achewa PIM became limited in their conception of the gospel.

Although Achewa PIM has been ill equipped to evaluate adequately new information that comes in, no havoc has been caused by sects and self appointed prophets because known have come APIM's way. Another reason might be that up to now Achewa PIM's church polity has not created room for outsiders to come in and impose themselves or misguide them. Achewa PIM has remained very much close to the Chewa culture such that it has copied almost nothing from other churches such as BACOMA and other evangelicals. In using the popular Christian cliche's such as "Amen, brother", "hallelujah", "praise God, amen", singing of choruses accompanied by clapping of hands and dancing, mass prayer, and theological debates on such issues as speaking in tongues that have opened doors to worldwide brotherhoods of believers. On account of not participating in inter-denominational meetings and the so called "fellowship" meetings of Evangelical and Protestant Christians, Achewa PIM has remained virtually unaffected by controversies in these churches, and its members being swept into the fold of some highly evangelistic sects or churches that are deviating from the normal.

Recommendations

Despite the obvious limitations, Achewa PIM provides a spiritual home for a group of people who live their Christian faith in that church. It is a church in which people are serving God and others. The result is fellowship and community. Most mission churches only meet for a short time and each member spends his/her time elsewhere outside the community of the church. Achewa PIM members have time for each other. Though local APIM congregations are independent and support themselves, they are responsible to and for each other. The emphasis of Achewa PIM is on building a community. Members of APIM see the unity of the church and of the society.

Achewa PIM members express their faith in ways that are familiar to them. They are uplifted because the Christian faith is integrated into their way of thinking and their approach to life. There is no gap between the gospel that is proclaimed and the gospel that is heard. Like those in the mainline churches, APIM members preach and hear the messages in the culture of their day. Since they have developed an indigenous liturgy, members of APIM are able to receive God's Word in word and in deed. They are able to pray and praise God and also to confess their faith. The Christian faith is spread by Africans amongst Africans. Though it takes a long time to penetrate, but when it does it is truly African; that is, it becomes truly indigenous.

APIM gives attention to the whole life. The society is analyzed and the messages are related to it. APIM members see the living relationship of the word and the social environment. They do not have the financial problems that some of the mainline churches in Africa have because they do not build or do anything for which the members are able to pay for. Therefore, their church buildings are poor, but they belong to them, so does the church, and that is independence.

There can be little doubt that the contribution of Achewa PIM to the Chilembwe heritage, and thus to the history (which is being written) of indigenous Baptist and evangelical churches in Malawi, and to the history of the nation, is by no means insignificant. Achewa PIM continues to contribute to the development and history of the Church and the world at large as it attempts to accomplish its duty and role as a church under the Lordship of Jesus Christ.

In addition to providing a spiritual home for a group of people, Achewa PIM contributed to the formation of several congregations in Lilongwe, Blantyre, Chikwawa, Phalombe and Zomba Districts, to the establishment of the Baptist Bible School and subsequently, another Baptist church, BACOMA. When BMIM realized that the greatest challenge to the spread of the Gospel of Jesus Christ lied in the villages, Albright cultivated the friendship of Achewa PIM. In the process of studying the Bible together, APIM started new congregation to the benefit of BMIM. Achewa PIM became the stepping stone for BMIM and the foundation for the Baptist Bible School from which the idea of a seminary came. Despite Achewa PIM leadership not being well drilled in English to enable them to study in that language, they contributed to the sending of the first Malawian for seminary training provided for by SBC outside the country. Since then, many people have come to know the Lord Jesus Christ from these humble beginnings. No doubt, that Achewa PIM has contributed to the history of Baptists in Malawi, especially that of African Baptist Assembly, Baptist Convention of Malawi and of Independent Baptist Convention of Malawi. The history of these churches cannot be complete without the story of Achewa PIM.

Bibliography

A. Primary Sources

Oral Informants

Banda, B. Kapalamula, *abusa*, BACOMA, Falls Baptist Church
Bikisoni, Linesi, *mkazi*, BACOMA, formerly APIM Mphindo
Butao, Christopher, *abusa*, BACOMA, Area 36 Baptist Church
Chakwala, Sitoliya, *amayi*, founder and member, Mphanje
Chalera, Nasoni, *abusa*, Mphindo
Chalinda, Beti, *amayi*, BACOMA, Mphindo
Chalosi, *abusa*, Mwala, Dedza
Chibwinja, Lefani, *abusa*, BACOMA, Chingira
Chimlozi, Anderson, CCAP, Kalumbu
Chimpesa, Peturo, former member of Achewa PIM
Chinsera, Shadreck M., church monitor, Nyanje
Chisemphere, Oliva, *amayi busa*, Kalumbu
Chisi, W.A.C., *abusa*, BACOMA, Lilongwe
Dooko, Letiya, *amayi busa*, Msemanjira, Nyanje
Fulanki, Linesi, *mkazi*, BACOMA, formerly of Mphindo APIM
Galatiya, Stephen, *abusa*, BACOMA, Senzani, Ntcheu
Gedeya, former member of BACOMA, Njovu Village
Gunya, Sonny, *abusa*, BACOMA, Soche
Kabaluka, Josi, *mlaliki*, Mgala
Kafulatira, Foulger, former member of PIM, Kalumba
Kakhobwe, Litida, *mkazi*, member of PIM, Katantha
Kamchedzera, Enita, *amayi busa*, Nsabwe
Kamchedzera, Dr. Garton, Lecturer, University of Malawi, member, BACOMA, Zomba
Kamchedzera, Sandifolo *abusa*, Nsabwe
Kamdolozi, Ezina, *mkazi*, member of PIM, Matapila
Kampangire, Adiresi, *mkazi*, member of PIM, Katantha
Kampangire, Naomi, *amayi*, member of PIM Katantha
Kamunthu, Magi, CCAP, Kalumbu
Kamunthu, Numeri, CCAP, Kalumbu
Kantefu, Simon, Mphanje
Kapatuka, Halisoni, *mlaliki*, Mphindo
Kasamu, Kamuikeni, member, Chinungu
Kaunde, Feliati Dirawo, PIM, Matapila
Kaunde, Velina, *mkazi*, PIM, Matapila
Khama, Velina, *mkazi*, BACOMA, formerly of Mphindo APIM
Kuthedze, Daulosi S., *abusa*, IBACOMA, Nyangu
Kuthedze, Emelesi, *mkazi*, IBACOMA, Nyangu
Lenadi, Alexina, *mkazi*, *mlangizi*, Kachala

Lipenga, Dalesi, *mkazi*, BACOMA, formerly Mphindo APIM
Longwe, Molly, *mkazi*, teacher, BTS, BACOMA
Makondesa, Patrick, PIM, Blantyre
Marudo, Eliya, *mlaliki*, Katunga
Masalaza, Oliva, *amayi*, chair, Mphanje
Matewere, Erika, *mkazi*, deaconess, BACOMA, New Jerusalem, Limbe
Maynard, Robert, *abusa*, Capital City Baptist church, Lilongwe
Mbalame, Julius, *mlaliki*, Chingoma
Mgala, Yulita, member, Mphindo
Mgawi, K.J., *abusa*, CCAP, Kasungu, formerly at Nkhoma
Mkaka, Redson, *abusa*, BACOMA, Mphindo
Mkhumbeni, Sefilina, *amayi*, CCAP, Kalumbu
Mlamba, Wyson, *mlaliki*, Mwase
Mnjolo, Jese, *mkazi*, Mphindo
Nyongo, Lefeyasi, member, Mwase
Mtsinje, Levi, former Achewa PIM member at Nyanje
Mwamuru, Rabson, chairman, Nyanje
NaBanda, member, Mphindo
Ndege, Yosofati, Bishop, Chalendewa
Ngalawo, Elikana, *mkazi*, BACOMA, formerly of Mphindo APIM
Njovu, chief, member of African Abraham Church, Njovu Village
Nyangu, Eliamu Mlongoti, Chijere, *abusa*, IBACOMA, Mtchinji
Nyengere, Kasinja, Roman Catholic Church, Likuni, Lilongwe
Peturo, Feliasi, *abusa*, Kachala
Phiri, Misinde, *abusa*, BACOMA, Senga Bay
Sandalamu, L.K., *abusa*, BACOMA, Kafumbula
Scott, Rue, Dr., former SBC missionary to Malawi, Oklahoma, USA
Sikatero, Nelson, Nyanje
Simoko, Navison, *abusa*, Phatha
Solomoni, Hawa, *mkazi*, new convert, Kakwere
Sopo, K., Vice Bishop, Gondwa, Nathenje
Thole, Dailesi P., *mkazi*, member of PIM, Katantha
Thomasi, Wiscot, *abusa*, Mwase
Tsokonombwe, David, *abusa*, Nyanje
Upton, Sam, Dr., BMIM, Lilongwe
Vizi, Lositala, *manejara*, Phatha
Wisikoti, Elenesi, *amayi*, Kamkalamba's niece, Nyanje
Yohane, Lemia, *mkazi*, formerly of Mphindo APIM

Church Documents

BACOMA' "An Extract of the First Meeting of the Baptist Convention of Malawi Held in Lilongwe on 26 May 1972"
BACOMA, E.C. Minutes, Lilongwe, 12.11.1973.
BACOMA Meeting Minutes, Lilongwe, 15.01.1975.
Baptist Mission in Malawi Primary Documents Manual 1995.

BIBLIOGRAPHY 165

Unpublished Material

Chaponda, Orison J.T., "*Gule wamkulu* in Catholic Lilongwe Rural: A Cultural Phenomenon and a Personal Problem," a paper presented at the postgraduate colloquium, University of Malawi, May 1998.

Chatepa, H.K., "The Containment Policy of the Zambezi Industrial Mission: The Denominational Balkanization of the Ntonda Lowlands", a research paper, Chancellor College, Zomba, n.d.

Chikanza, J.C., "Missionaries to Themselves: an Assessment of the Contribution of African Indigenous Churches to Christianity and Development in Malawi", Theology Conference paper, Chancellor College, Zomba, 1993.

"Civil Case No. 319 of 1977: The Registered Trustees of African Baptist Assembly and Rev L. Muocha in the High Court of Malawi".

Dambo, E., "Sectarianism in the Providence Industrial Mission: an Assessment of Background Causes", seminar paper, Chancellor College, Zomba, 1980-81.

Ellen, Mary, letter to Baptist Mission in Central Africa (BMCA) Families, Harare, n.d.

Englund, Harri, "Pentecostalism and Transnationalism in Malawi", a special paper presented at the postgraduate colloquium of the Department of Theology and Religious Studies, University of Malawi, Nantipwiri, May 1999.

Fiedler, Klaus, "Bishop Lucas' Christianization of Traditional Rites, the Kikuyu Female Circumcision Controversy and the 'Cultural Approach' of Conservative German Missionaries in Tanzania", a seminar, paper, n.d.

Garrett, Rev and Mrs Marvin L., letter to Baptist Mission in Central Africa (BMCA) Families, Chegutu, 29 January 1961.

Garrett, Rev and Mrs Marvin L., letter to the "Nyasalanders", Chegutu, 20 March 1961.

Goerner, H. Cornell, letter to Rev Marvin L. Garret, Richmond, 6 February 1961.

Kafulatira, A.H., "*Ciyambi ca Mpingo wa Achewa* Providence Industrial Mission *Kudera la Lilongwe*".

Kingsley, Beverly, a note to Hany H. Longwe, Ft. Worth, 1999.

Kingsley, Gene, a note to Hany Longwe, Ft. Worth, 1999.

Longwe, Hany H., "An Outline History of Evangelical Churches in Malawi", MA module paper, University of Malawi, 1997.

Makondesa, Patrick., "Christian Initiation Rites in Southern Malawi", MA module 1, Department of Theology and Religious studies, University of Malawi, 1999.

Matenje, Flossie, "African Independent Churches and Politics", seminar paper on New Religious Movements, Chancellor College, Zomba, 1980/81.

Mijoga, Hilary, B.P., "The Evangelical Lutheran Church in Malawi: its Development," Chancellor College, Zomba, n.d.

Mugabe, Henry J., "African View of Church Leadership and Polity", a paper presented at the National Churches and Missions in Partnership Conference, Harare, 24-28 November 1986.

Ndege, Yosofati, Portions of his Ruined Diaries.

Parratt, John, "Mbombwe Revisited: Dr. Daniel Malikebu and the Second Era of the Providence Industrial Mission", a history seminar paper, University of Malawi, 29 January 1985.
Phiri, D.D., *Let Us Die for Africa*, Blantyre: Central Africana Limited, 1999.
Scott, Rue, a note to Hany Longwe, Oklahoma City, 1999.
Shelburne, G.B., "History of the Church of Christ in Malawi", a paper presented at Namikango Bible School, 1976.
Swafford, Gary and Carolyn, a note to Hany Longwe, Montgomery, 18.03.1999

Dissertations and Theses

Alexander, Frank, "Missions in Malawi", MA, Fuller Theological Seminary, 1969.
Capp, Philip L., "Contextual Factors in Church Growth in Malawi", M.D., Western Evangelical Seminary, 1979.
Chakanza J.C., "Continuity and Change: a Study of New Religious Movements in Malawi, 1900- 1981", DPhil, Corpus Christi College, Oxford, 1985.
Church, Henry G. Jr., "The Impact of Theological Education Upon Church Growth in the Free Methodist church in Malawi", PhD, University of Malawi, 1999.
Kapito, Lucy K., "Women in African Independent Churches in Ndirande and Mbayani Townships, Blantyre City", BA, (Theology), University of Malawi, 1995.
Makondesa, Patrick., "The Life and Ministry of Rev and Mrs Muocha of Providence Industrial Mission", BA, University of Malawi, 1996.
Pauw, Christoff Martin, "Mission and Church in Malawi: The History of the Nkhoma Synod of the Church of Central Africa, Presbyterian 1889-1962", PhD, University of Stellenbosch, 1980.
Saunders, D.L., "A History of Baptists in East and Central Africa", PhD, Southern Baptist Theological Seminary, 1973.

B. Secondary Soures

Books

Anderson, Keith B., *Introductory Course and African Traditional Religion*, Nairobi: Provincial Board of Theological Education, 1986.
Baker, Robert A., *A Baptist Source Book with Particular Reference to Southern Baptists*, Nashville: Broadman, 1966.
Baptist Convention of Zimbabwe, *Programme Base Design*, Bulawayo: BCZ, 1984.
Barrett, DEB., *Schism and Renewal in Africa: An Analysis of Thousand Contemporary Religious Movements*: Nairobi: Oxford, 1968.
Baur, John, *2000 Years of Christianity in Africa: an African History 62 - 1992*, Nairobi: Paulines, 1994.
Bourdillon, M., *Religion and Society: A Text for Africa*, Gweru: Mambo, 1990.

BIBLIOGRAPHY

Brackney, William H., with Ruby J. Burke, *Faith, Life, and Witness: The Papers of the Study and Research Division of the Baptist World Alliance - 1986-1990*, Birmingham, AL: Sanford University, 1990.

Buku Lopatulika ndilo Mau a Mulungu, Bible Society of Malawi, 1997 Impression.

Carson, D.A., (Consulting ed.), *New Bible Commentary 21st Century Edition*, Leicester: InterVarsity, 1994.

Cauthen, Baker, J. and Others, *Advance: A History of Southern Baptist Foreign Missions*, Nashville: Broadman, 1970.

Chikanza, J.C., "New Religious Movements in Malawi: a Biographical Review", in A.F. Walls and W.R. Shenk (eds.), *Exploring New Religious Movements: Essays in Honour of Harold W. Turner*, Elkhart: Mission Focus, 1990.

Chikanza, J.C. and Kenneth R. Ross (eds.), *Religion in Malawi: An Annotated Bibliography*, Blantyre: CLAIM, 1998.

Church, Henry, *Light is Shining in the Africa I Know*, Indiana: Light and Life, 1987.

Daneel, Inus, *Quest for Belonging*, Gweru: Mambo, 1987.

Downs, Perry G., *Teaching for Spiritual Growth: An Introduction to Christian Education*, Grand Rapids: Zondervan, 1994.

Estep, W.R., The *Reformation and Protestantism*, El Paso: Carib Baptist, 1983.

Falk, Peter, *The Growth of the Church in Africa*, Grand Rapids, Zondervan, 1979.

Faw, Harold W., *Psychology in Christian Perspective: An Analysis of Key Issues*, Grand Rapids: Baker, 1995.

Fiedler, Klaus, "Power at the Receiving End: The Jehovah's Witnesses' Experience in One Party Malawi", in Kenneth R. Ross (ed.), *God, People and Power in Malawi: Democratization in Theological Perspective*, Blantyre: CLAIM, 1996.

Fiedler, Klaus, "The *Smaller* Churches and Big Government", in Matembo S. Nzunda and Kenneth Ross, Church, Law and Political Transition in Malawi 1992-1994, Gweru: Mambo, 1995.

Fiedler, Klaus, *The Story of Faith Missions*, Oxford: Regnum; Sutherland: Albatross, 1994.

Fitts, Leroy, *A History of Black Baptists*, Nashville: Broadman, 1985.

Gaebelein, Frank E., (ed.), *The Expositor's Bible Commentary Vol. 10*, Grand Rapids: Zondervan, 1976.

Gehman, Richard, *African Traditional Religion in Biblical Perspective*, Kijabe: Kesho, 1989.

Giles, James E., *Biblical Ethics and Contemporary Issues*, El Paso: Carib, 1994.

Green, Michael, *Freed to Serve: Training and Equipping for Ministry*, London: Hodder and Stoughton, 1988.

Haar, Gerrie ter, *Halfway to Paradise: African Christians in Europe*, Cardiff: University, 1998.

Hastings, Adrian, *The Church in Africa 1450-1950*, Oxford: Clarendon, 1996.

Hiebert, Paul G. and Eloise Hiebert Meneses, *Incarnational Ministry: Planting Churches in Band, Tribal, Peasant, and Urban Societies*, Grand Rapids: Baker, 1995.

Kholowa, Janet, and Klaus Fiedler, *Pa Chiyambi Anawalenga Chimodzimodzi*, Blantyre: CLAIM, 1999.
Lampert-Stokes, Barbara, *Blantyre: Glimpses of the Early Days*, Blantyre: Society of Malawi, 1989.
Langworthy, Harry, *"Africa for the African". The Life of Joseph Booth*, Blantyre: CLAIM, 1996.
Longwe, Molly, *From Chinamwali to Chilangizo*, Zomba: Kachere, 2007.
Lingenfelter, Sherwood G., *Transforming Culture: A Challenge for Christian Mission*, Grand Rapids: Baker, 1992.
McBeth, H. Leon, *The Baptist Heritage: Four Centuries of Baptist Witness*, Nashville: Broadman, 1987.
Mbiti, John S., *African Religions and Philosophy*, Oxford: Heinemann, 1990.
Mgawi, K.J., *C.C.A.P. Nkhoma Synod: Mbiri ya Mpingo ndi Mudzi wa Nkhoma 1896 mpaka 1961*, Nkhoma: Nkhoma, 1996.
Mijoga, Hilary, *Separate but Same Message*, Blantyre: CLAIM.
Minnis, J.R., "Prospects and Problems for Civil Society in Malawi", in Kings M. Phiri and Kenneth R. Ross (eds.), *Democratization in Malawi: a Stocktaking*, Blantyre: CLAIM, 1998.
Morcom, Dee, "What Do We Stand for as Baptists and as Evangelicals?", in Desmond Hoffmeister and Louise Kretszchmar, *Towards a Holistic, Afrocentric and Participatory Understanding of the Gospel of Jesus Christ*, Johannesburg: Baptist Convention of South Africa, 1995.
Muga, Erasto, *African Response to Western Christian Religion: A Sociological Analysis of African Separatist Religious and Political Movements in East Africa*, Nairobi: East African Literature Bureau, 1975.
Osei-Mensah, Gottfried, *Wanted Servant Leaders*, Achimoto: Africa Christian, 1990.
Phiri, Isabel Apawo, *Women, Presbyterianism and Patriarchy: Religious Experience of Chewa Women in Central Malawi*, Blantyre: CLAIM, 1997.
Poland, Harry and Ernest Adams, *Breakthrough: Sunday School Work*, Nashville: Convention, 1990.
Shepperson, G. and T. Price, *Independent African*, Edinburgh: University Press, 1987, first paperback edition, reprinted Blantyre: CLAIM-Kachere, 2000.
Sundkler, B.G.M., *Banthu Prophets in South Africa*, London: Oxford, 1961.
Swartley, Willard M., *Slavery, Sabbath, War and Women: Case Issues in Biblical Interpretation*, Scottdale: Herald, 1983.
Weller, John and Jane Linden, *Mainstream Christianity to 1980 in Malawi, Zambia and Zimbabwe*, Gweru: Mambo, 1984.

Journals, Magazines and News Publications

Chapman, Morris H., "Local Church Autonomy", *SBC Life*, December 1997.
Chakanza, J.C., "The Independency Alternative: An Historical Survey", *Religion in Malawi*, Vol. 4. (1994).
Chakanza, J.C., "Sectarianism in Joseph Booth's Mission Foundations, 1925-1975: the Search for Causative Factors", *Religion in Malawi*, Vol. 2 (1988).

BIBLIOGRAPHY

Chakanza, J.C., "Towards an Interpretation of Independent Churches in Malawi", *Africa Theological Journal*, Vol 11 (1982).

Commission, The, Foreign Mission Board, Southern Baptist Convention, December (1966).

Freemen, E., "The Epoch of Negro Baptists and the Foreign Mission Board, National Baptist Convention, U.S.A., Inc", Kansas City: Central University, (1953).

"Institute of Basic Life Principles", n.p., U.S.A. (1986).

Linden, Ian an Jane, "John Chilembwe and the `New Jerusalem'", *Journal of African History*, Vol. 12 (1971).

Pauw, C. Martin, "Independency and Religious Change in Malawi: a New Challenge for the Church", *Missionalia*, Vol. 21/2 (1993).

Macdonald, Roderick, J., "Reverend Hannock Musokera Phiri and the Establishment of the African Methodist Episcopal Church", *African Historical Studies*, Vol. 3/1 (1970).

Mijoga, Hilary, B.P., "Hermeneutics in African Instituted Churches in Malawi", *Missionalia*, Vol. 24/3 (November 1996).

Mwase, G., "Problems of Oedipal Historicism: the Saga of John Chilembwe the Malawian", *Journal of Black Studies*, Vol. 8/2 (1977).

Mtewa, M., "Tribute to Dr Malikebu", *The Enquirer*, Vol. 1 No. (6 September 1993).

National Statistical Office, *Malawi Population and Housing Census 1987: Summary of Final Results* Vol. 1, Zomba: Government Printer, July 1991.

Parratt, John K., "African Independent Churches in Malawi", *Journal of Social Science* (Zomba), Vol. 10 (1983).

Rainer, Thom, "Closing the Back Door of Our Churches", Baptist Messenger, (5 Novembor 1998).

Tengatenga, James, "Religious Pluralism in Malawi: A Challenge to the Church", *Religion in Malawi*, No. 8, (April 1998).

Tenney, Merrill C., *The Zondervan Pictorial Encyclopedia of the Bible*, Grand Rapids: Zondervan, 1977.

Index

1915 Rising, Chilembwe, 11, 13, 15, 22ff, 143
Achewa Baptist Association (ABA), 67
African Baptist Assembly, 164
Alaliki (preachers), 52, 74, 91, 113, 116f, 120, 124, 131, 133, 148
Alangizi (counsellors), 29, 31, 84f, 91, 116, 130ff, 133, 136f, 148, 153
Albright, Leroy, 57ff, 66ff, 70f, 75ff, 80ff, 88, 94, 94, 99ff, 102ff, 136, 164
Amayi busa (pastor's wife), 131
Associate, 8, 63ff, 65fn, 67, 86, 135, 147, 153, 155
Association, 60fn, 139, 153, 159fn
Attire, 29, 152f
Authority, 32ff, 35, 42, 46, 59, 104, 109, 148, 152
BMIM, 59, 62ff, 65ff, 68ff, 76ff, 79ff, 82ff, 85ff, 90, 93f, 96ff, 102ff, 110f, 119, 121, 140, 159, 161, 164; see also Baptist Mission in Malawi
Baptism, 25f, 41ff, 45, 56, 89, 94ff, 110, 113, 121ff, 124ff, 129f, 150
Baptist Bible School, 64, 66, 68, 72, 76, 96, 164
Baptist Convention of Malawi (BACOMA), 65, 76, 79, 82ff, 85ff, 87ff, 90, 93ff, 96ff, 100f, 111, 121, 126f, 136, 144, 150, 152, 158f, 162, 164
Baptist Mission in Malawi, 62, 85; see also BMIM
Baptist Theological Seminary of Malawi, 66
Booth, Joseph, 9
Celebrate, 56, 115
Celebration, 110, 158
Centralized, 33, 149
Chadza, T/A; Village, 27, 46f, 84, 90, 103, 106, 108, 135
Chalendewa, 52ff, 71, 73, 99, 106, 109, 130, 142f
Chalera, Nasoni, 69, 95f, 112, 141

Challenge, 34, 43, 59, 74ff, 78, 85, 89, 126f, 151, 161, 164
Chando, Simiyoni, 72, 142
Chief Nyangu Kabudula, 19
Chiefs, 20, 31, 37, 84, 90, 103, 105, 134f, 149f, 152
Chiipira Village, 13, 18, 26
Chijere, Eliamu Mlongoti, 19, 40
Chikadula, 53f, 142
Chikhanda, 17, 141
Chakwela, Siteliya (Mrs), 72, 107, 142
Chilangizo, 85, 108
Children, 12, 19ff, 22, 26, 29f, 44, 48, 62, 85, 91f, 94, 120, 126ff, 131f, 135, 137f, 144, 147, 162
Chilembwe, John, 9ff, 20, 22ff, 33, 150,158 and Joseph Booth, 67 Associated with Chilembwe, 67, 147 Era, 149 Heritage, 163 John Chilembwe Day, 89 Legacy, 55 Role, 149, 155f *Ubatizo wa* John Chilembwe, 41ff, 96
Chilonga, 143
Chimpesa, Peturo, 27, 59ff, 62
Chinamwali, 84f
Ching'oma, 122
Chinungu, 141
Chinsamba, 62, 71, 106, 112, 142
Chiphaka, 17, 26, 36
Chiriza (memorial pillar), 40, 51, 54, 103f
Chituwi, 142
Chiuzira, 51, 60, 62, 77, 105f, 112, 141
Chiwona, Jamison, 142
Chiwoza, 141f
Chizindikiro cha mpatuko, 16
Chonde, 129, 141f
Christianization, 160, 162
Church Planting, 71ff, 92
Communication, 15, 160
Companion, 61, 89, 147
Contribute, 21, 28, 55, 76, 78, 88, 101, 103, 106, 152, 154f, 160, 163f;

INDEX

171

Contribution, 76, 79, 98f, 104f, 121, 148, 163
Corporate; Cooperative, 82, 154, 159
Crusade, 78f, 86, 94, 100,
Culture, 16, 20f, 27, 29, 31, 101f, 106, 118, 122, 124, 127, 131, 138, 145ff, 148f, 151ff, 156, 160, 162ff
Damalekani, 142
Dedication, 68, 105, 113, 128, 130, 150
Dedza, 13, 15, 18f, 30, 35f, 106, 109, 111f
Development, agricultural, 12, 17, 21, 28, 44, 50, 55, 88, 99, 136, 158, 160, 162ff
Deviate, 19, 39; see also *Kupatuka*
Diamphwe River, 15, 35
Discipleship, 159
Dissociate, 80, 110
Divorce, 13, 22, 36, 48f, 52f
Doctrine, 43, 89f, 144, 158
Dress (dressed, dressing), 15f, 29, 41, 47, 71, 153
Dutch Reformed Church Mission (DRCM), 11, 36
Dziwe, 51, 91, 93f, 97f, 141ff
Dzoole, 18
Education, 20ff, 28, 30, 44, 46, 50, 55f, 57, 73, 86, 88, 134f, 138ff, 144f, 159ff, 162
Emasi, Makabisi, 69
Equip, 41, 136, 162
Ethical, 89
Ethnocentrism, 162
Evangelical, 43, 49, 79, 121, 153, 162f
Evangelism, 40, 44, 69, 77, 139f, 159f
Faith, 11ff, 13, 30, 44, 50, 63, 67, 75, 118, 134, 152, 155, 158f, 163
Faithful, 22, 28, 41, 47, 51, 77, 104, 129, 144
Fellowship, 19, 22, 25, 34, 44f, 51, 55, 58, 79, 92, 103, 105f, 111, 113, 116f, 136f, 144, 150, 155, 158, 162f
Folomana, Bezina (Mrs), 107
Fraternal, 159
Freedom, 81
Galatiya, Stephen, 63ff, 69, 81ff, 87

Gender, 150f
Gondwa, 107, 110, 112, 142
Gule Wamkulu, 20ff, 25, 27, 92, 127, 134, 145, 150, 153; see also *Nyau*
Headscarf, 16f, 47, 91f, 153
Identification, 16; Indentity, 38fn, 77, 96, 102, 109, 160
Immorality, 89
Independence, 21, 34, 44, 55, 58f, 67, 81, 87, 102, 110, 134ff, 147, 149f, 156f, 163f
Independent Baptist Convention of Malawi, 164
Indigenization of Christianity, 9
Information, 85, 119, 139, 148, 161f
Jesitala, Bobo, 142
Kachala, 122, 147
Kachiwanda, Bizai and Magareti, 18
Kadumbanya, Laimoni, 142
Kafulatira, Aziri, 17, 26f, 36, 40, 46, 51; Daren, 18; Foulger, 18
Kafumbula, 97ff
Kakhobwe, Aliyele Biswick, 26
Kakwere, 122, 130, 132, 143
Kalemba, Magireti, wife, 13;
Kalemba, Peter, 10-49, 51, 55, 91f, 102, 104, 109f, 121, 126, 134, 139f, 141, 147, 149, 160f
Kalonga, Feniasi (Peter), 27, 45f, 51, 63, 69, 71, 73, 78, 90, 93, 103, 105ff
Kalumbu, Chief, 37, 84
  Chidampamba, Chief, 11
  Church, 37, 51, 141f
  Station, 112
  Village, 10ff, 13, 19, 25, 40, 42, 45, 51
Kamchedzera, Crispin, 135
  Enita, 71, 107
  Garton, 135, 137f
  Sandifolo, 79, 91f, 107, 109, 112, 134f, 137, 142
Kamchiliko, Charles, 27, 98, 141
Kamkalamba, Aaron, 17, 36, 40, 43, 45f, 51f, 54f, 58ff, 61, 63, 66, 68f, 73ff, 75, 77, 79, 100, 103ff, 106, 110, 140f, 161
Kampini, 19

INDEX

Kamunga, 143
Kapatuka, Halison, 79, 95
Kaphala, Sikefa, 18, 142
Katunga, 51, 106, 142
Kokha, J, 17, 36, 73, 141
Kufula dziko, 135
Kuika Manja, 108; see also Laying on of Hands
Kupatuka, 19; see also Deviate
Kuthira Ndemanga, 108
Laying on of Hands, 108; see also *Kuika Manja*
Liberation, 8, 108, 152
Lilongwe Baptist Association, 93, 97; Lilongwe Urban Baptist Association, 97
Lord's Supper, 41f, 45, 113, 125, 158
Lumwila, 142
MCP Party, 93, 98, 103; Party Card, 59ff; Youth League, 93
Makhaya, Dafren, 63, 66, 69, 77, 80ff, 83, 95
Malikebu, Daniel, S., 9f, 23f, 26ff, 30, 32ff, 39, 45, 47f, 55ff, 110, 116, 147, 160 Flora, 23f
Mangoni, 8, 11ff, 14, 16ff, 19ff, 22ff, 25ff, 28, 30, 32ff, 36, 39f, 55f, 76, 102, 109f, 113, 134, 139f, 144, 148, 160f
Marudo, (Mrs) 107,
Matapila, 18
Matapila, Chief Batiwelo, 40
Matapila, Harison, 17, 26, 36; Joseph, 17, 36; "Kambanje", 17
Matapila School, 17
Maturity, 50, 69, 149
Mazengera, 37, 84, 103
Mbewa 2, 142
Mbombwe, Chiradzulu, 8ff, 11, 13, 23ff, 26f, 30, 32ff, 35, 37, 40, 45, 55ff, 59, 63, 86, 110, 160f
Mediators, 161
Memorize, 20, 119
Mgala, 71, 122, 142
Mitundu, 19, 27
Mkute, Andrew, 18
Mlaliki wa kumudzi, 27

Mnjele, 142
Modern, 39, 110, 134, 151, 154, 162
Movement, 67, 73, 94, 100, 102, 110, 157, 162
Mpango ku mutu, 16f, 38, 47, 91f, 122, 153; see also headscarf
Mpanyila (Mozambique), 14f
Mphambanya, 129, 142
Mphanda, 18f, 39f, 51
Mphanje, 72, 142f
Mphindo, 46f, 51ff, 54, 91ff, 97, 141f
Mpingo wa Mpatuko, 16ff, 19f, 22, 25ff, 28f, 31ff, 34ff, 37ff, 41, 46f, 55, 91, 105, 143, 160
Mpingo wa nkhondo, 15
Msendeli, 142; see also Nsabwe
Msondole, 17
M'mbalo, 129, 143
Music, 80, 120, 124, 138, 153f
Mwachilolo, 17ff, 48, 142
Mwala, 92f, 112, 142
Mwase, 93, 142
Mwinimudzi, 77, 93, 100
Naked, 15
Nambuma, 106
Nathenje, 58, 100, 105f, 109, 112
Nationalization, 82
Ndalama, Matthew, 27, 40, 46, 51f, 54, 58, 63f, 66, 69, 71, 73, 78, 83f, 89f, 92, 103, 106ff, 129, 142f; Kelita, 71
Ndege, Yosofati, 52ff, 55, 58, 63, 65f, 69f, 73, 78f, 81ff, 89f, 93f, 99, 103, 106ff, 109, 130, 132, 138, 142; Achenjakwapi, 53
Nkhalamba, (Mrs) 107
Nkhoma, 11, 17ff, 21, 26, 36f, 77, 85, 106, 109, 121; CCAP Synod, 22, 36f, 85; Mission, 17, 21, 26ff, 29, 36, 45
Nkhoma, Chidzanja, 58
Nkhosa, 18ff, 34
Nsabwe, 71, 122, 129, 135; see also Msendeli
Nyangu, Anderson, the second convert, 11ff, 14ff, 19, 26, 30, 39f, 110

INDEX

Annie, wife, 13; Milia, second wife, 13
Nyanje, 17, 19, 38, 45f, 51, 58, 73ff, 93, 99, 105f, 108f, 112, 141f
Nyau, 20; see also *Gule Wamkulu*
Opposition, Chilembwe's, 11ff; To partnership, 59
Ordination, 41, 73f, 108f, 112, 150;
Ordained, 27, 30, 33, 39, 41f, 45f, 50f, 54, 73, 105, 109, 112
Osametedwa, 134f
Paternalistic, 148
Phatha, 40, 51, 72, 75, 129, 141f
Phiri, Njolomole, 81ff, 90f, 95ff, 101f
Polity, 32, 43, 149, 162
Polygamy, 147
Power, 33f, 59, 78, 98, 106, 109, 136, 139f, 146, 149, 161
Preaching, 26f, 40f, 43, 46, 54, 89, 100, 108, 119ff, 128f, 137, 159; see also Ulaliki
Prison, 15
Re-baptize, 65; Rebaptism, 97
Regenerate, 26, 76, 128
Reinforce, 21, 59, 162
Relationship, 20, 22, 25f, 32, 37, 55, 58f, 61ff, 86f, 90f, 99, 101, 103, 110f, 128, 132, 149ff, 152, 159f, 163
Resentment, 88, 110
Resources, 34, 77, 79, 84, 127, 154, 161
Respect, Respected, 15, 18, 20, 29f, 35, 37, 49, 59, 64, 110, 122, 130f, 150, 152
Responsibility, 9, 14, 22, 29, 35, 43, 80, 85, 88, 137, 149, 154, 160
Sandalamu, L.K., 91, 97
Schism, 95, 158
Scott, Rue, 78, 89ff, 94, 97ff, 100ff
Sect, 162f
Section, 30f, 39, 78, 106f, 112f, 136, 144, 152, 161
Senzani, 19, 34
Separate, 36, 54, 61, 81, 86, 90, 150, 161f
Simoko, Peturo, 69, 79, 112f, 141

Social, Society, 20ff, 29, 32, 84, 92, 101f, 118, 134, 138, 144, 146ff, 151f, 156, 162f
Sopo, Seliyasi, 107ff, 112, 129, 142
Spirituality, 159
Structure, 103, 120, 131, 148, 154
Subordination, 72
Suspicion, 91, 109, 141
Syncretism, 145
Teacher of *alaliki*, 52
Theological, 33, 63, 65, 67, 95, 138ff, 144, 150f, 159, 162
Torture, 14
Traditional, 13, 22, 51, 72, 86, 111, 114, 126ff, 135, 145f, 152, 157f
Training, 10, 20ff, 25ff, 28, 32, 41, 48, 50, 52, 54f, 62f, 65, 68, 70f, 81, 85ff, 88, 113, 134, 136ff, 139, 161f 164
Tribal, 38f, 100, 110, 134, 139, 148, 156, 162;
Tribe, 22, 38f, 50, 100, 106, 160
Tsoyo, 13, 142
Ulaliki, 26, 108; see also Preaching
Umodzi, 90f; see also unity
Umodzi wa Amayi a Baptist ku Malawi, 86, 136
Unity, 31, 69, 105, 151, 155, 158, 163
Wedding, 136, 150
Witch-hunt, 14
Witness, 13, 37, 63, 68, 71, 76f, 79, 123, 126, 140, 159
Women, 15f, 25f, 28ff, 31, 40, 47, 49, 68, 71ff, 74, 84ff, 89, 91f, 98, 104, 107, 109, 111, 115f, 120, 122, 131, 133, 136, 140, 147, 150ff
Worship, 18f, 44f, 54, 62, 72, 100, 106, 116ff, 119, 121, 125, 137, 139, 152f, 159f
Youth, 116, 131, 154f
Zingano, Anderson, 27, 73
Zion Church, 42, 62, 64f, 74, 82, 108, 150
Zirombo, 134ff
Zomba, 8, 14, 23, 63f, 138, 163
Zomba Baptist Church, 138

www.ingramcontent.com/pod-product-compliance
Lightning Source LLC
Chambersburg PA
CBHW020616300426
44113CB00007B/661